The virtues of cooking

RECIPES & STORIES
TO UPLIFT FAMILY THROUGH FOOD

ELINOR ALLCOTT GRIFFITH

Designer: Alicia Tagliasacchi

Copy Editor: Joyce Altman

First Edition
Printed in the United States of America
Blurb Creative Publishing Platform, San Francisco, Calif.

To the bread-makers and pie-bakers of my childhood,
my parents John and June Allcott.
And to my own family's enthusiastic eaters and cooks,
Peter, Kathleen and Alex.

contents

Foreword

KATHLEEN GRIFFITH

*M*y activity seemed uncharacteristic. A hurried New Yorker, I was in the kitchen of my parents' home, elbow deep in olive oil with salt and pepper clinging to my fingernails as I worked on coating russet potatoes… at the speed of molasses. Soon the house began wafting rosemary; the crackle of a roaring fire drifted into my thoughts along with laughter, the deep belly-real kind. Every sense was heightened and everything slowed down.

I experienced all of this not because it was real or because I am crazy (it really was just my mom and me and a few simple potatoes!), but because my mom's cooking, even in the preparation, always makes you feel something. As I looked at her, I felt a wave of gratitude. I felt stillness. Peace. No thoughts of work or my to-do list. After a draining week, I needed to feel steadied, grounded and uplifted, so that is exactly what I got. More gratitude as I considered her desire now to pass along this gift—a keepsake of virtues wrapped in a cookbook—in a time when virtually no one passes anything along anymore. Hers is actually a new type of culinary movement, using recipes to evoke virtues like *gratitude* and *love* and *courage*. She calls it "Virtues Cooking," and it will unfold in the pages before you.

Growing up, our home was not as big as everyone else's, our gadgets less cool and while Mom's cooking was really tasty, it was not exceptional. And yet, our home was the center of gravity for everyone. In college my friends would come home for the holidays (even all the way from North Carolina), not because of me but because of what was brewing in her kitchen. They would share a note of gratitude at the dinner table, knead the Friendship Bread, throw together new granola combinations and experiment with pancake shapes. It was as if everyone was coming for the experience surrounding food versus the food itself.

Looking back on this repeated phenomenon I see my mom picked up on what our family was missing, a friend lacked or a stranger required and would serve up a recipe to fill that need. A food experience embedded with a virtue. It was, and is, both as simple and magical as that. If I was feeling uptight and stressed at school, she would create a recipe that was playful and sparked *creativity*. If a girlfriend felt like dating-life was too complicated, out came something that gave *hope*. If my brother was getting impatient, she would make a dish that taught *patience*. Often if a neighbor seemed isolated or sick, Friendship Bread would come knocking on their door. And so I began to see and learn about the virtues of cooking.

This is the way food was intended. Food that nourishes the heart and makes you whole. Food that imprints virtues that you can carry forward and easily call upon. Food that can produce an experience, an emotion and a guaranteed outcome.

The end result of practicing Virtues Cooking is not just hearing that laughter or feeling that stillness I felt that night in the kitchen, but in knowing you are cultivating something that can be used throughout a lifetime. Virtues nurtured over time at the table help you know who you are and what you stand for, so you can flow with change, without getting carried away by it or spun around in it. My hope is that this style of cooking will bring to your family all that it has brought to ours!

introduction

FINDING JOY {AND OTHER VIRTUES} AT THE TABLE

*A*ll too often well-meaning parents take what they see as time-saving shortcuts. Rushed and harried, trying to do their best, they give up family meals and grab fast-food or a few energy bars for their children, and everyone eats on the run.

Slurp, slurp, slurp, a few more French fries, burp.

If you've picked up this book, chances are you hunger for something more… less of a hectic, "hamster-wheel" existence and more time with kids, hopefully over yummy food. Well, those skipped meals at home *are* vital in nourishing a child's well-being. Food is truly one of the greatest experiences binding a family together. But the real culinary jackpot hasn't been well chronicled, until now. It turns out certain homemade meals are also ideal for spooning in the key ingredient for a happy, resilient and thriving family. I'm talking about VIRTUES—qualities like *love, honesty* and *resourcefulness.*

Simply put, specific recipes can serve up specific virtues. By experimenting with "Virtues Cooking," parents nourish not only a child's stomach, but also heart and spirit, and all-important character. It's a recipe for success. Parents can strengthen a family right away. They can course-correct and knit everyone back together. They can produce specific outcomes, including *joyfulness*. I'm jumping up on my soapbox here... jump, jump... to emphasize this process should be pleasurable and playful. So starting now, today, you can make your youngster more... well, fill in the blank with whatever virtues listed in the book's Contents seem in short supply.

For decades I was a working, time-starved mom juggling two kids, so I can speak honestly about how this works. As you'll soon see, each of the book's twenty-eight chapters serves up a virtue as part of one of my family's favorite food stories—all entertaining and insightful. To help elicit the virtue, there are easy, wholesome and delicious recipes. For more inspiration, quotes are sprinkled in, and sidebars reference studies on the benefits of family-time at the table. And the really good news now: for Virtues Cooking, all anyone needs is common sense and a fun plan of action. No workbooks, no headaches in the making. Just focus on a virtue, cook up a recipe, and make the idea sizzle and stick.

Here's what I mean by using Virtues Cooking with a child. When my neighbor said her young son would eat only the same sugary cereal day after day, I immediately thought of pancakes and using the virtue of *spontaneity* as a way to tempt him to try a different breakfast. "Hmmm, why not try Playful Pancakes?" I asked. "You know, make a big fuss over asking him what shape he'd like you to make out of the batter, his spontaneous choice. Maybe his initials. Or an animal like a dog. You then paint the animal with the pancake batter, or use a pancake mold." This nod to *spontaneity* opened the door, a silly one, so he would try new food and get a taste of this virtue.

Or consider the virtue of *friendliness*. A disastrous water leak in my girlfriend Nancy's apartment, now years ago, prompted me to search out my dad's recipe for Friendship Bread. My teenage daughter, Kathleen, soon enlisted, the two of us then baked bread and beaming widely, gave my friend a loaf, its golden crust scented with a slightly burnt note of molasses, yeast and butter. Without my having said much, Kathleen had soaked up the "bread-friendship" idea that a gift from one's kitchen can help someone rebound after a rough patch.

Virtues Cooking is really that simple—and, over time, it can be life-changing.

*T*he idea for *The Virtues of Cooking* started out quite by chance. Roasted broccoli, not book plots and plans, was on my mind. Garlicky, gingery, fired up by shakes of oh-so-hot red pepper flakes, the broccoli was for dinner. But where *were* the instructions?

I began to flip through my recipe folder: Spicy Chicken Enchiladas, Halibut with Sauce Diable, Chicken Satay.... What was this? Clipped to a recipe for Orange Cake was a questionnaire with these words, "Application for permission to date my daughter." Huh? How did that goofball test of love get there? I found Valentines from my kids. Photos of my grandmother. And next to a recipe for baked ziti, practically oozing with droplets of tomato sauce from many makings of the dish, I discovered my father's wonder-filled letter on his "cosmic encounter with primordial soup."

And then it hit me. This file wasn't merely a collection of recipes. It hinted at something special happening around the table, something beyond the food itself. Like a determined detective on an unsolved case, I started to sleuth my way through the rest of the file to see what had been added over time. I found a widely circulated email about what were purportedly the Dalai Lama's "Instructions for Life." My husband, Peter, and I had talked about it at a New Year's party. This perspective, especially Rule No. 19, explained why it had earned a place in my recipe folder: "Approach love and cooking with reckless abandon."

Next was a family photo from Thanksgiving. Peter was carving a scrumptious Worth-the-Wait Turkey Roast. My son, Alex, then eighteen, was back from college and, despite not being keen on picture-taking, he was caught grinning as he heaped food high onto his plate. Daughter Kathleen, also home from school, and I linger nearby. In a blink I was whirling in time back to that family gathering.

Inhale. I could practically smell the turkey, taste the pear-pecan stuffing.

Exhale. I felt the many blessings of the day. Our son had joined us for what weeks earlier he brushed off as an overrated holiday. Fortunately, food was a powerful magnet pulling us together.

The recipe for Roasted Garlicky Broccoli? It emerged eventually from amidst a cluster of my father's drawings. Heaps of 'em. Given on anniversaries, birthdays, holidays, really any ol' day, Dad spent many resourceful hours at our family's long kitchen table crayoning out special greetings. His cards often captured the klutzy happenings of Max, the talking dog, and Bear. (John Allcott's alter ego was John Bear, also known as "J.B.") His creative bouquet of bright flowers made me chuckle.

Eclectic and personal, sparkling with humor, creativity and love, this stuff in the recipe file still had me puzzled. More detective work would be needed.

*O*ne fall day I was visiting my childhood home in North Carolina, my parents long gone. I walked through the overgrown garden, once flush with super-sized Big Boy tomatoes, dangling green pole beans, rows of abundant basil. I rejoiced to find the grape arbor still bejeweled with bronze scuppernongs. Those grapes? I used them for food fights. I would dash full throttle down our dirt road after the neighbor kids and squirt out the gooey, seedy insides—gotcha, GOTcha, GOTCHA! Even recalling that high-spirited time made me feel sticky. And giddy. I felt a flash of something. But what? Springing to mind was the word "enthusiasm."

I was reminded of another wild time with the same kids. On that occasion, my father made a whimsical breakfast treat of Inside-Out Toast, ever so enthusiastically.

As I mulled over other experiences with food, and thought about my recipe folder with its sparkle of *humor, creativity* and *love*, additional words bubbled forth: *Gratitude. Idealism. Patience.* These were all... virtues.

Without realizing it—in cooking and eating and being around food—we four Allcott children were learning (often mischievously) and our parents were modeling (often imperfectly) various virtues. Later with my own kids, I must have done the same, like when Kathleen and I gave away the Friendship Bread. Under the magnifying glass of memory, I spotted a parade of horn-tooting virtues marching their way through my family's most-cherished food experiences.

Thinking my now-grown daughter might like a cookbook on Virtues Cooking, I looked in bookstores and online. I found nothing. I started to reflect more on the power of food, the process of cooking, and all the warmth and fun around the table as opportunities for true learning and transcendence; and how it's a process that actually, counterintuitively, gives back a sense of the fullness of time. (Bye-bye hamster wheel!) Other busy families might like to enhance mealtime, instill virtues and build up a child's character strengths... if only they had the idea.

The Virtues of Cooking is the result, the first of its kind. Part inspirational how-to, part culinary memoir, part cookbook, it's my family's unconventional recipe for a good life.

And there is magic in the recipes and stories. I've curated them carefully and can guarantee they can serve up the virtue. That's been my family's experience. For isn't one of the highest compliments a parent can hear simply this, they've raised very principled, value-driven children? That the family is tight and sticks together?

My hope is that *The Virtues of Cooking* will now stir up things wondrously in your home. Like a friend, I'll be cheering you on. I'll be sharing what I've learned, through trial and error, and hot-halibut-skidding-across-the-floor disasters. (That zany story heralds, rightfully, *simplicity* as its virtue.) I encourage reading through the book from the beginning to the end, applying a "virtuous" recipe a day for roughly a month. Or single out a specific virtue and focus on that chapter and its virtue-producing recipes. I can promise this. If you put all twenty-eight virtues into practice using the recipes, such as Circus Tent Apple Pie (think of the sense of *gratitude* everyone will feel as the ballooning tent-like crust gives way to the slightly tart, cinnamony apples), your family will be on its way to renewal and joy.

And, as you use Virtues Cooking, remember my little motto: salt for luck and thyme for love.

XOXO Elinor

P.S. If the sketch of the happy man clutching the flowers reminds you of the book's other illustrations, you're right. The artist is the same, John Allcott, my talented father. And the images are from my recipe folder, his numerous sketchbooks and the walls of my home.

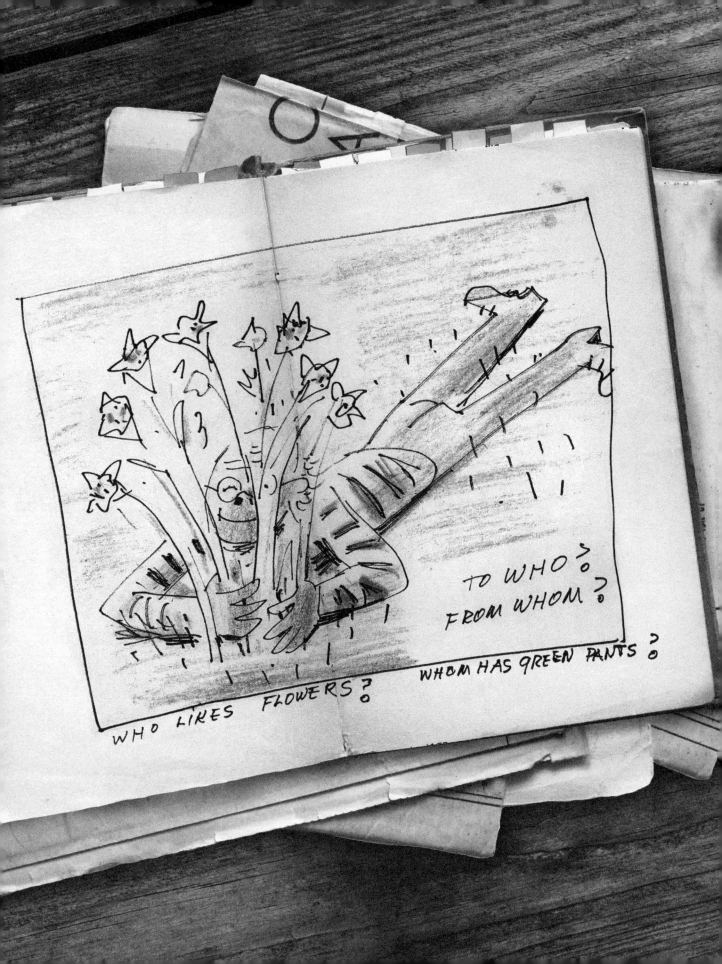

1) friendliness

No Loafing Around

Bread and friendliness. The confluence of food and virtue started most unexpectedly over the dough hook of my parents' KitchenAid mixer. What occurred next in the kitchen of our home in Chapel Hill, N.C., and how other transformative food experiences shaped me and my three siblings, is rather unusual. The following 28 stories chronicle what happened, beginning with a few extra loaves of what came to be known as "Friendship Bread."

*D*ad was often in the kitchen when I got home from school. Not threatened by wearing an apron, he had taken over our family's weekly bread-making after Momma's return to work. "How are things?" he'd ask simply, then scurry around assembling the ingredients: two packets of yeast, bags of bread flour and brown sugar, a bottle of molasses, leftover oatmeal from the fridge, a prized stick of Land O'Lakes butter....

Hovering behind him in our galley kitchen—fridge and stove on one side, sink and dishwasher on the other, shelves all around—I would pour out my worries. It was preteen stuff like no phone calls from Skip, the heartthrob who'd transferred to our junior high. Or not understanding my French teacher with her heavy Southern accent and lisp. Or a stern ultimatum from Momma to get rid of the mice caged on a shelf above her clothes closet.

On that afternoon I'd told Dad sheepishly, "I know they had babies suddenly. Occasionally litter flutters down, but the mice were for my science project. Remember? I got an *A*. Besides, I thought I had two females."

"Those mice babies could soon surprise us with their own babies," said Dad, now grabbing the salt. "I read someplace that mice reproduce in twenty days and if nothing is done there can be nearly one million of them scampering about in a year. A million, all above your mother's clothes."

The virtue of FRIENDLINESS consists of warm, affable behavior toward people.

Yikes, I thought, Momma must have warned him the mice had to go. I could almost hear her words still hanging in the air, "Today, John! It's your turn to convince her... today!" My usually laid-back father had clearly done some fact-finding on mice reproduction to make a stronger case.

"I know what we can do," he said. "I bet the students in my life-drawing class at the art department would like to sketch them. Mice models, you know, like Mickey and Minnie. Surely some student will want to take home such an adorable mouse family."

"Okay," I agreed, "as long as I don't have to let them go outside. I didn't know what to do."

Like butter melting on a slice of the soon-to-be-made bread, my worries disappeared, whatever they were that day. I began to help Dad regularly with his baking. A little scientist, I loved to see yeast bubble up after warm water and a teaspoon of sugar fueled its dormant cells. I gave weather reports for atmospheric changes over the KitchenAid mixer as we shoveled in ingredients: "Clouds are forming. Floury clouds." I used a stopwatch to time how long it took the mixture to inch up the dough hook, curl over the top and cling on tenaciously, the motor straining from such a heavy load. And on the dough hook chugged as we added more flour....

"Poke it down," Dad would tell me, stopping the mixer. As we stood side by side, it felt like his full attention was actually on me, not the bread. I cranked up Rod Stewart on the record player, sang along with the Temptations and danced about to the

Contours' "Do You Love Me?" Bobbing and twisting in the kitchen, I belted out: "I can mash potato, mash potato. I can do the twist, do the twist... Watch me now."

No longer feeling the outer wrappings of a self-conscious kid, I gyrated to the music and twisted down to the floor. Free, carefree. Exuberant. The transformation continued, and a lively magic surrounded us. My younger brother Gene, age six, banged away at the drums. And Dad matched our punched-up good mood as he extracted the sticky dough from the silver mixing bowl, heaped it onto a butcher-block counter and started to push it around rhythmically.

It was my turn next to knead the dough. "Lean down with the heels of your hands," he'd say. "Flip the far side in as you give a quarter turn, and toss in small handfuls of flour to stop stickiness." We stood together, him instructing, me hunched over the dough, Gene laughing, until I finally got a wild three-step going: *Push, flip 'n turn. Push, flip 'n turn. Push, flip 'n turn!*

Soon bread was rising in four pans and in a circular... flowerpot. Momma got the crazy idea for this eight-inch-wide clay pot from a cooking magazine. "Why not try it?" she had said with a shrug. "It's like the French bakeware of the nineteenth century." She immediately went to the garden store and bought one. That was the start of the whimsical flowerpot loaf.

"I'm going to take a tax." Dad would grin as he pulled out the now-baked bread, sawed off a crust and layered on butter. A large quarter chunk for him and the rest for me.

Dad never worried about the miles of mess he left behind. I headed up his cleanup crew, along with Gene and our older siblings Johnny (fourteen) and Liz (sixteen). We soaped up the mixing bowl. We wiped flour handprints off cabinet fronts. We scraped dried dough from the strangest places: the side of the Waring blender, the yellow breadbox painted with three smiling daisies, a flower vase left by the sink, and even removed chunks from the dog's dish.

Fortunately, Dad's oatmeal bread was divine. And that fresh bread and a large friendly dose of his attention while baking it were the best antidotes for preteen angst.

One day the flowerpot loaf disappeared. Out of the five loaves Dad and I had made, the round one disappeared. Vanished. No explanation.

Later that afternoon I pieced together what happened. Dad had picked up that loaf and headed out the door. Wearing red plaid pants and a madras shirt (looking unquestionably like an art professor), he'd headed through the woods behind our home carrying the bread and some recent sketches. He was going to visit Peg and Phil Rees, friends over on Oteys Road. As he told us later, his creation caused quite a stir. "No kidding," Peg had exclaimed. "Really? You and Elinor baked this round loaf in a flowerpot?" She wanted all the details.

That was the start of the giveaway loaves. Another day Dad smiled mischievously and said, "Our bread got rave reviews today at the White House."

"No kidding," Johnny yelled. He'd overheard our conversation from his bedroom near the kitchen. "THE White House?"

"Yup," said Dad. "They're calling it 'the Best Bread in America.'"

We knew he was kidding and had merely marched, bread in hand, down Chase Avenue to visit our neighbors, Tera and Sheldon White.

"The word from the White House is our bread has its seal of approval," he said, warming up ideas for a little story. "According to Sheldon, and he would certainly know, the White House seal of approval for the Best Bread in America is like a royal certificate in Britain. You know, pip pip and all that, by appointment to her Majesty's Service. It's what Queen Elizabeth gives to favored vendors. This is a very special Upper Crust thing, said Sheldon. He went on to tell me the endeavor was certainly not half-baked."

Feeling silly—after all, weren't we of the Upper Crust?—we decided there was only one thing to do: nibble on more of America's Best Bread.

Soon the giveaway loaves were known across town as "John's Friendship Bread." And bread-making took on a life of its own. A new baby, a sick husband, a promotion, or "just because…." With his arms full of bread, Dad would walk into Chapel Hill, then a small North Carolina town of 12,000 people, cross Franklin Street and drop off a loaf with friends such as Benjamin Swalin, the director of the North Carolina Symphony and his harpsichord-playing wife Maxine. On his way home he might scoot down Franklin to do his banking and give a small loaf to the teller. And stop at the bank's entrance to chat and make a sketch, and offer bread to the flower-sellers—a cluster of black women with bouquets of daisies, zinnias and roses.

Other days Dad and I would jump into his Datsun, me holding our still-warm bread, and we'd drive into Chatham County. On those visits to see old Mr. Shield, we seldom came back empty-handed. Accompanying us home were garden-fresh raspberries, butter beans, or a Mason jar of pickled okra, though I must confess I

> *Friendship is the most important thing—not career or housework, or one's fatigue—and it needs to be tended and nurtured.*
>
> *–Julia Child*

never took a hankering to this Southern specialty. And amazed by all the activity, eyes twinkling, Momma loved to remark that there was "no loafing around at our house."

Something as simple as Friendship Bread opens a door… an oven door… for friendliness to flourish and be stirred into countless lives.

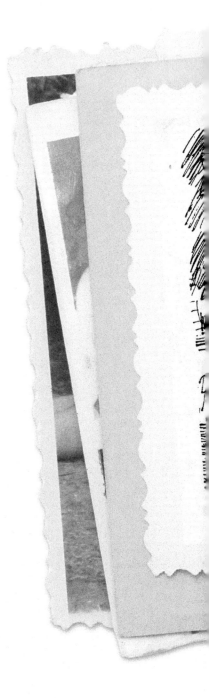

Franklin Street

FRIENDSHIP BREAD

yields 4 large loaves

A. 2 packets yeast
1 teaspoon sugar
¼ cup warm water

B. 4 cups warm water
4 cups bread flour

C. 1½ cups oatmeal *(make ahead and cool)*
5 tablespoons melted butter
1 cup brown sugar
5 tablespoons molasses
pinch baking soda
1 tablespoon salt
7 to 8 cups bread flour
(I often include a cup of whole wheat flour)

Instead of baking 4 loaves, try making
3 regular loaves and 2 smaller ones
to give away. That's Flour Power!

This recipe is like lyrics for the Jackson 5 song that goes, "All you gotta do is repeat after me! A, B, C! It's easy as one, two, three. As simple as do, re, mi. A, B, C. One, two, three." So then, it's actually easy to follow the ABC's and 123's of making Friendship Bread.

Here's what you do with your ABC's....

A. Combine the yeast, sugar and warm water in the large mixing bowl of a heavy-duty mixer, stir and let sit for 5 minutes.

B. Add 4 cups warm water and 4 cups bread flour. Now using the bread hook, stir the ingredients to form a sponge. Let double in size.

C. With the mixer running, add the remaining ingredients, including the flour—a cup or two at a time. Once ingredients are mixed and the consistency isn't too sticky (more flour may be needed), put the dough on a floured surface and knead for 10 minutes. Place in a clean, lightly greased bowl, cover with a kitchen towel and let double in size. Punch down. Divide the dough into four 9 x 5-inch loaf pans (prepare pans by wiping a trace of butter along the bottom and sides, then dusting with flour) and let the dough rise for about an hour.

Now the 123's of baking Friendship Bread: Preheat oven to 450 degrees. Bake the bread for 15 minutes. Then turn the oven down to 425 for another 15 minutes. When done, the tops should be golden brown and crusty hard. Just to be sure, though, thump gently on the top to check for a hollow sound. Cool on a rack.

Friendliness

Friendliness warms the hearts and joins the paths of people. So, to strengthen this virtue, bake up a batch of Friendship Bread with your children, and give away warm loaves.

2) humor

SNAKES... AT THE BREAKFAST TABLE?

"Sheldon just spotted a fat copperhead down the street near the persimmon tree where you were playing yesterday," said my mother, placing a glass of orange juice by my plate. "He phoned a few moments ago. He's heading back with a hoe to look for it again."

Suddenly my two brothers, sister and I were wide-awake, bug-eyed, as we sat at the kitchen table awaiting breakfast. I often played carefree games of kick the can around that tree with our neighbor Sheldon White's three children, so the thought of a harmful snake nearby caused me, then ten, to feel a rush of fear.

Momma started our day frequently with warnings about various dangers we might encounter. "Be sure to watch out," she continued. "That snake may have babies."

"Babies?" I repeated. "A pile of squirmy babies? Poisonous ones?"

She was clearly warming up, ready to launch into one of her impromptu lectures. "Yes, baby copperheads have the same nasty venom and sometimes a dozen or so are born at once," Momma replied solemnly. "Now remember to shuffle your feet as you walk in woodsy areas and make noise, maybe sing, and a copperhead will have time to disappear down its snake hole. And…."

Interrupting, not giving her a moment more for an anxiety-producing discourse about the remote chance of our being bitten, Dad broke in lightheartedly:

"Okay, now who wants my homemade bread?"

"I want to be first," I yelled drowning out my siblings' voices.

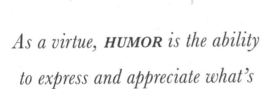

As a virtue, HUMOR is the ability to express and appreciate what's comic and amusing, even absurd.

He sat smiling mischievously at Command Center, his name for the "important" position at the end of the table, in charge of the old toaster. Holding gingerly onto the hot handle, he opened the door, pulled out a toasty slice and slathered on butter and jam. He circled his right arm dramatically in the air (his goofy version of a baseball pitcher's windup), and let the toast fly. It went sliding wildly across the table. I started to laugh. Globs of half-melted butter and raspberry jam clung tenaciously to the top as it sputtered to a stop, just inches short of my juice glass.

"Wow, Dad, that was cool," I said. It was slapstick humor like in the movies.

I was well-familiar with Momma's concerns about safety, but much preferred Dad's comic early morning antics. He was put off by seriousness, at breakfast. Emerging to eat after a night's sleep, a child shouldn't experience heavy, scary stuff, which would be hurled soon enough—at school, in the news or elsewhere. His tone was decidedly different from Momma's. How we began the day, he believed, would become the default setting, guiding us, steadying us, through whatever else happened later on. Dad believed in starting the day with humor.

Amidst our chatter, he now peered back into the toaster's scorched interior. "I spot a muffin," he said. "Who wants one?"

My younger brother Gene waved his hand energetically. "A muffin, a muffin, it's my turn," he said loudly. "Did you forget meeeee?"

Dad now did another windup, this time lobbing a hot muffin three feet into the air. My younger brother reached in and just managed to make the catch. He whooped in joy, and Momma found an indulgent smile curling up her face. We loved breakfast, with its muffin-tossing and toast-flinging.

And then—after reloading the toaster with more bread and muffins for my older siblings, Liz and Johnny—Dad reached beside him on the table for his ever-handy black felt-tip pen and a leather sketchbook. As he waited for us to eat, he turned to sketching as another way to ramp up humor. Most days he merely looked out the window for inspiration: a distant squirrel that turned out to be only a pine cone ("my glasses must be smudged"), a dog with a funny-looking spot shaped like a heart or, as was happening today, thoughts of a slithery reptile. With a few bold strokes of his pen, Dad created a coiled snake on the page. Even looking from across the table, I could make out its telltale triangular head, dark saddleback markings and two over-exaggerated fangs.

"Will Sheldon find the snake?" I asked, once more uneasy.

"Hopefully," said Dad finishing up the drawing and passing it around. "We'll have to wait and see." He'd sketched the worrisome snake, me, the neighbor's kids, all at the tree. "Fortunately, no one was bitten," he continued. "As the great playwright Mr. S. said... are you listening, Gene?... No, that's not what he said. Shakespeare said something that's quite wonderful to remember. He said, 'all's well that ends well.' It was the name of one of his comedies."

Somehow Dad's cartoonish drawing, his banter, made the snake situation seem much less threatening, almost fun. Still, to please Momma, I said earnestly, "I'm not going to play near that tree any time soon. I won't go back to gather the persimmons either. I tried one, and it was as mouth-puckering as a gulp from the Mason jar you fill with unsweetened lemon juice for our lemonade. Nope, not going back there."

"Why not ask the kids to play here?"

Momma liked me hanging out with Missy, Fran and Henry White. They were polite and well-behaved. When they talked to her, they said things like, "Yes, ma'am" or "No ma'am" or "Okay, Miss June." Their family's history in Chapel Hill went way

> *A person without a sense of humor is like a wagon without springs. It's jolted by every pebble on the road.*
>
> —Henry Ward Beecher

There once was a woman called June Bear,
Of amazing aplomb as you'll soon hear;
    She balanced her husband,
    4 children and onions,
And did this not once but all year.

back, and Sheldon was on the board of the historical society. Momma suspected that some of the townspeople didn't think we measured up quite so well, at least not by conservative Southern standards. She and Dad were outsiders. From Madison and near Chicago, my parents had headed south as newlyweds so Dad could teach at the University of North Carolina; he'd started the Art Department. But that didn't give us a lick of bragging rights when it came to a Southern pedigree....

And while truth was on the kitchen table, there was another thing: my parents were never too brave when it came to snakes. Good thing our fearless neighbor had a shed full of hoes.

Dad took a brief detour now to his study and came back hugging several volumes of the *Encyclopedia Britannica*. Another part of his breakfast strategy was sprinkling the morning with ideas, many of which were humorous. Purchased at a book sale for a few dollars, the encyclopedia had a copyright in the 1930s, but that didn't deter him. "A lot had already happened in the world by then," he'd once explained. "There's still lots for you to learn."

Spotting a picture of the Eiffel Tower, he leaned toward Johnny who'd recently started French. "Look," he said, showing the page, "Gustave Eiffel's iconic tower in Paris was once the tallest building in the world—1043 magnificent feet of iron— completed in 1889 for *L'Exposition Universelle*. And you know what happened after World War I? A journalist rode down a section of its stairs on a bike. Just imagine how this stunt caused plenty of laughs for the war-weary French."

In these morning treks through the old encyclopedia, Dad barely paused over the familiar (painter Claude Monet, for instance); he gravitated toward the unusual and arcane, things like a write-up on subcutaneous fatty tissue. (The word "fat" guaranteed a laugh from Gene.) Being susceptible to suggestion, I'm glad he never found a reference to "ophidiophobia," or a fear of snakes, and read about it. If so, I might have developed the phobia.

As for the worrisome copperhead, to my relief Sheldon took care of it. But, at least once a year, one of us would nearly step on one of its copper-headed babies or slow-moving cousins: near the tire swing out back, around the tomato plants in the vegetable garden, under a house window, and once doing an Olympic free climb up the stone steps toward the front door.

No surprise then; the next day over breakfast Momma would recite a "be careful, shuffle your feet" warning. Likewise, true to his beliefs, Dad would edge us onto a funnier track. That meant a merrier whirl of humor.

food facts:

MORE MEALS TOGETHER, BETTER GRADES

A survey by Columbia University extols the benefits of the food-family connection. Have dinner with your teen at least five times a week, it states, and the results are astounding: better grades (teens are 40 percent more likely to earn A's and B's), lower use of alcohol (42 percent less likely), cigarettes (59 percent less likely) and marijuana (66 percent less likely). Still, since only half of all teens have regular dinners with their family, according to the same survey, think of this alternative: family breakfasts.

VIRTUES COOKING TIP:

humor

Feed this virtue daily. **Humor** is a choice
before becoming a habit. And what could
be better to reset and elevate mood than
humorous toast-flinging or muffin-tossing
with kids at breakfast?

MADCAP MORNING GLORY MUFFINS

yields 24 to 30 muffins

2½ cups sugar
4 cups all-purpose flour
4 teaspoons cinnamon
4 teaspoons baking soda
1 teaspoon salt
1 cup shredded coconut
1 cup raisins
4 cups carrots *(grated)*
2 cups apples *(grated)*
6 large eggs *(lightly beaten)*
1½ cups vegetable oil
1 teaspoon pure vanilla extract
½ cup pecans
1 container cupcake liners

Preheat oven to 375 degrees. Line regular-sized muffin tins with paper liners.

In a large bowl, sift together the sugar, flour, cinnamon, baking soda and salt. Add coconut, raisins, carrots and apples. *(To grate the carrots and apples, I use my food processor.)* Stir well.

In another bowl, whisk the eggs, oil and vanilla; and then with a large wooden spoon stir this mixture into the dry ingredients, only until blended.

Fill each muffin liner three-fourths full and top with a pecan. Bake for 30 minutes until lightly browned, and cool on a cooling rack.

These muffins freeze and reheat well. Once when staying with my friend Peg, I smelled the enticing scent of cinnamon drifting down the hallway. I thought she'd been up baking since 6 a.m. "Much easier," she explained. "I made the Morning Glories earlier in the week and froze them, then reheated several this morning for a few minutes at 325 degrees."

3) spontaneity

POTS AND PANS, AND PANCAKES

"Can you make me pancakes?" I called out to my mother. "Like last Sunday?" My favorite breakfast was homemade pancakes in a puddle of Vermont maple syrup served up on Sunday before church. Wearing a green gingham apron to protect her colorful African-print dress, Momma pulled out her own mother's spattered recipe card. It called for two cups of rich buttermilk and whipped egg whites for puffiness.

But what mattered most to me was how Momma played with the batter. She'd recently come up with the idea for Playful Pancakes. She would tell us to request a specific shape and then use batter to paint it on the griddle. My father, the art professor, wasn't the only one in the house with artistic abilities; her palette just happened to be at the stove.

"What would you like?" she asked. "I can do just about anything."

"Hmmm, what about some big *E's*," I said, referring to the first initial of my name. "I'd like that a lot." Last Sunday I'd asked, "Momma, can you make me a chubby bear like the one in Dad's bedtime stories?" I was a preteen then into games and stories. Another time I had yelled out: "What about a snug house with a small window on the side—that's so the girl who lives there, me, can see when her friends come over and are playing outside."

Momma dabbed the hot griddle with a small spoonful of butter and carefully ladled out a line of *E's*. The batter shimmied and bubbled, and sizzled up around the edges. I soon had five super-sized, puffy *E's* stacked high on my plate. Maple syrup handy.

There's real virtue in NOT having every moment scheduled or planned, hence the appeal of...SPON-TA-NE-I-TY.

The design part was cool. I loved making these spur-of-the-moment decisions, which felt fun and empowering; it was neat being the center of attention. Momma had already reminded my three siblings, "Elinor is going first today. We've all the time in the world."

"Mom, Momma, a big furry dog for me," my younger brother Gene soon hollered. When she set down his plate, we burst into laughter. Despite her best efforts to use small spoonfuls of batter to draw the dog's head, body and four feet, the result was unrecognizable—more like a large ball surrounded by five protruding ball-bumps.

"Eat that one anyway," she said, always practical. "I'll try again. The griddle needs to be hotter so the drawing holds together." This time the result was a dinner-plate-sized pancake shaped more like a dog, with a distinct, crispy tail.

These Playful Pancakes quickly became a Sunday sensation. And there was a bonus. I learned that this activity around food helped address one of Momma's concerns in raising us. Much of our day, she believed, was too busy and overscheduled. A key to spontaneity, and developing other character strengths, was having loads of free time.

A sense of spontaneity, she knew, could belly up to the table with shout-outs for quirky Playful Pancakes.

*O*ur mother's Command Center was the old GE four-burner stove; her vision, though, went way beyond its ancient white top and foiled-lined burners. For 365 days of the year, she plotted and planned. She cooked delicious and healthy meals, and then layered on her Momma Agenda. With us kids held captive at the table, she used activities involving food to spotlight a virtue needing attention. For mini-lectures about dangerous copperheads. For discussions about social issues and foreign lands. For searching questions: "Sleeping better? Finished your essay? Another headache in Miss Hunt's class? Hung the laundry up outdoors yet?"

Some days at breakfast she'd settle heavily into discussions about politics, and even Dad's attempts at humor wouldn't divert her. Having grown up in Wilmette, Ill., a suburb of Chicago along Lake Michigan, my mother certainly never fit the image of a Southern Belle, not with her waist-length flame of red hair, her pronounced limp from a polio-type illness in childhood and, well, her gutsy outspokenness. Women's Rights, Civil Rights, entrenched Southern ways, she and other trendsetters had identified many areas ready for change. Everyone had a responsibility to make the world better. In a voice so serious that sometimes my younger brother Gene and I burst into nervous laughter, she would read us the latest letter to the editor she'd written to our town's newspaper, *The Chapel Hill Weekly*.

"It's horrible what is going on at the Long Meadow Dairy Bar," she'd say. "Coloreds can't eat in the dining area. Imagine that."

When not stewing over some local injustice, Momma's interests carried her far from Chapel Hill. She loved to talk about distant countries—and their cuisine. She gathered foreign professors and their homesick families, and served up an American version of their traditional meals. Our kitchen seemed to touch down magically all over the world. In France, for Julia Child–inspired boeuf bourguignon and coq au vin. In Switzerland, for raclette spiced with green cornichons and tiny, tangy onions. Egypt, for slow-simmered, oniony eggplant and chopped meat. China, for stir-fry meals loaded with crisp vegetables. And occasionally I would watch her break into a stash of imported chocolate, hidden away in the back of a cabinet, for a mousse au chocolat, a sure sign that she'd landed back in France.

About this time in the early 1960s—shortly after Julia's *Mastering the Art of French Cooking* had created a stir—my mother and I started to watch *The French Chef*. Momma identified with the chef's hard-working, fun-loving ways. Most of all, we were riveted by all the kitchen drama surrounding Julia who once described herself as "a large woman sloshing eggs too quickly here, too slowly there, gasping, looking at the wrong camera while talking too loudly and so on."

Soon I was stove-side flipping pages in Julia's cookbook. And my culinary coming of age—that moment I remember so well when I tentatively took her recipe for chilled pastry dough out of the refrigerator for my first solo attempt at dessert, an apple tart (the dough sticking occasionally but I repaired it, pinching and patting pieces into place)—was with Julia's warble of words in my ears. "The pleasures of the table," she said, "and of life, are infinite—*toujours bon appétit!*"

By now Momma had upgraded her cooking ingredients. The kitchen shelves held a stockpile of then-exotic Dijon mustard, Szechuan pepper, Indian sesame oil, Mexican vanilla and Greek olive oil. She'd exchanged margarine for butter, powdered milk for cream, dried herbs for garden-fresh basil, thyme, oregano and parsley. And she began making French dishes regularly such as Julia's omelets.

Sad to say, Momma's omelets, unlike Julia's noteworthy creations, were often speckled with what we called "questionable edibles." That meant food that had disappeared for days in the fridge's clutter of half-consumed jars and bottles, and plates of leftovers, only to resurface in this French dish. To my mother's ever-thrifty mind, omelets were an ideal way to repurpose food from refrigerator clean-outs: leftover round steak, sautéed onions, grilled red peppers.

These clean-outs were also how she continued to champion a sense of spontaneity from her perch at the stove. "Tooo-day," said Momma one morning, doing a silly imitation of a French accent, "for brake-fast you can 'ave a foamy om-e-let with, let me see what I can offer, jam-bon or cham-pi-gnons or poiv-ron rouge. What would you like?"

"I'll have jambon," I said, remembering the word from middle school French class. I knew she'd merely found a baggie full of Virginia ham slices. In this case spontaneity manifested itself in a little moment of time, with a choice for this or that.

And then Momma drifted off into thought and said wistfully, almost as if planting the idea so it could sprout eventually: "Some day, my sweet Bitty (my silly

The fun stuff comes when someone is not so strict on sticking to the script. You're allowed the spontaneity, and great moments can happen.

–Jennifer Aniston

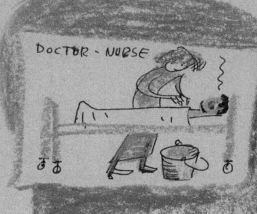

DOCTOR - NURSE

HORTI -
CULTIST

REGARDEZ LE LIVRE!

PROFESSOR

nickname), you will travel to Paris, a treat in itself with the Eiffel Tower, and then go on to the Normandy coast. You will likely head to Mont Saint-Michel, an impressive eleventh-century Benedictine abbey that sits atop stony cliffs on a tiny island. On one of the village's cobblestone streets you might notice a restaurant called La Mère Poulard. Your Grammy Chloupek still talks about her whirlwind trip to Europe in the 1930s and her favorite meal: an omelet at Poulard whisked to perfection in a copper bowl and cooked over an open hearth, a sprinkle of local sea salt tossed in for a crunch of the ocean."

As she slid her own frothy omelet onto my tan plastic breakfast plate, I felt transported to another country. "La Mère Poulard couldn't do better than this," she said. "It isn't hard becoming a decent chef."

You have to come on with a bang. You never want to go out with a whimper. Everything can have drama if it's done right. Even a pancake.

–Julia Child

*I*n the spirit of full culinary disclosure, Momma shunned Southern breakfasts. She never made me scrambled eggs and bacon, cheese grits on the side. Or biscuits with sausage gravy. Instead, she gravitated toward more unusual selections:

Hamburgers. "A little protein," she said, "gets your brain off to an excellent start."

Cream of wheat with ice cream. Vanilla usually. Chocolate sometimes. "No worries about anemia if you eat a cup of this cereal with its high iron content, about 50 percent of your daily requirement," said Momma. As for the ice cream, we knew her sweet tooth was speaking.

Oatmeal. Not ordinary Quaker, but John McCann's steel cut Irish oats.

Sliced apples cooked in brown sugar and Vienna sausages. Or fresh apple sauce piled onto buttered toast. Both dishes were made from Virginia winesaps picked at a friend's farm. The old "apple a day" adage, Momma told us, was rooted in solid research. "There's high vitamin C," she said, "as well as significant soluble fiber and antioxidants to boost your immune system."

Bircher-muesli. First prepared in Switzerland by Dr. Bircher in the 1920s, this cereal seemed over-the-top healthy: oats, almonds, yogurt, apples, bananas and oranges.

My favorite breakfasts, though, were quite simple: Playful Pancakes, Friendship Bread and Madcap Morning Glory Muffins. And at their respective Command Centers, my parents continued to dish out life's little lessons.

After all, spontaneity (and other virtues) can be quite a thrilling launchpad for the day.

P.S. Many years later my mother-in-law Grayce, nearing 100, whispered the secret of her good health: oatmeal and its cousin, Red River porridge (cracked wheat, rye and flax seeds, grown on the vast Canadian prairie); she developed this hot-cereal habit while growing up in chilly Saskatchewan. "Oatmeal is warming and is really good for you," she said thoughtfully. "It encourages you to have a good day."

food facts:

SKIP BREAKFAST? NO WAY...

In a 2008 survey, the International Food Information Council reported that "93% of Americans agree that breakfast is the most important meal of the day, yet less than half (44%) eat it every day." A sampling of research findings on the importance of this meal:

- *Better school performance: Children who eat breakfast have better reading, math and standardized test scores, according to the Journal of the American Dietetic Association.*
- *Boost short-term memory: The Journal of Adolescent Health covered a study of 319 teens (ages 13 to 20) that showed increased memory for those who ate a high-protein breakfast. Conversely, a high-caloric breakfast adversely affected concentration.*
- *Weight control: Breakfast-skippers are 4.5 times more likely to be obese, according to the American Journal of Epidemiology.*

Or catch this. In 2003, researchers at the UK's Reading University found that 9- to 16-year-olds who eat a sugary breakfast and fizzy drinks do tasks in school at the level of a 70-year-old!

VIRTUES COOKING TIP:

spontaneity

With all the daily hustle, it's easy to neglect the virtue of **spontaneity**. So free up time and make Playful Pancakes. A child will delight in choosing the shapes—his or her initials or a silly animal, for instance. Even teens find this fun!

PLAYFUL PANCAKES

serves 4 to 6

2 cups all-purpose flour
½ teaspoon salt
1½ teaspoon baking soda
1 teaspoon sugar
2 cups buttermilk
2 tablespoons vegetable oil
2 large egg yolks
2 egg whites

Mix the dry ingredients—flour, salt, baking soda and sugar—in a small bowl and set aside. In a larger bowl, combine the buttermilk, oil and egg yolks. Whisk the dry ingredients into this mixture and set aside. In the bowl of an electric mixer, beat the egg whites until stiff, then gently fold them into the pancake batter.

Heat a large sauté pan over medium heat, add a generous amount of butter *(it makes edges crispy)* and pour batter into two-to-three-inch rounds, flipping once; or, better yet, form initials or creative shapes. Serve with butter and real maple syrup.

If pressed for time, use pancake mix. My favorite is from New Hope Mills, operated since 1823 in upstate New York.

4) enthusiasm

The Inside Scoop on Toast

One Saturday morning Gene begged Dad to make his favorite breakfast, Inside-Out Toast. "Let's see if I've got the right ingredients and tools," said Dad scrunching up his eyebrows and looking around. He lifted a menacing-looking, eight-inch serrated knife from the breadboard near the toaster. Waving the knife theatrically in the air, he acted as if he were fighting with an imaginary burglar, and stabbed at the air.

"Be careful, John," Momma said. "Not too wild."

All four of us kids gasped as we watched the gyrations of the knife, our heads swaying and bobbing as we followed its movements up and down, and circling around. This could be quite a show, I thought, and it's not even eight in the morning.

"Good, my knife is handy," he said, now securing it back safely in a slot on the breadboard. "I'll need it later for several important steps."

Dad leapt from the table and walked a dozen or so steps in a crouched, policeman-on-the-prowl position; he stopped in our galley-shaped kitchen. Dad was on patrol. Glancing to the right, to the left, he walked a few more steps and then peered into the yellow tin breadbox painted with daisies. Out he pulled... a loaf of Wonder Bread.

All this high-stakes drama was because Dad liked our mornings to start with bucketfuls of... enthusiasm. Like his emphasis on humor, this virtue was key in setting an upbeat tone for the day. Soon back at what he called Command Center (actually only his seat at the head of the table), he used the long knife energetically to slash open the Wonder Bread. Out came several slices.

The virtue of **ENTHUSIASM** *brings out an electric, eager, excited feeling. Can't you just feel its EEEExuberance?*

"This white bread is essential for Inside-Out Toast," he said, again putting away the knife. "You'll soon taste the *wonders* of Wonder Bread."

Dad toasted two pieces lightly, and once more the knife came into play. Using exaggerated motions, he sawed a hot slice of the bread lengthwise, essentially down its inside. "I have only one more step to go," he said. "I need to heap on grease." That was his expression for butter. After smearing on several knifefuls, he added a swipe of raspberry jam and put the two toasted sides of the toast together, the greased outside now on the inside.

With great ceremony, Dad put this still-steamy concoction on a small tan plastic plate and passed it to the youngest among us, Gene. "Eat it before it cools," he said, as if instructions were necessary.

We all peered at Gene... waiting.

A true showman, our six-year-old brother lifted the Inside-Out Toast to his mouth, slowly bit down into the layers, slowly munched and munched and munched. Slowly bit again. Slowly passed back the plate and said, "Nice work, Pop."

Gene knew he was almost always the first stop when the plastic plate was passed, the *de facto* Little Prince of the Table. He had that winning position locked up. As for us, the hungry siblings, we were leaning so far forward in our chairs, so intent, looking so far down into Gene's grinning mouth as he'd scoffed the last crunchy bit of

Inside-Out Toast, that to ask for a slice ourselves at this point, well, forget it.

Our brother, legally blind and wearing coke-bottle-thick glasses, was empowered by family dynamics with his protective mother to his left and father to his right. Gene had been a premie, weighing only two pounds, fourteen ounces at birth (that's the weight of two containers of butter and a small apple or two) and had spent his first three months in a hospital incubator. Ever since then our parents had shoveled bucket-loads of food into him, today included. So, although his poor eyesight didn't exactly set him up as an example of survival of the fittest (Charles Darwin aboard *HMS Beagle*, please take note of the power of modern medicine and hovering parents), this evolutionary model with dutiful parents had merit, too.

Savoring the moment, Gene repeated, "Yup, Pop, nice work. Got more?"

Despite my having to wait many minutes more for Inside-Out Toast, I knew this was a standout breakfast. So one Saturday, Gene and I stepped over the makeshift train of bikes and wagons cluttering the driveway and marched up Chase Avenue, for some bragging. We banged on the door of our neighbors, the Whites, and confronted their children: "Our dad makes the best Inside-Out Toast in the world! Bet your dad doesn't know how to cook."

Of course, the three kids had never heard of Inside-Out Toast. But competition can be a heady motivator in the South, even among polite, well-mannered youngsters, and so not to be outdone, they rang our doorbell early the next Saturday and pulled extra chairs over to our long table and asked, "Mista Alllll-cott, can we try your Inside-Out Toast?"

Again, Dad made a big deal of vigorously cutting the toasted slices with "my dan-ger-ous, per-il-ous, haz-ard-ous knife." To his credit, he did show more restraint before dropping it with a big clattering clank onto the breadboard. He then schooled them on the grease. "Only use the best butter and then add raspberry jam."

"Thank you, Mista Alllll-cott," said Missy, the eldest, in her sweet Southern drawl, after all of them smacked their way through several pieces. And, presto, off they flew up the dirt road.

Less than an hour later, when Mom answered the doorbell, we heard, "Miss

> *Enthusiasm is a way of praying. It is what binds us to the Heaven and to Earth, to grown-ups, and to children; it is what tells us that our desires are important and deserve our best efforts. It is enthusiasm that reaffirms to us that everything is possible, as long as we are totally committed to what we are doing.*
>
> –Paulo Coelho

June, can we come back in?" It was the Whites... flecks of sugar now sticking to their cheeks, pinked up from running all the way to our house. They swaggered into our kitchen and announced: "Our dad's Inside-Out Toast is better than yours. He wins! He uses butter *and* sugar *and* cinnamon. Our grease tastes better than yours."

"My dad rules," Gene shouted fiercely. "He's the King of Inside-Out Toast! He's the... he's the... he's the inventor."

"Yeah," I yelled in support. "Our dad is king!"

Dad started to laugh. Once more he gathered us kids at the table; he wanted to placate the Whites; stop all the bickering. He fired more Wonder Bread into the toaster and located the sugar and a small container of cinnamon among the spices above the old GE stove. Out came his knife for another Inside-Out Toast taste-testing, this time to check out Sheldon White's sugary creation.

"Not bad, not bad at all," Dad grinned trying a sample. "The sugary crunch on the bread and that all-is-right-in-the-world smell of cinnamon *do* bring out the wonders of Wonder Bread. Tell your dad that we like this new grease. Tell him I approve."

All of the huffing, strutting, chest-beating over our fathers subsided. Vanished. At heart we knew it was all in fun, a high-spirited—very enthusiastic—commotion over toast. And there was nothing namby-pamby, wishy-washy, milk-toasty, about any of us. A little later that month we heard that Sheldon, who'd never done much cooking before, had started making breakfast regularly on Sunday for his family. He cooked up scrambled eggs and bacon, creamy Southern grits, and regular toasted Wonder Bread.

When it comes to enthusiasm playing out over breakfast, the possibilities are endless. But there can only be one true King of Inside-Out Toast... you hear!

" *Enthusiasm is the mother of effort, and without it nothing great was ever achieved.* "

–Ralph Waldo Emerson

food facts:

UNCLE ALCOTT LOVED BRAN AND RECESS...

One day Dad revealed several surprises about our family history. "Our distant relative Amos Bronson Alcott was an early advocate of healthy eating," said Dad. Alcott promoted eating bran, we learned, with all its vitamins and minerals. He didn't believe in the steak and mush pie breakfasts of the 1800s that contributed to widespread dyspepsia, a fancy word for gassy indigestion.

"Ahhh yes," Dad continued. "Uncle Alcott was the father of Louisa May Alcott who wrote Little Women. He was a well-known Transcendental philosopher and educator. Some called him 'America's Socrates' and 'the Plato of our time,' and he deeply influenced Emerson and Thoreau."

The part of the story we liked best, though, was that Uncle Alcott is credited with popularizing recess. "Alcott was the first in America to start recess in school. He thought children could learn better if they have time to play, socialize and eat well."

INSIDE-OUT TOAST

———

serves 4

8 slices thick store-bought white bread
4 tablespoons "grease" *(a.k.a., butter)*
¼ cup sugar
1 teaspoon cinnamon

Lightly toast two pieces of bread. Now rev up excitement by ceremoniously and carefully using a large serrated knife to split the toast lengthwise down the inside.

Add "grease" or butter to one of the still-warm toasted sides and sprinkle on small amounts of sugar and cinnamon. Put the toasted sides together and present to your family and friends. *Voilà*, Inside-Out Toast.

A family taste-testing is a great way to select the best filling. Our family preferred buttery "grease" and raspberry jam until neighbor kids suggested crunchy sugar and cinnamon.

VIRTUES COOKING TIP:

enthusiasm

From the Greek words for "god within" (en for "within" and theos for "god"), **enthusiasm** is the spark that ignites activity. When life is in a grey, dull zone use this virtue with kids to dial up enthusiasm, over goofy Inside-Out Toast.

5) resourcefulness

RAUCOUS AND WILD IN THE KITCHEN

"Shall we write a book this morning?" asked Dad. Wearing a sleeveless, ribbed t-shirt and baggy jeans hitched high by a belt around his waist, he was sitting at the kitchen table, a magical place where just about anything could happen—that is, for children encouraged to be resourceful.

Breakfast had finished long ago. The four of us kids had time, nothing planned and a ton of energy. There was no competition from TV (didn't own one then), telephone (only a black rotary phone on a party line), video games (not mass produced yet) or personal computers (ditto). With no school on the weekend, time played out before us in abundance. And Dad was at the idea switch, ready to kick-start our day and rocket our thoughts into high orbit like Explorer 1, the U.S. satellite still circling Earth.

"I've a suggestion," he said, pretending to be serious. "What about writing a little book called *How to Get Rid of Unwanted Household Guests?*"

I held my breath. Oh, no. Did Momma hear?

Just moments earlier she had placed two plates of hot Sticky Cinnamon Buns, bubbling with a caramel-raisin-pecan topping, to cool on the table. "No pinching at the edges!" she'd instructed before heading to her bedroom to put on a dress. "Those sticky buns are to welcome Great Aunt Mercedes when we return from the airport."

Having heard Momma's earlier admonition to "be resourceful," my older sister Liz and I had helped make those sticky buns. We'd shelled the pecans and dug out the meat, careful not to leave behind any bitter, tough pieces that might, as Momma had said, "send Aunt Mercedes, cracked tooth in hand, to the dentist." And while our mother had prepared the sweet dough, Liz had mixed the pecans with butter, brown sugar and raisins for the topping. I'd smushed spoonfuls of it around the pans, and kept imagining my first bite, so gooey and good. No mistake, these sticky buns were a rare indulgence, our mother's most-delicious breakfast treat.

*As a virtue, **RESOURCEFULNESS** digs deep in both mundane and challenging situations.*

Now what exactly had Momma overheard, I wondered anxiously. Was she sputtering mad at Dad for his stirring up trouble over the arrival of her relative, the matronly spinster from Minneapolis? Or possibly upset at my younger brother Gene for hearing him say, "Aunt Mercedes' corkscrew-curly hair makes her look like Puddles that old white poodle of hers." Fortunately, no fired-up reprimand burst from the bedroom, and I exhaled a long sigh. She hadn't heard anything.

Absentmindedly, Dad peered at a pile of nearby sketches he'd made. Still lost in thought, he reached then for some blank paper and a felt-tip pen, and drew a picture of us holding up the cinnamon buns as we greeted our rotund aunt and her headful of curls. But wait, he sketched her arms filled with packages, fancily wrapped presents. Suddenly, I wanted gift-bearing Aunt Mercedes to stay for a long time. Still, Gene had taken up Dad's challenge for a book about unwanted guests and was itching for trouble. "Yee-haw, here's an idea," he said boisterously. "We could start the book with our best technique, the No. 1 way to get rid of unwanted guests. Gather up all the dead flies on the window sills; you know, search behind the curtains. Dozens are there with bulging green eyes and stiff wings. Put them in ice trays, fill 'er up with water and freeze 'em. When the time is right, you toss the cubes into orange juice. 'Hello dear Aunt Mer-ce-des, are you thirsty?'"

Gene then made gulping sounds, as if imitating our spinster aunt choking after noticing an insect in her juice. He rolled his eyes back in his head, pretended to swoon and rousing himself said, "It would rid us of flies and keep that ol' lady from sleeping in my bedroom. She'd catch the next plane home."

Now we were actually worried about our orange juice. You never knew with Gene. I inspected the remainder of my juice for dark specks, for wings. Nothing. Liz took her spoon and stirred around the orange liquid, then leaned over and did the same with Johnny's glass. Again, nothing.

Dad's silly book-making projects were solely for personal entertainment, never professionally published. Most never went beyond the idea stage. They were part of our parents way to make us resourceful in dealing with new situations and ideas—and to let off steam. Still, Dad's "unwanted guests" idea had skidded way off track. Having some lighthearted fun with Aunt Mercedes's arrival was his intent, while keeping a close eye on Gene. Wild and rambunctious, quick to frustrate, Gene had only recently started elementary school and felt like an outsider, distanced from the other students by near blindness and thick glasses. Dad pulled out one of his sketchbooks and pushed it and a box of stubby crayons toward Gene. "Why don't you make some pictures for the book."

Just then Momma walked by, fastening her earrings. "I've a better idea," said Dad loudly. "Johnny, Gene and I can write a book called *The Boys' Book of Inventions.* You remember that flat tire on my Datsun last week? Our book could have a chapter about new-fangled jacks to lift cars."

"What about a device like a super-strong air mattress?" suggested Johnny. "You put it under the car and attach multiple air hoses; all six of us could have our own hose and blow at once. Psst, psst, as the mattress inflates, the car rises up. It's easy now to change the tire. This idea will be great for our book."

Using a black crayon Gene sketched the big bold outlines of a car perched atop an oversized air mattress, at least that's what he said the big black blob was. His head was tilted to the side so his good eye was close to the page and the center of his thick lenses focused on each crayon stroke, his head moving constantly. Meanwhile,

Johnny started to turn his idea into a story. "A dangerous flaw in the air chambers keeps the mattress swelling way beyond its limits," he continued. "The Datsun is soon looming way, way, way up. It's risen ten feet in the air."

"What happens next?" prodded Dad. "Anything exciting?"

"Pop, it's gonna pop," exclaimed Gene. "Watch out, Pop." He was aware of the funny repetition of the word pop. With that he picked up a red crayon and drew a jagged gash in his sketch of the air mattress.

"Oops," he shrieked, thinking of how the car would tumble. "Oops, oops. The car is falling. Car-ash! You'll need a new tire and a new rear end and a new chrome bumper.

"Hey, Mom," continued Gene; his arms flapped out toward the sticky buns like a hungry baby bird who'd just noticed the return of its worm-carrying mother. "We're starving here. Can't we have one sticky bun? Please, please?"

Unable to resist Gene's plea (after all, he was once an emaciated premie), Momma scooted one plate of sticky buns toward us. Eight hands dove in, followed by Dad's. All of us, even Dad, were in kiddie food heaven: enjoying a swirl of ooey-gooey sweet caramel and raisins, a crunch of pecan, and a warm smooch from the sticky bun. We munched. We chatted about chapters for the invention book... at this most wonderful table.

And what a table it was. When butter fell from Dad's breakfast toast-flinging or jam left a skittering smudge, when a tall plastic glass of milk spilled, no concerns. This was no 200-year-old antique from Colonial Williamsburg. Our table should have held a special certificate, though. Momma was that proud of her creation. For the design, she'd selected a ten-foot-long oatmeal-colored composite material and added a smooth wooden edge, and it sat atop two black sawhorses. A touch of modernism.

Big enough to seat twelve for a roast turkey Christmas dinner.

Big enough to hold dozens of dishes for Art Department parties.

Big enough to stage a one-ring circus. On a rainy summer day, after much parental prodding, again with resourcefulness in mind ("what are *you* planning to do indoors today?"), Gene and I had transformed the table into the setting for our own mini-Ringling Bros. "Greatest Show on Earth" extravaganza. In charge of the snack bar, Momma warmed milk for hot chocolate and opened tins of homemade cookies. And soon the show was on….

For the Awesome Allcott Circus, so named by Gene after our family, we festooned the table with posters. Dad did a picture of an always-in-trouble clumsy bear, "J.B." (That was for John Bear, the name of his alter ego's cartoon character.) Star billing also went to several dangerous animals that I singled out: to Miss Scamp, "a very small, very ferocious lion from far distant Siam"; to Misty, "a bad-tempered ghostly dog whose history of nasty bites can be traced back to Weimar, Germany"; and to "an American viper with piercing fangs and a fast-acting poison."

"Look closely at this wicked, this venomous snake from the U.S. of A.," I said in what I hoped sounded like the deep voice of a circus ringmaster. I strutted alongside the table, and in my hand I bounced a very thin, very scared, very harmless snake. "It was captured on a dried-up creek bed in the woods behind the house and may look like a garter snake, but it is... DEAD-ly. (Dramatic roll of the eyes.) This snake is more poisonous than all the copperheads in Carolina."

"Watch me," insisted Gene. He gave a shove as he pushed past me. "Are you watching me?"

He'd stuck the family's Siamese cat in a doll stroller and did a loop around our Weimaraner dog sleeping on the floor. "Watch this man-eating, this child-eating... oops, drat. Watch this hot-milk-drinking lion!"

As the cat landed on the table, next to Gene's mug of chocolate milk, Dad couldn't resist the fun. "Just a minute," he said. "I want you to see my favorite circus." On a small ceramic side table he dug among several books and pulled out a catalogue for New York City's Whitney Museum. What did he show us? A photo of a miniature wire-and-paper circus by artist Alexander Calder. "For his circus, Calder created tiny lions and trapeze artists, and an ambulance for injuries. Other performers, too."

With that Momma went to the craft shelf in her sewing closet; she pulled out pipe cleaners and telephone wire, glitter, and piles of red, yellow, green and brown construction paper. Inspired thus, we created our own troupe of clowns, acrobats and lion-tamers, and encircled them with wooden blocks, like in a real one-ring circus, all created (resourcefully) on Momma's magnificent table.

*T*he table's blank surface offered armloads of possibilities beyond food. It could be an art studio, a lecture hall, a publishing house for zany books. A library stacked with magazines, textbooks, and space for homework. An atelier to sew dresses, or for jewelry-making and basket-weaving. A petting zoo. A sports arena—our heads tilted toward the radio to better hear UNC's high-intensity basketball games. Or an opera house with live FM broadcasts from New York's Metropolitan Opera, on Saturdays. And, of course, the home of the Awesome Allcott Circus.

We grew ever more resourceful around that ordinary, extraordinary table, pursuing our own interests... all together. And it was here more than elsewhere—daily, weekly, monthly, yearly—that our parents launched ideas to feed resourcefulness. This transformed us, especially Gene. "Mr. Watch Me" wasn't a bad apple; he was merely an insecure little guy who needed guidance in order to become a fearless, ever-resourceful tamer of life's lions.

As for Great Aunt Mercedes, we greeted her with the remaining plate of Sticky Cinnamon Buns and gave her a truly warm, bun-sticky welcome.

STICKY CINNAMON BUNS

yields 18 buns

buns

5½+ cups all-purpose flour, *unsifted*
¾ cup sugar
1 teaspoon salt
3 packages active dry yeast
½ cup butter *(1 stick)*, room temperature
1 cup very warm water
3 large eggs, room temperature
2 tablespoons butter, *melted*
½ cup dark brown sugar
1 tablespoon cinnamon
½ cup raisins

pecan topping

½ cup butter *(1 stick)*
1 cup dark brown sugar
1 cup pecan pieces

You can freeze the second pan for up to a month. Before the dough has risen cover the pan tightly with plastic wrap and aluminum foil, and freeze. When ready to use, remove and let stand for about 3 hours to defrost and then follow direction for rising and baking.

First, prepare two 9-inch round cake pans with the **Pecan Topping** *(see below)* and set aside. Then in the bowl of an electric mixer, mix 1¼ cups flour and the sugar, salt and yeast. Add butter, stirring. Slowly add warm water and beat on medium for 2 minutes. Add eggs and ¼ cup more flour, scraping sides. Beat on high for 2 minutes more, again scraping. Stir in several more cups of flour until a soft dough is formed. Knead on a floured board until elastic, about 10 minutes. Take half the dough and roll into a rectangle *(about 9 x 14-inches)*, brush with melted butter and sprinkle with brown sugar, cinnamon and raisins. Roll up from one of the 9-inch ends and form a tube; cut into nine 1-inch pieces and seal edges. Put pieces in a pan, spiral side up, atop the Pecan Topping. Repeat for second pan.

Rising and Baking:

In a warm area, let the buns double in size, about an hour. Bake in preheated oven at 375 degrees for 25 to 30 minutes, until golden brown. After cooling for 10 minutes, flip the pans over onto a plate and scoop out any remaining caramelized topping for the top.

Pecan Topping

In a small saucepan, melt butter over low heat. Add brown sugar and stir until sugar is dissolved. Pour into cake pans. Sprinkle the bottom with pecan pieces and set aside.

VIRTUES COOKING TIP:

resourcefulness

Think about it: this prized virtue, **resourcefulness**,
frequently hides from sight. It needs discovery. To
encourage this virtue ask children to be your "helping
hands" and make Sticky Cinnamon Buns.

6) hope

The Soup Factory on Chase Avenue

My mother's relationship with soup was both practical and mysterious. And if things got really rough—that choppy "white rater rapids" stuff of life—then she returned to soup, for hope.

Early on in her years of cooking, Momma discovered a simple truth. You could either make a meal with, say, a meat, two vegetables and something starchy like potatoes, messing up four or more pots and pans, or you could heap it all together and, *voilà, potage.* We had lots and lots of soup growing up.

As to the mysterious part, the rare winter snowfall where we lived in the South somehow triggered Momma's "time to make soup" button. It was like a mathematical equation: 2 inches of snow = 8 quarts of Russian borscht.

The hope part? That will be cleared up shortly.

One day, a few weeks before Christmas, snowflakes started to fall. Momma was recovering from hip surgery, still achy and only recently out of bed, but she asked

Dad to get out her soup pot and set it up on the stove; it was so large (16 quarts) that it looked like a witch's caldron. She slowly ladled in cup after cup of beef stock and heaved in six large beets oozing with bright-red juice. She shredded a human-sized head of cabbage. She hacked into several pounds of still-frozen beef, likely a chuck roast pulled from the depths of the ancient freezer. Carrots, onions and potatoes also bobbed in her brew.

None of these ingredients were exactly kid-friendly, and actually the thought of eating it was stomach-churning. Besides, with reports in the news about the Cold War and Khrushchev saying that the Communists would bury America, it seemed to us kids that fixing Russian borscht—and eating it—was, well, un-American.

HOPE is a virtue full of expectation and desire.

"What's wrong with a can of Campbell's chicken noodle soup?" I asked Momma real politely. "Or plain ol' Campbell's tomato soup with grated cheddar on top?"

I got that look, as if I didn't know what was good for me. Still, I'd heard that Commies and witches were close by. We needed to be vigilant. A classmate, who'd heard it from another friend, told me that FBI agents were at the University of North Carolina going through student records, looking for suspicious left-leaning political activity. Then my middle school teacher had shocked our English class by saying her daughter-in-law was a witch, a member of Wicca. And now with strands of red hair popping out of her usually meticulous French twist, Momma looked questionable herself. She was turning our home on Chase Avenue into a soup factory and churning out buckets of soup, in a worrisome witch-like pot.

I told Momma my concerns. "Once again, Bitty, your over-active imagination is hard at work," she said with a sigh, using her nickname for me. "Grammy Chloupek made this soup, as did her mother and grandmothers. It's among the hearty meals made by our Czechoslovakian ancestors. Calling it Russian borscht is just easier."

There was a weariness about Momma these days, an impatience. She had always been the no-nonsense, get-the-job-done-now parent. Dad was more for humor, enthusiasm and day-dreaming, an extra hug. He always found time for sketching, storytelling and piano-playing on the upright Chickering in the living room. But Momma's mood was wintery. Her newly fused hip had required her to spend months flat on her back in a body cast, from just under her shoulders to down past both knees; and now she expected us "to get with it" and "please, not another one of your wild flights of fancy, El-in-or."

So as she limped over to the kitchen table to put out a large blue Jugtown bowl filled with borscht, along with a smaller Jugtown dish of sour cream and an even smaller one with dried dill from our garden, I became quiet. I was skating on thin ice. Again. I ladled out just enough soup in my dish so as not to look ungrateful, hiding those bloody-looking beets under a topping of sour cream and dill, which I did like. Cautiously, I peeped out, "After soup, I can go outside by myself and sled." I finished eating as fast as possible.

As I put my bowl into the kitchen sink, a few beets still clinging stubbornly to the bottom, I overheard Momma say to Dad, "What should I do now? Making this soup and doing a little cooking helped. But how can I get our family back on its feet after my surgery has disrupted everyone's life, especially my own? I need to sink my teeth into something substantial."

*T*he previous Christmas was when Momma first told us about the operation. "I'll spend about a month in the hospital before recuperating at home," she'd said matter-of-factly. She then clammed up and slowly studied each of our four faces. And just like the lyrics of "Silent Night," all was calm, all was bright, at least on the surface. Talk about a surprise, though; none of us kids had known she needed surgery nor did we suspect her right hip throbbed constantly as the joint deteriorated. Her pronounced limp, we were merely told, was caused by a disease similar to polio that had kept her bedridden as a child for months.

Noticing our puzzled looks now and Momma's silence, Dad gave a half-smile and picked up the conversation. "Aunt Jo will move in during that time," he said, referring to a friend's aunt who helped out in emergencies. "Grammy Chloupek will also come from Illinois for several weeks, and Millard will drive Nannie over each day in his big Cadillac, to clean and cook. With Nannie in the kitchen the food will be

Southern—crispy fried chicken, pork chops covered in gravy, shrimp and grits.

"All families go through rough patches," he continued. "You should know that after surgery Mom will be in a cast for about nine months. That's where hope comes in. Sometimes to make things better, people have to endure difficult procedures, hard things like operations. Hope is what keeps you going."

During the following glum meals without Momma around, Dad reported on her progress at the hospital and gathered up our homemade cards to cheer her. We tried to be hopeful. But the hours dragged. Finally, our six-foot-long "Welcome Home Mom" banner greeted her as she was brought up the front stone stairs on a stretcher, step by careful step. Momma was settled into a hospital bed in a bedroom at the end of the house, and we dutifully went to visit and did homework next to her and tried to chat; we folded endless Japanese origami birds with her.

"It doesn't feel right," said my younger brother Gene. "Mom never laughs any more, and she looks white, like a ghost."

One day while helping my older brother Johnny burn trash outside, a chore he did weekly, an airborne piece of paper set my tights on fire. I had to be rushed to the hospital's emergency room. Second degree blisters bubbled my right kneecap. After I got home that afternoon I hobbled to Momma's bedroom, a thick gauze bandage immobilizing my knee. I wanted to be brave, too.

"It was an accident, Momma," I said soberly. "A gust of wind picked up some burning trash that landed on my clothes. Johnny was smart. He told me what he'd learned in Boy Scouts, to 'stop, drop and roll.'"

"I heard your screams," she said softly. "I'm so sorry. There was nothing I could do."

Out of sight in my bedroom I cried. When I walked, even slightly bending the knee cracked open the raw skin. Dad found me red-eyed. Again, he talked about hope. "Mom's long and painful recovery doesn't lessen your burned knee and all the hurt it's causing you," he said. "You need time to heal but, trust me, you and Mom will both get better.

"Let me think," he continued. "Dr. Dad orders, hmmm... a large piece of

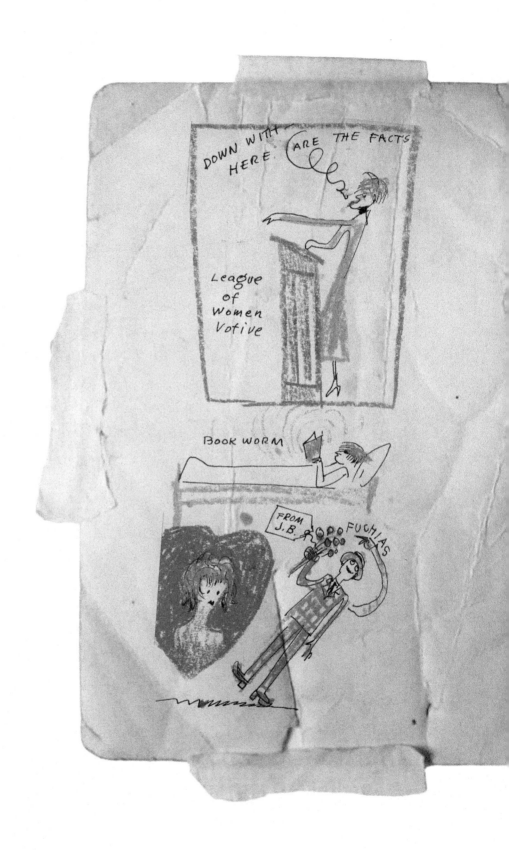

Nannie's freshly made pecan pie, right now."

*D*ad's confidence, his silly prescription for dessert at four o'clock that miserable afternoon, helped me latch onto hope… by eating pie. For Momma, hope sprouted many months later in that unexpected December snowfall and it started to blossom around her making borscht. For a precious few hours, she returned to her Command Center in the kitchen with kids close by.

A week later another culinary tradition fortunately jump-started hope: Christmas cookie-baking. On the screened porch off the kitchen Dad had stockpiled five-pound bags of flour; boxes of white, brown and powdered sugar; bags of nuts and candied and fresh fruits; jars of fresh spices—cinnamon, cardamom, cloves and nutmeg—and vanilla from Mexico. My sister, Liz, and I picked up nutcrackers and shucked pecans and walnuts. Johnny greased cookie trays and popped paper liners into muffin tins, and Gene, who'd truly been out of sorts for months as Momma lay immobilized on her back, volunteered to be the "Boy Taster" for any cookies she might make.

Momma hobbled over to the turntable in the living room and had a record soon spinning of soprano Leontyne Price's "O Holy Night." We watched her lean into a bowl of cookie dough, the toes of her right foot bouncing lightly to the music. And then drawing us in, she said, "Can you beat these egg whites until they're stiff?" And "Dust the chocolates in a few shakes of powdered sugar," and "Chill this batter in the fridge and then we'll bake it."

Our home filled with aromas. It was the cinnamony and cardamomy smell of Christmas. The scents curled into the rooms; they wrapped welcomingly around us. After years of pain, Momma was coming back to life. She read us Christmas stories. She sang carols that Dad played on the piano. And she invited an elderly church friend, Miss Doak, to join us for Christmas Eve supper.

"We wouldn't want her to be alone, would we?" asked Momma. "Our Christmas Eve meal is so special to me."

By Christmas Eve, our Southern Part of Heaven, as Chapel Hill is known, had warmed to a glorious nonwintery sixty degrees. With Momma we decorated our tree—actually three scrawny pines that we'd cut with Dad on the hillside below our home and wired together—with colorful origami cranes, all hand-folded while she was in bed. She reminded us merrily, as we hung up dozens of the colorful paper birds, that we'd once festooned a Christmas tree with white sand dollars and large shark teeth found on North Carolina's Outer Banks.

"That's weird," said Gene. "Sand dollars? Shark teeth?" He was too young to remember those decorations, but was now happily filling the tree's lower branches with the origami cranes.

Again Dad brought out Momma's super-sized soup pot, this time for Pea Soup. Hearty and tasty, our family's traditional Christmas Eve meal, the soup swirled soon with green peas, orange flecks of carrot and salty ham chunks. This time her soup-making felt festive, for everyone. And we watched her roast up a tray of garlicky croutons.

"Make special wishes as you toss the croutons onto the pea soup," Momma said lightly that night. We were gathered, finally, for Christmas Eve supper. Miss Doak sat at the other end of the kitchen table, which was decorated now with leftover origami birds, strings of red cranberries and white popcorn, and an assortment of ornaments. "A head start on wish-making for the New Year, on resolutions, would energize us all. Personally, I'm thinking of something big...."

"And Elinor," she said as we finished the soup, "can you put together a large plate of cookies?" A heaping platter of those cookies was the traditional companion food for Christmas Eve Pea Soup. Heading to the porch, I picked up an armload of tins stacked on the picnic table and opened them. I stood still, uncharacteristic for me, and counted the varieties: chocolate Toffee Bars, our neighbor Tera White's mouth-puckering Lemon Bars, tiny meringues, crunchy Springerle, itsy-bitsy fruitcakes, intoxicating rum balls (or so I thought), rich gingerbread, hazelnut sandwich cookies, apricot thumbprint cookies and the real standout, Aunt Dorothy's Holiday Cookies (more on them later)....

Thanks to culinary traditions, hope could make a most wondrous appearance.

hope

Hope is fragile at times and needs encouragement. Lift family spirits by talking over comfort food like Pea Soup. With each warm spoonful, your kids' dreams can take hold. So divine, soup.

PEA SOUP

serves 6

1 pound dried split green peas
1 cup onions, *chopped*
2 cups carrots, *diced*
1 cup celery, *diced*
2 cloves garlic, *minced*
⅛ cup good olive oil
4 cups chicken stock
4 cups water
1 bay leaf
1 teaspoon sea salt
1 teaspoon freshly ground pepper

If you don't have split peas and want something quick, what about **Ginger Carrot Soup**? Chances are the ingredients are handy: 1 medium onion *(diced)*, 4 – 6 cups of carrots *(sliced)*, 1 tablespoon *(or more)* fresh ginger, 1½ quarts chicken broth and 4 ounces of cream cheese. Sauté onions and add carrots, ginger and chicken broth; cook for half an hour until carrots are tender. Stir in cream cheese and, using an electric emulsifier, liquefy the soup. Salt and pepper to taste.

Put the split peas in a strainer, rinse under cold water and set aside. *(Note: be sure to check the bag for special cooking instructions.)* In a 4-quart stockpot, lightly cook the onions, carrots, celery and garlic in olive oil for 10 to 15 minutes. Add the split peas, chicken stock, water and seasonings to the pot and, after bringing to a boil, simmer for 40 to 60 minutes. Skim off any foam. Peas should end up soft but not mushy. The soup can be served as is or, for a creamier texture, do several short bursts with an electric emulsifier. Serve with garlic croutons.

Garlic Croutons

Preheat oven to 350 degrees. Use seeded rye and other bread, whatever is in your refrigerator. Dice bread into 1-inch pieces—about 8 cups in all—and set aside in a bowl. In a large metal roasting pan, add ¼ cup olive oil, 4 tablespoons butter and about 5 cloves of minced garlic. Set the pan in the oven for several minutes until butter melts, then remove. Add the bread cubes and stir. Bake for 20 to 30 minutes stirring occasionally. The croutons should be crispy and golden. They keep well in a ziplock bag in the fridge and are superb also on salad.

cookies:
sweet hope for
the holidays

LEMON BARS

yields 24 bars

crust

1 cup butter or margarine, *room temperature*
2 cups all-purpose flour
¼ cup powdered sugar
⅛ teaspoon salt

filling

4 large eggs, *room temperature*
2 cups granulated sugar
1 teaspoon baking powder
½ cup all-purpose flour
1 teaspoon corn starch
4 lemons: *zest the rind and squeeze for 1 cup juice*
¼ cup powdered sugar

Preheat oven to 350 degrees. Line a 9 x 13 x 2-inch baking pan with aluminum foil. In a small bowl, mix the butter with 2 cups of flour, powdered sugar and salt. Use two knives and cut back and forth with the same motion as if making a pie crust; aim for pea-sized lumps. Pack into the bottom of the pan. Bake for 15 to 20 minutes until lightly golden; remove pan from oven and cool.

In the bowl of an electric mixer, beat together the eggs, granulated sugar, baking powder, ½ cup flour, corn starch and lemon juice and zest. The filling should be light and foamy. Pour over the crust and bake for 30 to 35 minutes until firm. While still warm, cut into squares, dust with powdered sugar and store in fridge.

TOFFEE BARS

yields 24 bars

1 cup butter, room temperature
1 cup brown sugar
1 teaspoon pure vanilla extract
2 cups sifted flour
½ teaspoon salt
6 ounces semisweet chocolate bits
1 cup pecans, chopped

Preheat oven to 350 degrees. Cream butter, brown sugar and vanilla in a mixing bowl until light and fluffy. Add flour and salt, and mix well. Stir in chocolate bits and pecans. Spread into a 9 x 13 x 2-inch baking pan, either greased or lined with aluminum foil. Bake for 20 to 25 minutes. While warm, cut into bars and then cool in the pan.

7) idealism

MOMMA STIRS THINGS UP

In the early 1960s, on a summery evening that seemed just like the previous one and the one before it, a half-eaten apple pie still on the kitchen table, Momma said, "I've something to tell you, something exciting for me."

Well, the thought of something E-X-C-I-T-I-N-G got our attention. But what she said next set off firecrackers of worry. "Like you, I'm going to be a student this fall," she explained. "I'm heading back to college."

There was a long pause, Gene looking at me in disbelief. With our college-age sister Liz off painting houses at an American Friends Service work camp in Mexico, the three of us still at home were spread between elementary, middle and high school—all with different needs and perspectives. Gene, the youngest, was first to voice his concerns. "No way," he blurted out. "Who'll look after me?"

I piped in rapid-fire with my own worries: "This isn't a good idea. We've just got you back in our lives, Momma. For a horrible year you were in bed after hip surgery and couldn't do neat stuff or drive us around. No, this isn't good for us."

"I guess it will be okay," said Johnny. In high school, he had been reading about women's growing dissatisfaction with stay-at-home lives and knew that changes were happening across the country. "You'll be one of those new feminists, won't you?"

Seeing such frowns of concern made Dad laugh. Not in a mean way. His levity merely signaled that all would be fine. "She'll be helping me, well, bring home the bacon," he said with a chuckle. He reminded us that not only did Momma have a B.A. in Art History from the University of Chicago, but she had an advanced degree from the Winnetka Graduate Teachers College and had been an instructor at an experimental school in Menlo Park, Calif. "It hasn't been easy for your mother in the South," he added. "She's a go-getter, and while most women around us don't have jobs she misses the sense of accomplishment that comes with work. Remember, before you were born, she was a teacher."

The virtue of IDEALISM aims high with a vision of what might be.

"After surgery and months of time flat on my back to think," explained Momma, "you might say I got a bee in my bonnet. More women students than ever are attending UNC, and I started to dream about applying to the university myself. It's idealistic, I know, but I want to become a guidance counselor and help young coeds, young men too, make smart career choices."

This wasn't a situation, we realized, where we got a vote. We'd just have to adapt. She was always giving us orders about what to do, and now she could be like a boss to hundreds of college students. "I'll still be home a lot," said Momma. "And your Dad has flexibility in his teaching schedule. He'll be only a five-minute drive away. You'll barely know anything has changed."

One other thing was stressed. Since Gene was still in elementary school, one parent would always be home to meet his bus, someone who would also get him a... snack. Always hungry, already back to thinking about his stomach, Gene asked, "Is there more pie for me?"

And that's how an earthquake of change—a magnitude 6.0 on our home

Richter scale—rattled 301 Chase Avenue. The news shook up the household: a big idea, a plan of action and change.

Our entire southern world, where men in Chapel Hill still tipped their hats on Franklin Street to white-glove-wearing ladies, was rocking. Momma was part of a vanguard of local women starting to pound their pots and pans—personally and politically—for a new order with women as equals. Feminists such as Betty Friedan, Gloria Steinem and others became national role models. And Momma's idealistic commitment was as simple (and as difficult) as having the courage to take off her apron, push up her sleeves, and rethink how best to nurture herself and her entire family.

Shaken by Momma's dream, all of us shifted. Kids in the kitchen cooking; doing dishes; planting the garden with tomatoes, lettuce, basil and sugar snap peas; hanging laundry to dry on the clothesline over the rock wall that Dad was building. And like the stones he crowbarred out of the ground and set one by one into the wall, we kept applying the necessary building blocks for our new lives: idealism, backed by a mix of friendliness, humor, spontaneity, enthusiasm, resourcefulness and hope.

Dad understood Momma's struggle all too well. He had once had what he described as the perfect job: a piano-player for silent movies. As proof, he'd pull out and play from the stacks of sheet music—for romance, suspense, danger, silly stuff—stashed in a living room cabinet. But when movie sound tracks came along, he had been forced to rethink his future. With a Bachelor's degree in Philosophy from the University of Wisconsin, with sketches in the university yearbook and humor magazine, he wondered about something to do with art. Perhaps teaching art history.

In his own leap of faith Dad had landed in Italy. He pursued a certificate program at Florence's Royal Academy of Art and then a Master's of Art History at the Art Institute of Chicago. Afterward, a dashing, thirtyish, single professor teaching now at the Art Institute, he regaled June Chloupek (soon to be Mrs. John V. Allcott III, our mother) and other students with his stories. Unbelievable stories of how in Italy he studied daily in the shadow of Michelangelo's creations—like the magnificent sixteen-foot sculpture, *David*. (During WWII's aftermath, Dad returned to Florence to teach

Campus Parking Lot.

John Allcott, 1976

at the GI University; young soldiers awaiting ships to take them home took monthlong classes that helped replace years of missing education.)

Yes, Dad knew about idealism, and change. So the man of the house grilled up hamburgers as before, but now he stepped inside to make more "soul-i-cious" entrees such as Chicken Bino. Our commiserating neighbors, the Whites, had suggested this easy garlicky and mushroomy recipe. Bread-baking and apple pie-making, too. And in December of that year Dad enrolled in night school and took an Italian cooking class taught by chef Marcella who was, as he said, "the real thing from Torino."

"This is *Pasta alle Vongole*," he explained one night, ladling clam sauce over spaghetti, as Momma tapped away at the typewriter at the far end of the kitchen table. Or another time, over our boisterous snickers, he said: "Nothing poisonous about the white button mushrooms in my *Risotto coi Funghi*. They're different from the large veiny mushrooms our neighbor Phillips Russell found in the woods that ended up causing us all to have such unpleasant stomachaches."

Ever-so-proudly that Christmas Dad gave us copies of recipes from his Italian cooking class, "somewhat corrupted, *si*, but *Buon Natale* to you, nevertheless."

For her part, "June Bug," Dad's nickname for Momma, flew home from her morning classes so they could lunch together. She replaced time-consuming dishes from around the world with simple, make-ahead casseroles, stir-fry dishes and hearty salads. And while wearing black knee-high gardening boots ("better for avoiding a copperhead than open-toed sandals"), she encouraged us to grab an immense bouquet of basil and we'd scrunch the green leaves into the blender along with walnuts, parmesan and olive oil.

"Look," she'd say, "a quick pesto." An extra container of the aromatic green sauce would then be frozen for an even busier day.

Not surprisingly, activities in our home continued to revolve around the kitchen and the table: eating, reading and writing, sketching, and always time to talk. But now discussions poked into feminist books such as Friedan's bestseller *The Feminine Mystique* and Simone de Beauvoir's *The Second Sex* with its "one is not born, but rather becomes a woman" viewpoint.

" Far away there in the sunshine are my highest aspirations. I may not reach them, but I can look up and see their beauty, believe in them, and try to follow where they lead. "

–Louisa May Alcott

PASTA ALLE VONGOLE
Pasta with clams

Cook GARLIC, 3 cloves,
chopped, in OLIVE OIL.

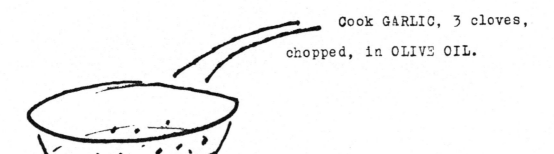

Add large can of TOMATOES,
squashed. Cook 10 - 20 min.

Add a can of CLAMS. SALT,
PEPPER.
Cook 15 minutes.

Add pasta, cooked and drained.

One morning we heard a whoop outside: "I'm done! I'm done!" We dashed to the windows and saw Momma at the mailbox, holding a white envelope. Her grades, delivered by the mailman. There was so much commotion soon on the front stairs, so much jumping up and down by Gene and me, that even our Weimaraner began to bark nonstop.

Later I overheard her talking on the phone. She always spoke a little louder and faster when making a long distance call, as if it would help bridge the miles and cut the costs. Who was it, I wondered. "I've my Master's degree," she said. "I'm so excited. I'm waiting to learn about a possible job at UNC's Guidance Center."

Momma was telling her mother. (A homemaker, Grammy Chloupek liked to tell us how, long before she'd had Momma and adopted another daughter, Ellen, that she was a career woman. "I trained as a nurse at the Battle Creek Sanitarium in Michigan and worked for a while," she'd say. "I was ahead of the times. I learned how the school's founder, Dr. John Harvey Kellogg, thought that for optimum health people should follow a regime of low-fat, high-protein and fiber-rich foods. No coffee; instead drink soy milk, and eat lots and lots of nuts...") And so it was in 1964 that our hard-driving Momma got another degree and soon landed her coveted job as a guidance counselor and librarian. I wasn't upset this time. Instead of heading off to a day of classes, she merely went to work. Not a change in her luncheon plans either; Momma still came home at noon, ate with Dad and relaxed. Call it a gracious nod to feminism, Southern style.

More excitement four years later. To help other women redefining themselves and their futures, she and a colleague designed and taught a pioneering course at UNC for homemakers yearning to relaunch professional careers. "We're going to call it, Expanding Opportunities for Women," she said proudly.

By now Momma had schooled us quite well in kitchen time-savers. Her make-ahead "Going Green" Pesto, a family favorite, was perfect for a variety of fast meals: for a Sugar Snap Pea Salad, which I adored, or over plain pasta. Or, better yet, over steaming shrimp and linguine.

Or she'd turn to her stockpile of Mason jars. With our help in the summer,

> *An idealist is one who, on noticing that a rose smells better than a cabbage, concludes that it will also make better soup.*
>
> –H.L. Mencken

when extra daylight seemingly lengthened time, she'd fill jars with corn relish, hot red-pepper jelly or dilly green beans. "Since it's your turn to cook tonight, you can use a jar of pepper jelly to jazz up the roast chicken," she told me. "The chicken will only need a few minutes of prep time." And following her advice, I simply tossed several chicken breasts—skin on and bones in—with olive oil, sea salt and pepper. I put them on a metal tray in a preheated 400 degree oven, basting occasionally, and an hour later when the tops were golden, we had a delicious dinner. The meal's piece de resistance was, of course, the pepper jelly.

When she or Dad baked bread, they made five loaves and froze some of the extras, which still tasted delicious....

No question, Momma's announcement rocked the family. Idealism's trumpet encouraged her to fling wide the doors of transformation. And thus prodded, the rest of us once tied to her apron strings adapted—and grew.

food facts:

MAKE IT COUNT

On average, Americans age 15 or older spend 67 minutes daily eating and drinking as a main activity. —U.S. Department of Agriculture

"GOING GREEN"
PESTO + SUGAR SNAP PEA SALAD

———

serves 4 to 6

½ pound baby spinach

1 *(10-oz.)* package frozen baby peas, or use fresh ones

½ cup sugar snap peas

½ cup pesto

1 teaspoon sea salt

½ teaspoon freshly ground pepper

2 tablespoons nuts *(pine nuts, pecans or walnuts)*

a wedge Parmesan cheese

In a large salad bowl, place the spinach, defrosted peas, fresh sugar snap peas and pesto, and toss well. Season with salt and pepper, and top with nuts and long, thin slivers of Parmesan.

The Formula for 5-Minute Meals: Pesto

To make pesto you will need: ½ cup toasted walnuts *(or some other nut)*, 3 to 5 peeled garlic cloves, a large handful of basil *(about 4 cups of leaves)*, 1⅓ cups good olive oil, 1 cup grated Parmesan cheese, salt and pepper. In a food processor mix the nuts and garlic, and then add the basil; pulse quickly. With the motor running pour in the olive oil, processing for 10 to 15 seconds, then add Parmesan, salt and pepper.

Remember, air blackens pesto. So put it immediately into small containers and add a thin skin of oil on top to prevent oxidation; either refrigerate or freeze.

VIRTUES COOKING TIP:

idealism

Idealism's companion is "change," a partnership. My mother was motivated by Women's Rights. Often today it's the Green Movement—a mindfulness of our planet. To help children cultivate Green IQ, why not "go green" by planting basil and clipping leaves later for a tasty pesto?

8) creativity

HOT DIGGITY DOG—A TRIP TO THE MOON

"Expedition to the Moon. Hazardous, spectacular, historic, entertaining—profitable. Those persons interested in joining, apply at the airport."

One Saturday morning, as I eased into a chair at the kitchen table, still heavy-headed from a lingering migraine, I read these words in a little book. To my surprise, Dad had written up a recent bedtime story. And the thought of an expedition to the moon, even an imaginary one, definitely helped dull the lingering pain.

Dad loved to splash around in creative thinking by making up stories, often involving the adventures of Dr. Max, the talking dog. (Conveniently, our Weimaraner just happened to be named Maxine.) His story was only sixteen pages, but it was a book because there was a cover, a stapled spine and typed text. Illustrations on every page. Copies were at three places, for each kid at home, and Dad had stacked extra ones on the table to send to our sister Liz at college and to other relatives: Grammy and Grampa Gene in Illinois, Aunt Ruth in Wisconsin, Great Aunt Mercedes in

Minnesota and Aunt Ellen in Washington, D.C.

"You wrote us our own book?" said Gene, noticeably pleased. The title on the cover was *Max, the Talking Dog: The Trip to the Moon*. Gene peered through his thick glasses to examine the book, turning his head from side to side. "And I'm one of the main characters?"

"Yes, yes," said Dad. "It's a very limited edition. Only a dozen copies in print. I self-published it by making copies yesterday at Kinkos. I hope the story will cheer you up, Elinor."

As I sipped a soda ("the caffeine may clear up your headache," said Momma who was hovering nearby and rarely let me have a soft drink), I began to rebound. Suddenly, after not eating for a day, I craved granola. I had made some with Momma earlier in the week, adding two sorts of oats, coconut and several ladles of honey; she'd let me select my favorite nuts (pecans) and dried fruits (cranberries and figs)—each time it was different, a nod to creativity. And so now I got up, filled a bowl with the Granola-tivity (so-called because I created it according to my own personal taste) and settled back at the table, ready for the fun to begin.

CREATIVITY takes what is known and makes a virtue out of creating a snazzy, razzle-dazzle new something.

"The purpose of the trip is to gather cheese," said Dad. "Everyone knows there is cheese on the moon. You kids are going to collect that cheese and sell it."

"What's that smelly cheese that Mom buys?" asked Gene chuckling. "Camp-on-Burt?"

"That is camembert," I said, eager to show off my knowledge of French, now that I was studying the language in middle school. "It comes from a town near France's north coast, in Normandy. And, Gene, you don't pronounce the final T."

At nine, Gene certainly didn't care about my mini-French lesson. But he did care about a good story and was still small enough to spring onto Dad's lap. "Hot-Diggity Dog," he exclaimed. "Read us your story, Pop." I pulled over my chair as did Johnny. And Dad related how Dr. Max, the "big cheese" so to speak, a brilliant dog, was interviewing three of the Allcott children to determine who might join him:

> *"The trip will be long and hard-u-ous," says Dr. Max. "Every one of us will have important tasks to perform. As a group we must have many talents, special abilities. So, I want to know how each of you thinks he can be valuable on the trip. Elinor, what can you do?"*
>
> *"I can speak French. Je suis… Je suis."*
>
> *"Excellent!" responds Max. "It is important that we be able to talk by radio with many different countries. Johnny, do you speak French? What can you do?"*
>
> *"I can speak French and Latin," says Johnny.*
>
> *"Marvelous! Way out there in space, we will doubtless be in contact with the dead as well as the living! And, Gene, what languages do you speak?"*
>
> *"I speak the language of the animals," says Gene.*
>
> *Max, raising his ears, "You do? Say something Gene."*
>
> *Gene: "Bark, bark, bark!"*
>
> *Max, jumping over the table: "Bark, bark, bark, bow-wow-wow!!"*
>
> *They all dance in a circle and shout, "We are all going to the MOON!"*

And so began Dad's story about a lunar adventure in search of cheese. Over the years Dad told us hundreds of stories. About *naughty* characters who lived far up in Carolina's Blue Ridge Mountains, like Beasle Weasel and Tweezle Weasel; while their parents were out, they did their house-cleaning chores by hauling a garden hose into the living room and… psst, psst… spraying off an old dusty piano and swamping the family sofa. ("Okay, I'll help out more around home with Momma at work," I promised after hearing that story. "And I'd never do something so awful.") About *smart* characters who constructed a Rube Goldberg-type machine that spray-painted the family car each day to match the owner's dress, fuchsia one day, chartreuse the next, just like our mother's bright clothes. ("Okay, Dad, I'll consider being a scientist when I grow up.") And *creative* characters with names just like ours: Liz, Johnny, Elinor and Gene.

6 *Creativity is contagious, pass it on.* 9

-Albert Einstein

Without warning during his storytelling, Dad would call on one of us. "What do you think happens next? You're the storyteller now." And so we would jump in, taking a dash of his story, adding a shake of our ideas, and create a new storyline.

Though always funny, Dad's stories tended to carry an underlying instructive message. Once earlier that year, at the impressionable age of thirteen and against my parents' instructions, I'd stayed out well past ten o'clock with some supposedly cool kids, not my normal, nose-in-a-book crowd. Fifteen of us had taken flashlights and gone to the Girl Scout shelter in the woods below our house. Some drank beer, held hands, smoked cigarettes. It was North Carolina after all, where big-eared brown mules still tilled tobacco pastures on the road to Pittsboro, and smoking was not then considered a serious health risk. I was less than a block from home, glints of our house lights shinning through the trees. Later, when I crept up the back stairs and opened the door expecting everyone to be asleep, Mom and Dad sat hunched, weary, at the kitchen table.

No welcoming breakfast pancakes or granola. Lots of explaining. A curfew (my first and last). Despite a slightly rebellious nature, I was ashamed. I really hadn't enjoyed myself. And the following week I overheard snatches of Gene's bedtime story, with Dad relating how a silly girl remained out past her bedtime and ended up in jail.

"No, she didn't stay in the dark, dank jail cell for long," he explained. "Her parents *who love her deeply* (did he know I was listening?) had rushed around for bail money and finally scraped up sufficient cash."

How could a kid rebel for long when a story awaits? Or when she or he is asked to tell one? Uneasy at school? Missing a sister at college? Concerned about the Datsun breaking down, again? Creating a wacky story safely explores emotions or possible outcomes while having fun. Likely without realizing it since our parents didn't read self-help books or have a TV to watch pediatricians ladling out sound bites of advice, this storytelling and book-writing became a way to help us kids make sense of what was happening at home or in the wider world, such as wild things like astronauts rocketing into space.

As for that memorable day around the table when Dad read us *Max, the*

66 No chaos, no creation. Evidence: the kitchen at mealtime. 99

—Mason Cooley

Talking Dog, we were captivated by hearing what we had supposedly discovered on the moon—"yup, gooey, ripe cheese with horrible cheesy fumes"—and learning about our spaceship's touch-and-go return:

> *All of a sudden the motor stops humming. The ship slows down. Max, alarmed, says, "Johnny, do something!"*
>
> *Johnny: "Nothing to do; we are out of fuel."*
>
> *Elinor, hysterical: "Will we have to spend the rest of our lives out here in space?"*
>
> *Max: "Don't worry, we have plenty of food."*
>
> *Johnny: "It's a pity we can't use some of it—ugh—for fuel." They haul out a box of cheese, rip open the lid, heave it into the fuel compartment and slam the door real quick. Instantly the motors start up again. The ship begins to move. It goes faster, faster, faster.*
>
> *Johnny: "We are getting to Earth, and I can't stop the ship." They go whirling around and around Earth, unable to stop. But finally the cheese, a solid-state fuel, subsides and they land at an airport. Spotlights, TV cameras, a great crowd of people awaits them.*
>
> *Dr. Max: "Are you from the International Cheese Association? We haven't tasted the cheese yet. It is probably a little strong...."*
>
> *The men: "We are the government delegation. President Kennedy sent us on a secret mission, and we want to buy the cheese to use for rocket fuel. We'll commission you as a general."*
>
> *The children's mother pushes through the crowd, holding a handkerchief over her nose. "Children, you have missed your supper. It is time to get home and to bed."*
>
> *Children, all: "And take a bath first!"*

Yes, home-told tales can be a little cheesy, a little goofy. One thing is for certain, though: the act of telling a story (and tossing together granola) makes everyone, adult and child, feel very creative.

creativity

Creativity takes same-ol' and spins
it. You can kick-start creativity with a
breakfast-pleaser like homemade granola
(aka, Granola-tivity). Give a child carte
blanch to add favorite nuts, fruits and other
ingredients.

GRANOLA-TIVITY

makes 12 cups

5 cups old-fashioned,
whole-grained oats, *not instant*
1 cup steel-cut oats
(try John McCann's steel-cut Irish oatmeal)
2 cups slivered almonds
2 cups shredded coconut
¾ cup vegetable oil
½ cup honey
1½ cups dried cranberries

Preheat oven to 350 degrees. In a large roasting pan *(11 x 16-inches)* mix the oats, nuts and coconut with the vegetable oil and honey. *(Or, if you're not counting dirty dishes, whisk the oil and honey in a small bowl before adding to the oats.)* Mix well. Bake for 25 to 30 minutes until golden brown, stirring every 10 minutes. Remove from oven and add the cranberries. Once cool, store in airtight containers.

Be creative and toss in other favorite
ingredients. Perhaps cashews,
pecans or hazelnuts. Or replace
the cranberries with dried cherries,
raisins, apricots or figs.

9) patience

PRETZELS AND PATIENCE

When Dad wasn't teaching summer school, he and Momma liked to head off on short, art-related trips: the National Gallery of Art and the Phillips Collection (Washington, D.C.), the Cone Collection (Baltimore) and the Art Institute of Chicago. One day they asked my sister, brothers and me if we'd like to visit their favorite destination for art, New York City.

"I'll need to be at the New York Public Library again this summer doing research for my book on UNC's campus architecture," explained Dad. "But you'll have time to explore with your mother, and I've planned a surprise for you."

Dad's friend Dorothy Knowles, an arts educator at the Museum of Modern Art, somehow made space in her teeny-tiny, one-bedroom apartment in SOHO to accommodate us, six more people. The first thing Gene and I did was to stick our heads way out her second-story living room window and look up Sullivan Street.

"Hello there," Gene shouted to people walking by, among them our high-school-age siblings, Liz and Johnny, who had already ventured out for a look at the Big Apple. Gene's head bobbled as his thick glasses took in the oddly dressed pedestrians below.

"Everyone, can you see me?" he yelled. "I'm up here. I can see you."

Our parents didn't seem to mind his shenanigans. Dad was heaping *pâté* onto a cracker and helping Dorothy uncork a wine bottle labeled Pouilly-Fuissé. Around Chapel Hill many counties were dry, no wine or alcoholic beverages sold, so wines from France were virtually unknown. My parents raised a glass with Dorothy to toast their weeklong stay. Momma's face seemed flushed. It was hot in the small living room, but not that warm. Something was up, but what?

"I'm glad to be in Manhattan," I heard her say. "Chapel Hill keeps testing my patience. Still, some good things are happening. In the Eastgate Shopping Center there's a Greek restaurant with a section in the front selling international food like olive oil, hummus and vine leaves. And on campus we've more women students, and black undergraduate enrollment is picking up, too."

"It sounds like mountains of change, and don't forget it was John who started the Art Department," replied Dorothy. "Tell me, June, how is your new job at the guidance center?"

"Not many coeds are stopping in yet to see about graduate programs in medicine or dentistry," replied Momma with a sigh. "It's just that, as Northerners, John and I feel that we've flapped our way to the South, stirred things up and still don't see much results. We expected more, faster. Honestly, we're often looked at like odd ducks."

"Well, you're not quacks, that's for sure," laughed Dorothy. "You're movers and shakers, and only need a little recharging of your batteries."

"I don't know what I'd do if we didn't have these trips," said Momma. "It gives me something to look forward to...."

These snatches of conversation—Momma sounding happy at times, then wistful, and her intense feelings evidently turning her face the color of her red hair—

*The virtue of **PATIENCE** is the ability to endure delay, trouble or hardship.*

floated over to my hangout at the window. And then off I trotted on a mission: sizing up my first New York apartment.

Everything seemed to fit in, on or under something. Rolled-up sleeping bags for Liz, Johnny, Gene and me, for instance, were already under the living room table, ready for an indoor campout, with Momma and Dad on a pull-out sofa. The table itself had two extensions that could be raised, enabling up to ten to eat together. An exotic flower—"it's a white Dendrobium," explained Dorothy matter-of-factly, as if everyone had orchids—was perched on art books stacked on the same table. As for her six-foot-long galley kitchen, it had floor-to-ceiling metal shelving layered with dishes, spices and condiments, all arranged alphabetically. Jars with tahini, tarragon and truffle paste, for instance, were at my nose level.

That night Dorothy prepared a gourmet French dinner, starting with what she said was baked *chèvre* or goat cheese on a bed of watercress. Alas, no food adoration from Gene. "I don't like cheese from a goat!" he blurted. "Don't like watercress. At home Mom gets it from the stream in the ravine behind our house." For once Momma couldn't get a restraining hand on him. And in a chain reaction Johnny looked at Liz who looked at me, and then we all looked at Dad whose mouth started to stretch into what at first appeared to be a yawn, followed by a smirk, and then a deep "ha-ha-ha-ha" broke loose.

"Sorry, Dorothy," he said shaking his head. "Our country boy eats beans normally, and isn't used to such high living."

By the time the main course—a poached salmon with a tarragon and green parsley sauce—arrived, Gene was ravenous, which put a stop to his outspokenness. Nevertheless, he rolled his eyes dramatically as he took in the food and its colors: a silver tray holding a pink fish topped with dollops of a green concoction. The dessert, a mousse au chocolat, albeit brown, was a different story, and after one bowlful Gene slowly spelled out these two words: "M-O-R-E, P-L-E-A-S-E."

I helped Momma with the dishes. "I don't know why your Dad didn't marry Dorothy years ago when he was teaching here at Hunter College," she said. "She's such a great cook, and they both love art." What? We knew Dad was thirty-six when he married Momma and that they were eleven years apart in age, but I couldn't fathom Dad dating Dorothy, breaking up and then remaining friends.

The next day our family strolled over to Dean & Deluca, the nearby gourmet food store. Momma was gleeful as she loaded a basket with cardamom and coriander, dark Belgian chocolate, a jar of tahini and an 18-inch-long pan for baking baguettes.

"Look," she said. "It's made in France and is for double loaves of French bread." She also discovered professional sheet pans, which "are perfect to keep our Old-Fashioned Holiday Cookies from burning," and a large stainless steel roaster with a rack. (I now use it for making my family's much-loved Worth-the-Wait Turkey Roast.)

"This cooking loot," said Momma with delight, "is coming with me back to Carolina."

I asked daily about Dad's surprise and was told it would be soon. Momma subwayed with us north to 79th Street at Broadway: Zabars. Time for our first bagel, hot and chewy, and poppy encrusted. We went rowing in Central Park, and afterward Dad joined us on Fifth Avenue at "Uncle Solomon's Garage." That was the name, he explained, that critics gave to the Guggenheim Museum. "It took architect Frank Lloyd Wright fifteen years, 700 sketches and countless full-scale designs to get approval," he told us. "It required tons of patience. Wright envisioned the museum, with its unusual circular ramp-gallery—so you could always see where you were coming from and where you were going—like a temple of the spirit."

Finally, around noon one day toward the end of vacation, Dad met up with us for our surprise. "It's not a food treat," he remarked. "It's not shopping on Fifth Avenue, or a handful of dollar bills; not on our shoestring budget. We'll meet Dorothy shortly at her office in the Museum of Modern Art. We're going to experience something together that's, well, quite special—a very, very famous painting."

I felt disappointed. Seeing art was his surprise?

With Dorothy in the lead and Gene bringing up the rear, we trudged silently up a side stairwell and rounded a corner. And there, no missing it, was a massive twenty-five-foot-long painting. It was longer than the length of our living room at home. Women shrieking, a dead baby, mayhem with soldiers, a horse contorted in

> *The sea does not reward those who are too anxious, too greedy, or too impatient. To dig for treasures shows not only impatience and greed, but lack of faith. Patience, patience, patience is what the sea teaches. Patience and faith. One should lie empty, open, choiceless as a beach—waiting for a gift from the sea.*
>
> –Anne Morrow Lindbergh

pain, hands outstretched from the carnage as if asking for mercy.

"This is Picasso's masterpiece, *Guernica*, which he entrusted to our museum for safekeeping," said Dorothy. "It's the artist's condemnation of the German and Italian bombing of Guernica, Spain, in 1937, following orders from the Nationalist forces. They killed an estimated 1600 people, many of them women and children. Later, during World War II, when Spanish-born Picasso was living in Paris, a Nazi officer surveying his apartment saw a photo of *Guernica* and asked, 'Did you do that?' He is said to have responded, 'No, you did.'"

Dad then picked up the story. "Every time I see the painting, it knocks me over, all the raw, brutal emotion used by the artist to inform viewers of atrocities in the Spanish Civil War. This painting was first exhibited at the Paris International Exposition, then in England and elsewhere, and Picasso is impatiently awaiting what will happens next in his homeland. He has stipulated that the painting can only go to Spain when General Franco is gone, and when liberty and democracy are established, and the republic restored.

"By raising awareness, his art is making a political statement for peace," continued Dad, now choking up, overwhelmed, still grappling with the monumental power of art. "It's changing the world. I've waited a long, long time to share this painting with you."

Guernica definitely surprised us. Somehow we ended up feeling quite grown up seeing such a famous painting. After all, it was our art professor father's long-awaited treat.

Dad wasn't quite finished with us, however. On our last day in Manhattan, a steamy Saturday, he asked, "Would you like to see two lions?" Now that *did* sound like fun, especially since we'd already spotted the Central Park Zoo.

A sense of mystery surrounded the event. We trailed him from Dorothy's apartment north up Sixth Avenue, crossed east over to Washington Square and then prowled our way up Fifth. After crossing 41st Street he stopped in front of a large columned building, the New York Public Library.

This was where he was doing research for his book, and there on the front

"The two most powerful warriors are patience and time."

—Leo Tolstoy

An Outing on the East River.   Xmas 1985

steps were two marble lions. They were the guardians of the library.

"That's Patience on the south," he said, as Johnny and Gene scampered up onto their backs and roared playfully at each other. "Fortitude on the north."

Dad paused. "Do you know what those words mean, patience and fortitude? In the 1930s, those were the names given to the lions by New York's Mayor Fiorello LaGuardia as qualities needed by New Yorkers to withstand the economic depression. It seems to me both words, especially patience, or the ability to withstand delays or setbacks, is always important."

That was it, nothing else said. The moment passed. We spotted a food vendor, a last opportunity for another signature New York experience, and so I raced to the cart yelling, "Dad, can I have a pretzel? A hot pretzel with mustard?"

"Yes," he said, "let's get several and share them."

Still, what he said lingered on. Dad's sidewalk comments tied together a string of impressions spotlighting patience: His commitment over time to patiently research his book on UNC's architecture; Momma's patience while promoting social change; Frank Lloyd Wright and Picasso awaiting the right timing for their dreams (*Guernica* finally arrived in Madrid in 1981 and was viewed by a million people that first year); and, in fact, all us kids as we anticipated our New York surprise. Every Thanksgiving I'm reminded of these impressions when I make my Worth-the-Wait Turkey Roast with its delectable pear-pecan stuffing, using Momma's large New York roasting pan. Despite the dish's complexity, I know that, with patience, the recipe can be prepared effortlessly over several days… while I recall that special trip.

A marble lion, Patience, on the steps of the country's flagship public library remains a regal remembrance of this virtue. Food lovers, though, might like our family's sillier reminder, of pretzels and Patience.

food facts:

ONE MARSHMALLOW OR TWO?

Neuroscientist Sam Wang, co-author of Welcome to Your Child's Brain: How the Mind Develops from Conception to College, says, "One of the major capacities that predict life success is self-control." The marshmallow test given to preschoolers, according to his findings, is twice as predictive as IQ for SAT scores. Originally conducted at Stanford University, this test places a marshmallow (or Oreo or pretzels) in front of a four-to-six-year-old child who is told he or she can have the treat immediately or be given twice the amount in fifteen minutes. (Think about the virtue of patience.) Subsequent tests show a surprising correlation between the results of those kids who could wait and their later success. A follow-up study, for instance, found this delayed gratification equates with higher SAT scores.

"Engaging in mentally demanding activities can increase self-control," says Dr. Wang. "You can build it up like a muscle."

WORTH-THE-WAIT TURKEY ROAST

serves 8 to 10

1 eight-pound turkey breast *(ask butcher to butterfly and pound to ¾-inch thickness)*
1 teaspoon sea salt
1 teaspoon freshly ground pepper
2 tablespoons butter
½ cup orange juice
4 cups chicken broth
kitchen string

stuffing

1 large onion, *chopped finely*
3 large stalks celery, *chopped finely*
1 cup butter
2 tablespoons flat-leaf parsley, *chopped*
1 teaspoon sea salt
1 teaspoon freshly ground pepper
2 cups chicken broth
1 *(15-oz.)* package dry bread crumbs
½ cup pecan pieces
2 firm pears, *chopped into ⅓-inch chunks*

gravy

3 tablespoons butter
3 tablespoons flour
1 teaspoon sea salt
1 teaspoon freshly ground pepper
2½ – 3 cups chicken broth

This elegant dish is perfect for holidays or entertaining large groups. Serve the turkey on family heirloom china.

Preheat oven to 350 degrees. With the turkey breast skin side down, put a generous amount of stuffing *(see recipe below)* on an imaginary line down the center of the breast. Using skewers, roll up and form a long tube and tie with kitchen string every 2 inches. Season with salt and pepper. Place seam-side down on the rack of a large 11 x 16-inch roasting pan. Melt the butter and orange juice, and baste the turkey breast. Before putting in the oven, loosely tent turkey with aluminum foil and add two cups of chicken broth to the bottom of the pan. *(Add more broth when the pan dries out.)* Bake for 2½ hours; remove the foil and baste again. Now roast uncovered until the top is golden brown and a kitchen thermometer inserted in the turkey registers 150 degrees. Remove from oven, re-tent to keep warm and let sit for 10 minutes before carving.

Stuffing

The stuffing and gravy can be made a day early. Using an eight-quart stockpot, sauté the onions and celery in the butter until soft. Turn off heat and stir in the remaining ingredients. Mix well and refrigerate until ready to use. Any unused stuffing can be cooked separately in a small covered casserole for 30 minutes at 350 degrees.

Gravy

In a small saucepan, make a "roux" by melting the butter over low heat and adding the flour, whisking for 1 minute. Add salt, pepper and 2½ cups broth and stir until thick. Cool and refrigerate. Once turkey is nearly finished the next day, reheat gravy on low and add turkey drippings from the baking pan; if needed, work in more chicken broth.

OLD-FASHIONED HOLIDAY COOKIES

yields 6 dozen cookies

1 quart dark karo syrup
½ pound light brown sugar
½ pound white sugar
¾ pound lard
1 teaspoon salt
¼ cup flour
¼ pound citron, *chopped finely*
¼ pound candied lemon peel, *chopped finely*
¼ pound orange peel, *chopped finely*
10 teaspoons ground cardamom
1 teaspoon powdered ginger
3 teaspoons cinnamon
3 teaspoons nutmeg
1½ teaspoons ground cloves
½ pound slivered almonds,
chopped and toasted at 200 degrees for 1 hour
3½ teaspoons baking soda
1 lemon, *zest the rind*
1 teaspoon oil of anise or 3 teaspoons anise extract
12+ cups all-purpose flour

What makes a house smell like the holidays? In our home it is Old-Fashioned Holiday Cookies. Patience is required.

Combine karo, the sugars and lard in a large saucepan and bring to a boil *(but don't boil)*. Set aside and cool, and then add salt. Next, in the large bowl of a KitchenAid or similar mixer, stir together a little flour with the candied fruits. Add the remaining ingredients, and then work in one cup of flour at a time.

Refrigerate the dough for several weeks so the flavors can "bloom." When ready to bake, remove the dough from the fridge so it warms and becomes more elastic. Preheat oven to 350 degrees. On a floured surface, roll out dough so it's thin; use cookie cutters and place cookies on an ungreased baking pan. Bake for 8 minutes; the dough will puff up and then resettle. Don't overbake.

Using cookie cutters, you and your family can assemble an edible winter village, with Santa, his reindeer and sleigh; houses and children; snowflakes, stars and candy canes.

VIRTUES COOKING TIP:

patience

Patience is the glue in accomplishment. Spotlight patience by making a Worth-the-Wait Turkey Roast. The recipe can be broken into easy steps; your kids can prepare the stuffing and gravy a day or two in advance—and everyone feasts at the end.

10) purposefulness

GRAMPA COOKS UP A PARADE

I was pushing the shopping cart for Grampa Gene on his Saturday trip to the supermarket. He stopped to pop in vanilla ice cream and chocolate pudding, both for my dessert. As we walked through the store we passed kids galore: a red-faced infant strapped in a baby seat, an unhappy toddler clutching a stuffed bear, a little boy asking repeatedly for "candeeeee."

Suddenly Grampa Gene patted his shirt pocket this way and that, found a two-inch harmonica and tooted out a little song. "I'm Gene," he said cheerily to the astonished boy who'd stopped reaching for the candy. Grampa handed the kid some wooden castanets, also plucked from his pocket. "Want to join me and tap, tap, tap out a tune?"

A salesman for Mirro aluminum cookware, Gene Chloupek had a fun-loving personality and was guided by a sense of deep purposefulness, to bring joy and happiness to others. He enjoyed staging musical performances such as this impromptu one for a kid in a supermarket, near his home in Wilmette, Ill. Or much bigger events at hospitals, for sick children or for disabled veterans. For those happenings he'd pack up his musical instruments, more than 100 in all—flutes, clarinets and ukuleles, miniature violins and trumpets, concertinas and drums—and load the back of his silver Buick station wagon. It took 22 cases to hold everything.

Gene's Crazy Quilt Band, as he called himself, eased aches and pains, loneliness and boredom, and created cascades of laughter. His music was off-tune, his lyrics corny. His black top hat bobbled with fake bumble bees and fluttered with a yellow canary. His vest blinked with tiny colored lights and surprised kids with squirts of water. Sometimes, like singer Bob Dylan, he'd fasten a large harmonica around his neck and blow out a tune, his hands free for a shake of a tambourine. Or he'd attach cymbals to the knees of his pants, pin a tail of bells on his backside, and then place seed-filled painted Mexican gourds on his shoes, each step thus making a lively and boisterous clang, jingle, shake.

As a virtue,

PURPOSEFULNESS

aligns goals with action,

vision with accomplishment.

Grampa Gene's mini-performance that day created a traffic jam of smiling people with their carts; children clapping and giggling and wanting a turn with the castanets. He pulled a little flute out of his coat pocket for several lively tunes. And before long I heard him croak out lyrics to a favorite song, "I'm a lonely little petunia in an onion patch."

As for me, my eleventh birthday recently celebrated, I was taking a summer school typing class while staying with him and Grammy. But this showmanship, this off-key singing and spur-of-the-moment harmonica-playing left me embarrassed. Actually mortified. I was ready to slink for cover behind the towering display of Scott paper towels.

"Let's go, Gramps," I said tugging at his hand, which still held the harmonica. "It's time to go."

I was used to colorful characters at the university back home in North Carolina. This behavior, though, was over-the-top. Singing in a supermarket? And I was very aware that I wore a homemade jean skirt, not something fancy from Marshall Field's in nearby Chicago. Even though Grammy had taken me to the department store for my first permanent earlier in the week, that experience had ended in a mess. My frizzy ringlets, again a source of today's insecurity, resulted from us not knowing to use rollers when my hair was still wet. Truth be told, I was tall enough to look like a grown-up but I was only a homesick kid. I didn't care if I ever ate chocolate pudding layered with softened vanilla ice cream ever, ever, ever again.

"Can't we get out of here?" I begged. "We've got to leave."

The summer had been a series of disasters. I'd already gotten in a monkey's heap of trouble... a week of 6 p.m. curfews, for instance, after splashing around on Wilmette's 16th Street with the Patten kids when a flash flood backed up storm drains and left knee-high water. "You might've been sucked into a drain or cut your foot on glass," sighed Grammy when she'd found us in the downpour, jumping about. Her normally elegant bun clung limply to a few wet hairpins.

Another time, as Grammy and I headed for a picnic and swim along Lake Michigan, she was driving so slowly, so very, very slowly, that I eased my left foot over from the passenger's side and gave what seemed to be a tiny bump to the driver's pedal. Like a Kentucky racehorse galloping from the gate, the car surged forward, then stopped. "I'm sorry, Grammy," I sputtered, not realizing at the time that this seemingly outgoing woman, born in 1889 prior to the invention of automobiles, dreaded driving on city streets. That horrible, unacceptable behavior landed me more curfew, two weeks of dish duty and I was required to make a long-distance call to my parents to promise, "I would never, ever press Grammy's car gas pedal again."

And now, head down, shoulders slumped, knees practically jiggling with unease, I heaved myself into the backseat of Grampa's car. As he loaded in the groceries, I started to cry. I made big feel-sorry-for-myself slobbering sobs. No words came from him until we returned to his home and I was on the walkway bordered with thick rows of parsley, planted by Grammy so I could grab a healthy snack. (Grammy, a nurse trained at John Harvey Kellogg's famed Battle Creek Sanitarium, knew that parsley was high in iron and good for a growing body.)

> *For me, I am driven by two main philosophies: know more today about the world than I knew yesterday and lessen the suffering of others. You'd be surprised how far that gets you.*
>
> *–Neil deGrasse Tyson*

"I wish... I wish I could make *you* happy," Grampa Gene said softly, looking down at the parsley, not me. "What can I do? You have great food and new friends, and you can all bang, screech and honk endlessly on the musical instruments in the basement." He stopped and looked up at my eyes. "My hobby is to bring people joy, and I can't even please you."

I was embarrassed again; this time differently. I'd somehow felt that I... Miss Nearly-a-Teen... was the one on center stage. And it was so strange being 800 miles away from home. But I loved my Grampa. I realized I was actually proud of his zany music wherever it happened. And I definitely wanted to be part of his harmonica-playing, Saturday-shopping trips.

Lifting a bag of groceries from his arms, I burst into dramatic sobs once more. But I still managed to gulp out, "I'm so... so sorry Grampa Gene. I am happy here with you and Grammy. So happy."

"Well, well, well," he replied with a gigantic smile. "I'm no longer blue. I feel suddenly as cheerful as my friend Urple the Purple, the pigmy elephant who lives in Happy Spot, America." Grampa Gene was referring to the made-up elephant in his funny stories, which he wrote and then photocopied to mail to hospitalized boys and girls, and veterans. Over the span of several years he'd send off monthly installments to several hundred people.

"Urple," he now said, "would like this news that you are happy. He would chirrup and wiggle his ears in delight. He'd squeal and roll his eyes, snort and jiggle his feet and swish water out of his trunk!

"Oh boy," continued Grampa, "if there's anything I like next to eating, it's a show. So let me tell you all about Urple and the Happy Spot Circus Parade. Let's go inside and have some lunch with Grammy, and I'll tell you that exciting tale." I followed Grampa Gene inside, and as I put the groceries on the counter next to a dessert that was cooling in an upside down angel food cake pan, he whispered and whispered some more into Grammy's ear; and then we walked into the dining room. He picked up a story from a two-inch stack on the table and started to read about the circus parade:

HELLO TO ELLIE & PETER, TOO — S.B.

Now you'll know right away what animals come first. They have long scrawny
necks. When they swallow an orange it has a long way to go and you wonder if it
will ever land in their tummies. I'm talking about giraffes. Three of them: the mama,
daddy and their girl. Folks called her Silly Neck, and she has all sorts of colored
ribbons hanging from her neck. When Silly Neck sees children eating ice cream or a
hot dog she sticks out her long tongue and grabs it. Then, in thanks, she slobbers a kiss
on the child's neck.

Ahhh, the high school clown band with Octopus Pete. He has eight mouthpieces
all connected to a large center horn. Eight clowns march along, each one blowing a
different tune into a mouthpiece. The sound? It's like a bunch of caw crows, hee-haw
donkeys, squealing pigs and yelling parrots are all trying to sing simultaneously.

Next, the circus floats. One has teenage girls wearing strange hats. The hats
are really cages with birds! Oh my word, have you ever seen such hats? In one cage
is a little rooster that cocks up his head with a "cock-a-doodle-do." Another hat has
a bantam hen that moves off her little nest and lets out a "cluckidee-cluck-luckidy-
cluck." And, can you believe it, she has just laid an egg!

The parade gets even more exciting, he explained, as along marches "twelve
Indian majorettes with make-believe papooses, all holding dolls having the cutest
colored hair: pink-poo; blue gurgle-bla; sunny-sue; iggly-egg and other splash-'em-up
colors. Fatso the Clown comes next and reaches into his hobo bag and tosses out bags
of caramel corn and salty honey-coated peanuts…."

Grampa's stories always contained references to food so I was practically
licking my lips when Grammy placed a roast beef and coleslaw sandwich before me.
Then with much to-do, she swished back into the kitchen and emerged carrying a
spectacular white-topped, red-studded dessert on her finest cut-glass, heirloom cake
platter.

"For dinner tonight I was going to have a Hazelnut Torte, one of my
family's best-loved recipes from Czechoslovakia," she said. "But we decided to have a

celebration right now. I quickly frosted the torte with whipped cream and dotted on fresh raspberries from your shopping trip. It's a treat for our special granddaughter. I've been making a bunch of Czech recipes so you'll know about the foods Grampa and I had growing up."

By the time Grampa Gene reached his story's finale, I was spooning up the last streaks of sweet whipped cream and the Hazelnut Torte crumbles. I listened intently as he read how he was the one riding "gleefully, gloriously, joyfully" at the end of the Happy Spot Circus Parade—high up on Urple the Purple's back. As for me, once a disgruntled preteen exploring new boundaries far from home, I had found a "happy spot" right in the midst of their home. Four more weeks remained with my wonderful grandparents. Mind you, add the words "delightfully wacky" for my grandfather.

It's really pretty cool, how purposefulness can bring happiness to others.

Urple The Purple Pigmy Elephant

HAZELNUT TORTE

—

serves 8

1 cup hazelnuts, *skins removed, toasted and chopped*
1 cup slivered almonds, *chopped*
1 cup grated Zwieback
1 teaspoon baking powder
8 large eggs, *room temperature and separated*
1½ cups sugar
½ teaspoon cream of tartar
¼ teaspoon salt

Preheat oven to 325 degrees. Use a 10-inch springform angel food pan. First, chop toasted nuts in a food processor until small bits form *(not a powder)*. In a small container, mix the grated Zwieback and baking powder. Now in the large bowl of an electric mixer, beat egg yolks until very stiff. Add ¾ cup sugar, beating for a minute. Set aside. Using a second mixing bowl, combine the egg whites, ¾ cup sugar, cream of tartar and salt, and beat until very stiff. Using a whisk, stir small amounts of the stiff egg whites into the egg yolk mixture, alternating with additions of the zwieback and the nuts; repeat.

Pour into the springform pan and bake for 45 minutes to 1 hour; top should be lightly golden and spring back to the touch. When cool, turn torte out onto a plate.

A dollop of whipped cream or creme fraiche atop each slice is divine. Or for a fancier look, frost the torte with whipped cream and decorate artfully—chopped toasted hazelnuts on the sides along with a sprinkling of whole nuts on top.

VIRTUES COOKING TIP:

purposefulness

Purposefulness is a virtue that can cause head-scratching. What is it exactly? Think of it as a special ingredient that supports your interests. Indeed, what about making a recipe loved for generations, like a Hazelnut Torte, and over dessert talking about your ancestors?

11) joyfulness

SIMPLE PLEASURES AND SECOND DESSERTS

One Saturday Gene and I set off on foot with our parents for the
Community Church, just across the woodsy ravine from our home. On most
weekends my gangly twelve-year-old brother could be found painting in the
basement, but on this morning he wanted to enter the church's pancake-
eating contest. How many Aunt Jemimas could he eat?

With our sister and brother away at college we represented the
Allcott kids. I was a weight-conscious high schooler and would only end
up eating four. Gene had other plans. Encouraged by a raucous group at
the griddle—volunteer cooks who were UNC professors in the philosophy
department, business school and elsewhere—Gene had a second plate of
four, then beckoned boldly for another, less maple syrup this time, more
butter. His count was soon up to twelve.

"Why stop now?" someone asked. "Eat two more and you'll break the church record."

Another serving of pancakes faced him on the table. By now Gene was being egged on by our minister, Rev. Charlie Jones, as well as the griddlers and a gaggle of his friends who were chanting, "Go Gene, Go Gene!"

He raised his fork to shoulder height, sent it zooming toward the plate and speared a pancake. Up came the fork to hover in front of his mouth. Soon in popped No. 13. He paused, watching everyone with a smirk, and then, after what seemed like minutes of chewing and swallowing and swallowing again, he repeated the dramatic plunge. In went No. 14.

"That's it, boys," said Gene with an audible burp, not minding the attention from several teenage girls. "Can't find NO MO' ROOM. Now call my agent if you want an interview or autograph." And he laughed and laughed some more. Always one to love a crowd (and food), the church's new Pancake Champ was a born showman. He was just like Grampa Gene, his namesake, both full of stories and jokes, and laughter.

*The virtue of **JOYFULNESS** has an easy equation: simple pleasures (think food) = JOY.*

Before Gene could change his mind and go back for yet more attention and pancakes (and potentially a gut-busting stomach ache), our parents rounded us up. In a light drizzle, we headed toward home. Approaching the Clay Hills, the name we'd given to a play area, actually just a bare red-clay hillside sloping down from the church parking lot, Gene couldn't stop himself. The mud appeared to have the ideal slipperiness for clay sliding. He dropped to his backside, raised his feet and tilting back—oblivious to Momma's commands to "Stop! Right now!"—he pushed himself off as if on a sled. Gene slid on his jeans down the muddy slope, bumped past a small carved-out fort that kids had constructed in the gully and came to a choppy stop.

"WHOOPIE!" Gene yelled. "WHOOPIE! This is the BEST SLIDING HILL, with the BEST SLIDING CLAY, in all of NORTH CAROLINA."

Simple pleasures were the heartbeat of this warm, drizzly day. Nothing special on the family agenda, yet everything was special, just because our parents were letting the day unfold around us with its own rhythm of joy.

Picking himself up Gene asked, "Wouldn't it be neat to climb to Elephant Rock?" This ten-foot-high stone outcrop was the site of another favorite hangout.

"Yes, let's go to Elephant Rock," I agreed.

We picked our way along a nearby stream, me first, then Gene and Dad. In the back Mom held tightly to a cane to steady herself after hip surgery several years earlier; she also kept a sharp lookout for snakes. Suddenly, she stooped over. Alongside a spring bordering the stream, she poked at something. "Aha," she said, holding up her cane. It wasn't a snake. It was a clump of wild watercress. She stuffed a handful into her raincoat pocket. "Watercress is expensive at the grocery. I love its tangy taste in sandwiches."

Up the embankment we headed now toward Elephant Rock. "This rock probably started inauspiciously as a seam of metamorphosed strata along the Triassic Sea," said Dad who always had a way of enlarging our vision. "As time went by erosion weathered it into a ridgeline holding up the progression to flat land. And you, lucky kids, get to climb it.

"People in our church call it Memorial Rock," he continued, referring to how the ashes of some members who'd passed away were scattered nearby. "It's a peaceful place where families can gather and memories replay."

Gene and I climbed up the rock, past the bronze plaque that Dad had helped erect with words chosen from Ecclesiastes 3: "To everything there is a season, and a time to every purpose under the heaven." Reaching the top, a few crows cawing out, I felt a rush of teenage spookiness and thought, if ashes were scattered, could ghosts be far away? Are those cawing crows the guardians of this place?

There was no time for more reflection. For standing at my side in full play mode was the Pancake Champ. Gene's stomach was extended, his pants muddy, his motto in life straight out of *Mad* magazine: "What, me worry?" Nothing existential or otherworldly was on his mind.

He quickly morphed into Gene, King of the Mountain. Taking a deep bow to our parents below, he gave a silly wave and then feeling invincible sprang skyward,

> *The kitchen really is the castle itself. This is where we spend our happiest moments and where we find the joy of being a family.*
>
> —Mario Batali

arms now outstretched, and flew out birdlike. Somehow Gene landed on his feet in the mud. There was a massive thump, his all-too-full stomach jarred. A sorrowful moan escaped, the first of many.

"Oh no, oh no," he said barely smiling. "I must go home and rest."

With Momma in front, we resumed our walk homeward through oak and pine forest, always watching so as not to plant our feet on the leaf-brown, diamond crosshatch of a copperhead. "Oh no," croaked Gene again rubbing his belly. "I've eaten way too much. No painting for me today." Once home, he headed to his room for a nap (another simple pleasure) and, fortunately, before long our Pancake Champ recovered completely.

*T*hat same spring inspiration came for an unusual simple pleasure. It might have started with all the art books Dad read after dinner, all those realistic still-life depictions of apples, oranges and grapes. Soon his stomach would rumble, and up he'd hop to check the kitchen for something sweet. All it took was the squeak of the opening refrigerator door, that crackling of an oh-so-stealthily unwrapped bar of chocolate, or the gentle tapping sound to release the top of a cookie tin, and homework would be dropped. A bedroom door would open along the wide corridor leading to the kitchen.

"Hey Dad," Gene would say, "whatcha doing? Found something good?"

At one of these late-night, food-fueled powwows, Gene tossed out an idea. "Shouldn't we have something sweet at this time *every* night?" he asked. "You know, several hours after eating and after homework is done? We could come back to the kitchen for an extra treat."

And so our father dreamed up the idea of Second Desserts.

Around 9 p.m. we'd convince Momma to let us spoon into remains of a French mousse au chocolat or scoop up leftover apple pie. More often than not, though, Dad was on his own. He came up with a delicious threesome: "Second Desserts" Pound Cake, vanilla ice cream and chocolate syrup. Toasting each slice left the pound cake crispy and crunchy; ice cream added a cool velvety embrace and syrup was splashed on in an artsy design. Joy guaranteed.

As for the "Second Desserts" Pound Cake, it was either bought at the

> " *If most of us valued food & cheer & song above hoarded gold, it would be a merrier world.* "
>
> –*J.R.R. Tolkien*

Carrboro Farmer's Market, or homemade. For once Mom, who usually shunned Southern cooking, didn't mind making the recipe the way it was done in the South. That meant using an often-shunned ingredient: lard, for lightness. Mom preferred Effie's recipe; she was the cook of her friend Trudy Taylor, whose son James went on to garner fame as a singer. His toga-wearing performance at our high school talent show was a preview of what was to come a few years later, with James's "Carolina on My Mind." Mom told us that Effie made a pound cake a day for the five hungry Taylor kids.

Throughout the rest of my high school years we continued to gather for Second Desserts and late-night talks: about the Vietnam War and Civil Rights; about my election as student body president of the newly built Chapel Hill High School and how to handle the exciting (and at times difficult) first year of full integration with all-black Lincoln High School.

Over Second Desserts Gene told us the exciting news of his first big art commission. He'd bartered with a local restaurant. (Notice the word "art" in the word, bartered? Or rearrange the letters and form the word "eat.") The Ranch House restaurant agreed to give him $50 in food vouchers, a mountainous amount of money in the 1960s, in exchange for his painting a gigantic billboard on the highway between Chapel Hill and Durham. His vouchers would buy cheeseburgers and pizza, and endless vanilla milkshakes.

It was over Second Desserts that Dad and Mom confronted Gene about another entrepreneurial venture, this one gone horribly awry. An acquaintance from school encouraged Gene to join him in a marijuana mail-order business. "This is asking for serious trouble," said Dad sternly when he found out. "It's a stupid, idiotic, harebrained idea. Besides, you'd do better selling art or bartering it, and then you wouldn't have to deal with gun-carrying Chapel Hill police." Months later Gene was back on track, and Dad was able to joke with him, saying, "I'm glad we didn't see a headline in *The Chapel Hill Weekly* stating, 'Young Artist Caught Selling Dope.' You escaped an entanglement with serious, life-changing consequences."

Soon enough Gene and I would be launched out of the Allcott nest. Like our siblings Liz and Johnny, we'd no longer be fed and course-corrected daily. But we were already fortified with one of the most important life lessons....

It's deeply satisfying if you can find enJOYment in simple pleasures.

VIRTUES COOKING TIP:

joyfulness

Joyfulness nestles in daily
happenings and elevates mood. You
and your kids can find immense joy
in making—and munching on—
Second Desserts.

"SECOND DESSERTS" POUND CAKE

serves 8

1 cup Crisco
2 cups sugar
6 large eggs
2 cups sifted all-purpose flour
1 teaspoon lemon juice
1 teaspoon pure vanilla extract

Preheat oven to 350 degrees. Grease the bottom *(not the sides)* of a 10-inch round tube pan. With an electric mixer, cream together the Crisco and sugar, and then add eggs one at a time. Beat hard. Next mix in the flour, again blending the ingredients. Not to be forgotten: a heaping teaspoonful of lemon juice and vanilla, stirred in well. Bake for 1 hour. Let the cake sit for 10 minutes before removing from the pan and cooling completely on a rack.

Don't open the oven and peak. Fortunately, most ovens today have glass doors so you can easily see if the cake is done.

12) faith

WHITES ONLY: FOOD FOR THOUGHT

The sign over the water fountain said: "Whites Only." Over another: "Colored."

As youngsters, we sensed something wasn't right at the Long Meadow Dairy Bar, a restaurant on Franklin Street where the town of Chapel Hill edges into Carrboro. But we didn't know what. We loved sipping frothy chocolate milkshakes at the ice cream counter. Occasionally we'd spot Negroes or Coloreds, as African-Americans were then called, though only whites were in the dining room. For the longest time my sister Liz, seeing the world through her then naive, artistic eyes, thought the signs over the water fountains meant white water came out of one and from the other, a rainbow of colors.

Not so, as we learned in the years ahead when racial tensions heated up the South. Not when restaurants, schools, churches and buses were at the center of deepening controversy.

Liz's view of the drinking water got an eye-opening new interpretation from Rev. Charles M. Jones, the pastor of the Presbyterian church attended by our family. "Integration" was a word he used over and over. Those water fountain signs were symptomatic of discrimination facing the community. He announced his support for testing the Supreme Court decision to bar discrimination in interstate bus travel.

The conservative Orange Presbytery, which oversaw the church in our area of North Carolina, wasn't thrilled with Rev. Jones's ministry and appointed a Special Judicial Commission to investigate. Despite a 156 to 14 vote of confidence from our local church members, the Presbytery got the last word. Charlie, as we called our beloved minister, was booted out.

FAITH, the belief in a higher spiritual power, is a virtue that sets our moral compass.

A small group of UNC faculty and their families soon met with him for informal Sunday services at Hill Hall, home of UNC's music department. "What can the churches do to promote justice, equality and brotherhood?" he asked one day in a sermon. "Words, deeds, preachment and practice must go hand in hand." And before long a new Community Church was built in the woods across from our home; this answered his call for a permanent, non-denominational spiritual home for all people, regardless of the color of their skin.

On February 1, 1960, our family was at the kitchen table eating and listening to nightly news on the radio. The announcer reported that four African-American university students had ordered coffee at the "whites only" counter at Woolworth's in Greensboro and staged a sit-in, all less than an hour away. "The concept of the world as one family, one brotherhood, is no longer just an ideal," said Charlie in another sermon. "It is a realistic demand."

For our family this was powerful food for thought.

The following New Year's, just after returning from the Community Church, the phone rang. We had one telephone only, a standard black rotary device on a party line. This meant that when we picked up the phone and heard Tera White two houses down talking to her aunt in the Deep South, we could listen for a second or two, then place the phone quietly back on its cradle; wait a sec, then pick up, listen: "Henry spotted a garter snake near the swing set... More racial trouble at the bus station and Long Meadow Dairy Bar... Bugs ate the okra plants." Whenever she caught us listening, Momma would flap her arms about and mouth silently, "Put that down," and then hiss an exaggerated "NOWWW." No TV reality show, no computer game, no video today could be as entertaining as party-line eavesdropping.

So when our phone rang, a number of people on our party line were likely listening... and shocked. We were just starting lunch with family friends Maxine and Ben Swalin who shared our parents' wedding anniversary, January 1. On the kitchen table a pot bubbled with oil. Nearby a sunburst of yellow forsythia, which Mom had forced into bloom in the warm basement, seemed to sprout from a green "frogskin" Jugtown vase. Mom had just finished saying: "We're having a festive Indonesian meal. Use one of these long forked skewers to spear a piece of chicken or shrimp, sizzle it up in the oil and then dip it into the creamy peanut satay sauce."

Dad was the one to answer the phone. "Yes, I'm Professor Allcott. Yes, I'll speak to him."

A puzzled look transformed our father's face as he paced about, stretching the phone's twenty-foot-long cord to its maximum. "What? Peter, you're calling from jail? That's awful. Well, of course I'll come right away."

"That's a darned shame," said Dad hanging up. "One of my art department graduate students, a mild-mannered, bright young man from Pennsylvania, was arrested in a Civil Rights sit-in at a country restaurant on old Pittsboro Road. He spent the night in jail and doesn't sound good. I need cash to post bond for his release." With no ATMs back then, we raced to our rooms to find stashed-away allowance money and with each of us contributing including the Swalins, Dad managed to collect about fifty dollars.

"We'll eat when you return," Mom said. She blew out the sterno under the oil and placed the chicken and shrimp back in the fridge. Our parents didn't usually hold hands or show signs of affection in front of us, but Dad lingered at the front door for a kiss. "Please bring Peter back with you," we heard Mom say. "He must be mighty upset and surely needs some good food."

> Faith and prayer are the vitamins of the soul; man cannot live in health without them.
>
> –Mahalia Jackson

An hour and a half passed before we heard the beep of Dad's Datsun as he rounded the bend of Chase Avenue. We raced down the stone stairs and formed a line. Dad's brave graduate student should have a warm welcome.

"I hope you're okay," said Mom. "What happened?"

A tired smile lit up Peter's face. He told us he'd gone with half a dozen people, including two African-Americans, to a small restaurant where they'd picketed before. "This time we entered and sat on stools at the lunch counter," he explained. "We asked politely for coffee. When the cook started shouting, we moved and sat cross-legged on the floor, our arms linked, and started to sing, 'We Shall Overcome.'"

Peter was sheet white and kept pausing, as if watching a replay in his head of the events. "Enraged, the cook turned from the grill where she'd been frying sausages and started yelling the "N" word, as well as other insults. 'Git out of here,' she shouted lunging toward us. 'Git out. NOW GIT OUT!'"

He stopped talking. We thought Peter had finished; but, no, there was more: "Rushing over, the woman slapped one of our group on the head, then squatted near him, lifted her skirt slightly and… I can't believe this still… she urinated. A puddle spread from around his shoes onto mine. She peed on us. Another employee then took the remains of dirty floor moppings, a bucket with ammonia, and heaved it. The splashes burned our legs, our arms."

Police were called, we learned. Peter and the other "bad guys" were yanked and pulled and dragged outside before being hauled off in squad cars and jailed for the night. "I never thought this could happen, not here in this progressive part of the South," Peter said. "If you don't mind, can I wash off the mess?"

After showering, after putting on a clean pair of Dad's pants and a shirt, Peter joined us for the long-delayed anniversary lunch, the Skewered Chicken Breasts (or Shrimp) with Satay Sauce. We had so many questions. His horrific experience stomped around in our heads like an irritated Carolina mule, but Momma insisted he needed to eat in peace. (We read more of the ugly details in *The Chapel Hill Weekly*.) So, along with Maxine and Ben, and Peter from Pennsylvania, we were unusually quiet as we skewered shrimp and chunks of chicken, and swirled it around in the deliciously tangy

Every man must decide whether he will walk in the light of creative altruism or the darkness of destructive selfishness. This is the judgment. Life's most persistent and urgent question is, 'What are you doing for others?'

–Dr. Martin Luther King, Jr.

satay sauce. We knew that faith—a spiritual commitment to doing the right things in life—demanded more.

Our family joined peaceful protests. We went to a friend's home who had a color TV and, with of hundreds of thousands of people nationwide, saw the 1963 March on Washington galvanize the nation. We listened to Dr. Martin Luther King's "I Have a Dream" speech. We heeded King's, "We must learn to live together as brothers or perish together as fools." My sister Liz, by then a high school senior, joined weekend work groups to renovate housing for African-Americans. Johnny walked in marches and attended rallies at black churches. In middle school, I picked out the notes on my guitar for "We Shall Overcome" and played the song endlessly.

Rev. Charlie Jones's idea for humanity with "one family, one brotherhood" began to take hold. Chapel Hill started to live up to its nickname, the Southern Part of Heaven. The "Whites Only" and "Coloreds" signs came down; restaurants opened their doors wider, even the Long Meadow Dairy Bar's dining room. And a few years later, when I was president of the Chapel Hill High School—at a new campus to fully integrate with all-black Lincoln High—my sense of faith underscored the need for us to work together mightily to keep everyone respectful and calm, and to heal communities too long apart.

As for Dad's graduate student, Peter came back many times. Inspired by our Indonesian meal, he asked if he could build an Asian rock garden in front of our home—a way of saying thanks. Around a wisteria bush full of waving purple blooms, he added pathways of white crushed stones and hauled in several massive granite boulders as meditative spots. Always, the garden was peaceful. He claimed us as his Chapel Hill family and visited to clip vines in the rock garden, talk art and eat family dinner, including chicken with satay sauce, a dish that lends itself to having leisurely and thoughtful discussions.

Faith teaches us to do our part in making the world a better place. Our blessings are many, our abundance unprecedented. We are one family, in one large (earthy) home, with extra room at the table....

SKEWERED CHICKEN BREASTS WITH SATAY SAUCE

---

serves 6 to 8

4 lemons, *zest and juice*
¾ cup good olive oil
1 teaspoon sea salt
1 teaspoon freshly ground pepper
2 pounds chicken breasts, *in large chunks*

satay sauce
(makes 1½ cups)
2 tablespoons olive oil
1 small onion, *grated*
2 cloves garlic, *minced*
2 teaspoons fresh ginger
¼ teaspoon red pepper flakes
2 tablespoons wine vinegar
3 tablespoons light brown sugar
2 tablespoons soy sauce
⅓ cup chunky peanut butter
¼ cup catsup
1 tablespoon fresh lemon juice

In a large bowl or 1-gallon freezer bag, mix the lemon zest and juice, and add olive oil, sea salt and pepper. Toss in the chicken breasts. Marinate for several hours and skewer chicken before grilling.

Satay Sauce

In a small saucepan, add the olive oil and sauté the onion, garlic, ginger and pepper flakes for 10 minutes. Stir in the rest of the ingredients, cook for a minute and cool. The sauce is ready to serve with grilled chicken.

Satay Sauce can be made a day before and reheated. Extra sauce can be used for a week, adding pizzazz to other foods.

faith

Like a brilliant star, **faith** steers us to do what's right. And talking about faith over food (think Chicken Satay) reinforces beliefs. To deepen faith through action, your family might eat an inexpensive meal weekly and contribute money saved to a family-chosen charity.

13) wonder

PRIMORDIAL SOUP

"Big news here is the soup on the kitchen ceiling," wrote Dad in his weekly letter to family and friends. "The providing hen was the one hibernating in the deep freeze for eighteen years."

So began a letter about food Dad sent to us, his now-grown children. Still, to better appreciate his funny culinary tale, we'd best back up in time. You see, my parents had an ancient, open-from-the-top-and-try-not-to-tumble-in chest freezer. For years Mom had packed it with homemade bread and cinnamon buns, orange juice and vegetables. Her real stockpile, though, was in poultry and beef supermarket "Specials of the Week." Always looking for a good deal, Mom had accumulated quite a collection of whole chickens, three-pound slabs of chuck steak and an occasional leg of lamb. This was fine as long as her booty remained in one of the three wire baskets across the top of the freezer, where food was easily accessible.

But some of these treasures got moved out of the baskets and sank deeper and deeper into the lower freezer. Labels smudged and smeared. Ice crystals layered the tops. Meats changed color from deep reds to dismal browns. Truth was, if I was visiting and looking for something to fix for dinner, I didn't dare venture beneath the baskets, into the frosty Freezer Neverland.

In this virtue, WONDER, there's surprise and a sense of admiration in encountering the unfamiliar and inexplicable in life.

One day catastrophe struck. A hurricane slammed the Carolinas. The electricity went out, and the freezer slowly began to thaw. When power was restored my mother said to my father, "Quick, let's invite friends over and eat up this food. I can make stews and casseroles, and use the ground beef for pasta sauce or, better yet, our family's recipe for baked ziti."

Only problem was the stuff at the freezer bottom, the mystery meat. A neighbor who'd stopped over was leery of this food; he suggested a triage approach. "June," he said pragmatically, "if you can't ID the food, chuck it. You'll need to toss almost everything."

"To make this more bearable," added my father, by now resigned to eating what he called prehistoric meat from a long-lost mastodon, "can you at least make chocolate chip cookies? We need something to look forward to."

Several black plastic garbage bags soon bulged with evil-looking remains from the freezer bottom. Items from the upper baskets made it into pots and pans, and all the stove burners got a workout. At her kitchen Command Center, mother was turning out lamb and beef dishes, baked ziti and cookies.

What happened next, however, signaled trouble. Mom was clutching a dubiously misshapen, semi-frozen chicken… an old hen. She put it temporarily in the sink. From her waist up she then disappeared into the far back reaches of a kitchen cabinet bordering the stove. She emerged triumphant, hoisting her very dusty, very ancient and very gigantic (16-quart) pressure cooker, something her father, a salesman for an aluminum cookware company, had given her when she got married.

"It will be perfect for making a large soup," she said.

But it's one thing to age food intentionally and eat it. Chinese pidan, for instance, or what's called 1,000-year-old eggs, is considered a delicacy, at least in China. The aged duck, chicken or quail eggs, however, are rarely more than 100 days old. But a hen hibernating for nearly two decades in the Arctic depths of a freezer, our freezer, was another story.

And this chicken soup-making was where my father resumed his family letter. He wanted to tell what our mother did ever so innocently:

> *June whittled the frozen hen into slivers and put them in the pressure cooker and turned up the heat. The bird, now soup, was held in the cooker by grace of this soft-metal washer on the cover that can resist only so much heat and pressure. When June stepped up the heat, the soup became primordial, a seething mass of subatomic particles dancing at millions of vibrations a second. It was then that the soft-metal washer gave up and did what it was programmed to do. It melted. And the soup shot ceilingward at a speed of thirty miles per second.*

It was, as Dad proclaimed, "The Big Bang all over again."

Our father was a quiet art historian normally, a university professor. Now, suddenly, he found himself struggling to explain theories about the Big Bang and Black Holes, and the origin of the universe going back 13.8 billion years… and how all of this related to his own cosmic culinary experience. He checked his study for science books and dug through the recycling bin for articles in the science section of *The New York Times* about the Big Bang. His reaction to the soup-splattered ceiling brought to my mind Thomas Aquinas, a thirteenth-century theologian who believed that "poets and philosophers are alike in being big with wonder."

Yes, that explained Dad's response: big with wonder. But shouldn't Aquinas have included artists, too? (The saint is also credited with saying, "How is it they live in such harmony, the billions of stars, when most men can barely go a minute without declaring war in their minds about someone they know.")

In the family letter, Dad played on in pure wonderment and concluded:

TO MRS. B.

Hercules could bend a pipe
   And often did so in sheer spite
     to show his might!

Merlin predicted the eclipse of the moon,
   And correctly divided pie with a spoon!

Democritus divined the structure of matter
   As Atoms and Newtons and things even flatter.

Moses said to the waters, "RECEDE!"
   which they did with a swish
     and all deliberate speed.

I'm not one with such tricks
   by sun or by moon
But I really don't care, —
   — I've got June

     with love from J.B.

11/68

Scarcely one-twenty-fourth of a second after release from the cooker, the primordial soup rained back down as a slippery lake on the floor. Apple sauce, from a similar catastrophe several years ago, is much better to use in this experiment. It sticks to the ceiling, transforming it into edible stalactites. The soup, on the other hand, lacks credibility and even Abby, the dog, backed away from it.

Fortunately, two dishes from the hurricane aftermath—Mom's baked ziti and chocolate chip cookies—were hits. (I now use my mother-in-law's healthier baked ziti recipe using ground turkey, not beef.) As for the primordial soup, clearly kitchen calamities don't always cause gustatory delight, but they definitely, definitively, can cause wonder.

BAKED ZITI

serves 6

1 large onion, *chopped*
3 cloves garlic, *minced*
1 pound ground turkey
1 (24-oz.) jar tomato sauce *(Classico Four Cheese, for example)*
1 pound dry ziti pasta
1 (8-oz.) block of mozzarella, *cut in chunks*
1 (8-oz.) container ricotta cheese
1 teaspoon sea salt
1 teaspoon fresh ground pepper

Preheat oven to 350 degrees; butter a 9 x 9-inch baking dish. In a large skillet, brown onions, garlic and turkey over medium heat. *(A little olive oil may be needed.)* Add tomato sauce and simmer 10 minutes. Meanwhile, bring a large pot of lightly salted water to a boil. Add ziti and cook until al dente, about 8 minutes; drain. Put a little sauce on the bottom of the baking dish, then layer as follows: ½ of the ziti and make little pockets of sauce and cheese. Repeat. Salt and pepper the top. Bake for 1 hour or until cheeses are bubbly.

Relax; everything can be done ahead, then baked just before you need it.

VIRTUES COOKING TIP:

wonder

As a virtue in the kitchen, wide-eyed **wonder** can transform the day into a big hit, perhaps with the entire family making Baked Ziti. Infuse the basic recipe with zingy flavors… hmmm, ever wonder about adding garden-fresh cherry tomatoes or chunks of cooked Italian sausage?

14) empathy

THE FRENCH CURE FOR HOMESICKNESS

During my sophomore year in college I debated applying to a study-abroad program in Lyon, France. The program offered by the University of North Carolina was targeted for French majors who had a B average or above. Alas, that wasn't me. I was an honor's student in Political Science but only had a casual knowledge of French. Should I still try?

If I could finagle it, studying abroad sounded cool—a definite upgrade from previous travel experiences. Better than my family's typical isn't-this-fun-camping-in-an-old-army-tent trip. Or the Manhattan excursions with us kids under a table in sleeping bags at a family friend's apartment. Or the previous summer's babysitting gig in Switzerland running after two energetic children. Besides, Paris would only be a train ride away. As the French writer Stendhal said: "Life is too short, and the time we waste in yawning never can be regained." I could use Lyon as a travel launchpad. And, as the same French novelist said in *Memoirs of a Tourist*, "I know of only one thing that you can do well in Lyon, and that's eat particularly well."

I could eat. I could learn more about preparing food. Julia Child had already introduced our family personally (or so it seemed because of her super-size personality on *The French Chef*) to cooking in France. I would be living in the gastronomic center of France.

Eagerly, I filled out the application and waited. And waited.

Toward the end of the spring semester a letter arrived. "I regret to inform you," it began. The letter ended by saying I was on a waiting list "in case something changes." June came and went, as did July. And in steamy August—my life seemingly a series of Stendhal's dull yawns, and just twenty-four hours before my parents and I were leaving to visit friends in Vermont—the phone rang.

The virtue of EMPATHY creates a deep understanding of another's situation and feelings.

"There's a place for you in Lyon," exclaimed a secretary in the French Department. "Someone dropped out. Can you be at New York City's Pier 92 on September 4? The group sails on a magnificent ocean liner, the *SS France*."

It is amazing what can be accomplished in a day. But after months of dreaming of France, and while girlfriends Carol and Connie heaved a year's worth of clothes into two suitcases, I wasn't so sure about spending nearly a year overseas. My girlfriends were my support group. I was close to my parents, and my brother Gene was still struggling in school. Did I really want to be that far away... 4,241 miles, to be exact?

"Try it out" was Momma's simple advice. "Give Lyon a chance. I think you'll end up finding a lot to like."

During the five days of our transatlantic crossing my worries subsided. It was easy feeling comfortable with a boatful of new friends—Rosemary and Laurie; Patsy, Diane, Teresa and Mary Ann; and some really cute guys—as we all leapt (inexpertly) into the lifestyle of sophisticated travelers. We dined on outrageous haute cuisine, the most extravagant food imaginable. An elegant Belle Epoque menu with thirteen courses for dinner: *hors-d'oeuvre, potages, oeufs, entrées* (the *Delices de Sole Bretonne*, for instance, was scrumptious beyond words; so delicious that I was reminded of Julia Child's first meal of sole en route to Paris that, as she said was, "the most exciting meal of my life"), *legumes* and *pâté, roti, buffet froid, salade, fromages, entremets, fruits, infusion, vins*. I tried them all.

Upon arrival, Rosemary, Mary Ann and I rented two rooms in a large apartment on Cours Franklin Roosevelt, a seemingly ideal half-hour walk from the university. But, with the others in dorms across the city, we were isolated.

And there followed soon a series of other eye-openers. I heard that a French friend, who was queasy in the mornings, suspected the culprit was all the rich food we'd been eating together; the doctor's diagnosis was... morning sickness. Another friend, saying he was "trying a little weed for fun," was surprised by our director stating at a weekly meeting, as if reading his mind, "The American consulate can do

nothing if anyone is caught smoking dope and jailed." What? He could end up in jail? Outside our main classroom at the University of Lyon picketing French students waved about placards and yelled concerns about a near doubling of tuition; outrageous, or so I thought, until I learned fees were still very reasonable, at least by U.S. standards—only about $100 a course.

Nothing was quite as it seemed, except the food.

The city's omnipresent cafes, bakeries and bistros offered incredible meals, even on a pauperly student's budget. Soon I put a hip-bulging, butt-bouncing thirty-five pounds onto my small frame. And, finally, I comprehended the real meaning of the word "moderation" as in food in moderation or more specifically, *Stop! No more than one croissant a day*, Elinor!

Still, as I walked along the Rhone River after classes, I couldn't resist one bakery. Jean-Jacques, the young owner, always greeted me with an exuberant, "*Bonjour, ma petite Américaine.*" Stopping there for a food pick-me-up became a daily ritual: Monday, a mini-bacon quiche; Tuesday, a delicate tomato tartlet; Wednesday, a lemon confection….

"*Merci beaucoup*," I'd say pushing several francs across the counter for my purchase. And then, thinking about my Dad's bread-baking, I'd pull out another coin and get a baguette. Before I'd leave Jean-Jacques would scoot into the back and emerge with something on the house like raspberry-flavored macaroons. Slightly crisp on the outside and chewy inside, a breath of sweet raspberries, they held a surprise taste of crunchy pistachios. The baker's attention felt heavenly for a girl (me) edging on homesickness.

One rainy fall day, my roommates off exploring, I looked glumly out my bedroom window and watched brown leaves from the planetrees spiral to the sidewalk. My French landlady had removed two lights from the chandelier over my bed, and only four tiny bulbs remained. It wasn't the first time Madame Loir had done this. I slipped momentarily down the hall to locate a vocabulary book and upon my return found Madame barring the door.

"*Fermez la lumière*," she scolded. "*L'électricité coûte beaucoup.*"

Her words were clear: Turn off the light. Electricity is costly. And I detected an unspoken message as well. *I wish you weren't here. I don't like having boarders in what used to be my in-law's luxurious apartment that we now must share with three strangers.*

At age nineteen, I was supposed to be having the time of my life, but her words were curt, and as the saying goes, it was the straw that broke the camel's back. I burst into tears. Not quiet sniffles, but blubbering sobs of anxiety that had built up over the past six weeks and surprised even me.

Back she came. "*Voulez-vous manger quelque chose avec moi?*" she now asked

> " From morning till night, sounds drift from the kitchen, most of them familiar and comforting…. On days when warmth is the most important need of the human heart, the kitchen is the place you can find it; it dries the wet sock, it cools the hot little brain. "
>
> –E.B. White

tentatively. She gestured toward a frying pan in her right hand that held sautéed onions.

I followed Madame Loir (yes, after turning off my light) into the kitchen. On the counter were chunks of potato and carrots floating in a bowl of water. Drying on the edge of the sink were chopped leeks. And in a stockpot, chicken bones fluttered around in a dance with celery and parsley. What was she cooking? She added the leeks and the onions and was soon making her family's version of Potato Leek Comfort Soup.

As we wobbled around in our own worlds—countries, ages and interests apart—her potato-leek potage, a classic French comfort food, turned out to be a peacemaker. We had to blow on each hot, velvety spoonful and talk. For the first time we pushed ourselves to communicate. Her husband's family, she said enunciating slowly in French so I could understand, was once very successful in the silk business until synthetic fibers became the rage. She said Roger was away on "business." But the sadness in her eyes indicated something more than tough financial times and watching francs misspent on electricity; her husband, it turned out, was a Frenchman secretly on the prowl.

As we talked more, I didn't feel so alone. It was as if her soup contained a secret ingredient—empathy, that elusive quality that can lessen problems and burdens, and build up friendship. (Soup is also an excellent way to elicit empathy's companion virtue, hope; see "The Soup Factory on Chase Avenue.") I searched for the French words to tell her about my facing so many confusing situations and missing my friends, parents and siblings. In halting French I explained: "My younger brother Gene is nearly blind and just wants to put paint on everything: canvas, plywood, cardboard, old T-shirts, basement walls. Art is the only thing he wants to do, and he writes occasionally that he is failing two courses in high school. Gene counts on me to help sort things out, but it's way too expensive to phone."

"Keep writing to him," she said in French. "A letter can be more useful than a hurried call."

A few weeks later she made another potage, this time with me next to her peeling the potatoes and carrots, our talks continuing. And in the months ahead—after a weekend in Paris and finally seeing the glorious Eiffel Tower; or visiting my Swiss friends; or spending two weeks in Russia with other political science students traveling behind the Iron Curtain; and especially after my excursion to Mont Saint-Michel and a most memorable foamy omelet at La Mère Poulard, first mentioned by my mother when I was much younger—I couldn't wait to return to my French home. I wanted to imitate Madame Loir's veal chops and salad vinaigrettes, her *pâté de campagne*, and, most of all, talk.

Salt is born of the purest of parents: the sun and the sea.

—*Pythagoras*

Toward the end of the school year Madame Loir invited me to make chicken crepes with her. As she went to add a pinch of sea salt, a little clumped and fell on the counter. She gathered it up quickly and threw it skyward.

"If you spill salt in my country, don't forget to toss it over your shoulder," she said laughing. "That way you hit the devil in the eye. We're a superstitious people, and it prevents further mischief."

"In America we toss salt for good luck," I said. "It's a similar superstition. I must have tossed around a lot of salt to be lucky enough to learn how to cook in France with you."

Funny, how shared soup (or crepes), served with sympathetic chatter, can banish the blues. And empathy's alchemy over food works any place in the world.

VIRTUES COOKING TIP:

empathy

If given a chance, the virtue of **empathy** produces unexpected results. Healing a lonely soul, for a start. Your kids can chop vegetables for a potato leek soup and surprise someone going through a rough patch with an offer for lunch.

POTATO LEEK COMFORT SOUP

———

serves 6

1 bunch leeks *(3 to 4 in all)*
1 medium onion, *diced*
3 tablespoons butter
1 cup carrots
4 medium Yukon gold potatoes
6 cups chicken stock
1 teaspoon sea salt
½ teaspoon freshly ground pepper
½ cup heavy cream *(optional)*

Wash the leeks carefully under running water to remove any sand. Discard the thin outer layer and, using only the white and light green portions, cut into half-inch sections. *(If you detect any hidden dirt, re-dunk leeks for another bath.)* In a 6-quart saucepan, sauté the leeks and onions in butter, roughly 8 to 10 minutes. Meanwhile, peel and dice the carrots and potatoes, which can be put in a bowl of cold water to prevent discoloration. When the onion-leek mixture is golden, add the carrots, potatoes, chicken stock, salt and pepper. Bring to a boil before simmering for about 20 minutes, until potatoes are tender. Use an electric emulsifier to purée the soup, and, if desired, add cream. Either serve immediately or cool and refrigerate. Gently reheat before serving.

Madame Loir's French Salad Dressing, so delicious it must be shared. In a glass container with a top, mix 2 tablespoons Dijon mustard and ½ cup balsamic vinegar; shake until the mustard dissolves. Add 1 cup good olive oil, and season with sea salt and freshly ground pepper. Shake firmly and refrigerate until ready to use.

15) loyalty

MEETING THE PARENTS, CHAPEL HILL STYLE

Alerted by the beeping of a taxi coming up Chase Avenue, I saw my father fly out the front door. And then I really saw him. He was wearing a ribbed sleeveless t-shirt, his dirty-kneed Levis cranked above his waist by a belt; his fringe of white hair, rumpled and uncombed. Dad had been baking bread for tonight's dinner and had hastily shoved the five loaves into the oven. I watched him stop to hide some messy mahonia leaves behind a bush and then bolt down the stone stairs.

What sort of first impression, I wondered uneasily, would he make on Peter, my new boyfriend?

Peter was from a very button-down, conservative, proper Toronto family. And there stood Dad in work clothes. A smear of flour was even imprinted on his bald forehead. It was like a sign that spelled out, "we're uncool." But it was too late to urge him back indoors to wash up and put on respectable clothes.

As for me, in a prim Villager dress and my best Pappagallo shoes,

I followed my father down the steps. I was starting to fume like an annoyed movie director who'd lost control of the production and sensed the film would be a flop.

"I'm John Allcott," he said, as if there was any doubt. "You'll meet my wife later this afternoon when June finishes work. Welcome back to Carolina."

Dad knew I'd met Peter earlier in the school year, among twenty students who were on a weeklong visit to the University of North Carolina, and that our group had reciprocated with a trip to the University of Toronto, in January, when his parents had me over for dinner. Both groups had made the same "will we EVER get there," twenty-three-hour bus ride. And he was aware that, of all crazy things, Peter and I had taken a fancy to each other over fiddle-playing and square dance do-si-doing at a UNC party.

As a virtue, LOYALTY stands steadfast, faithful to a person, ideal or custom.

Before I could sprint Peter off for a tour of the house and a chance to catch up alone, Dad launched into a story that left me gasping....

"You won't believe what happened earlier this week," he began, a glint in his eye. "The mailman knocked on our door saying $22 in cash was needed to pay for a C-O-D package from New York City. So I checked my wallet and found $11, then remembered $6 in my raincoat pocket, and dug into Elinor's brother's old piggy bank for five singles. All the time I was thinking, it must be something neat June ordered from an ad in *The New York Times*."

"Ripping open the package, out tumbled five cardboard boxes," he continued. "All contained men's underwear. Can you believe it? I've five of those fancy, low-cut bikini briefs."

Glancing at Peter, I suspected he had already sized up my father with one word: weird. An uncertain smile curled his mustache. And as I sucked in a quick breath of hot, humid Carolina air, I could see Dad was enjoying his performance. Perhaps he saw this as an icebreaker and didn't want us to appear stuffy. Or maybe this was his idea of a boyfriend initiation rite to test humor, or commitment. But whatever his reasoning I was aghast. I didn't know where this was going, nor could I stop it.

"Now, Peter, wouldn't you like to have one of the bikinis?" Dad asked. "All you have to do is quite simple. At dinner tonight, when my wife says something like 'We're soooo delighted to meet you finally,' you just make a burping sound."

"Well, I, hmmm, I... pretty house, so green... well, hmmm" were the nonsensical words bumping out of Peter's mouth as he looked around, no life-raft way back to the shores of a safe conversation.

But then, magically, a buzzer rang from the depths of Dad's right pocket. He pulled out a large, white kitchen timer. "Oops, that buzzing is for my bread," he said, striding two steps at a time up the stairs. "Gotta turn down the oven to 425 degrees while Elinor shows you our casa. And its color, one of June's favorites, is not really green but is a more artsy chartreuse."

If I'd somehow given Peter the impression on his earlier visit—during the square dance, barbecue and hand-clapping Baptist church service, during political science classes and pumping up "my dad as the head of UNC's Art Department," or during a glass or two of late-night bordeaux, "like the wine I had as a student last year in France"—that I was raised in a typical Southern home, well, that illusion just crashed. No, Robert Young *Father Knows Best* TV family either. And no stay-at-home mother.

To soften my family's zany ways, I wanted, desperately wanted, to appear conventional. Normal. And no question: this awkward boyfriend-meets-father moment was a killer. But one thing I knew with certainty. I was loyal. I would defend and uphold my father and my family even if it meant I had to put an end to this romance with Peter, the Canadian.

We walked quietly into the house. As I readied my defense of my fun-loving father, Peter surprised me. "What an awesome dad," he said. The youngest and most freewheeling of his four brothers and sisters, Peter told me that he liked my father's high-spirited ways. He liked the liberated dynamic of a woman working and a man in the kitchen. Most of all, Peter liked Dad's offbeat humor and quirky look.

"For his classes at UNC," I then explained proudly, "he often wears plaid pants and an untucked colorful Guayabera shirt under a brown corduroy jacket. It

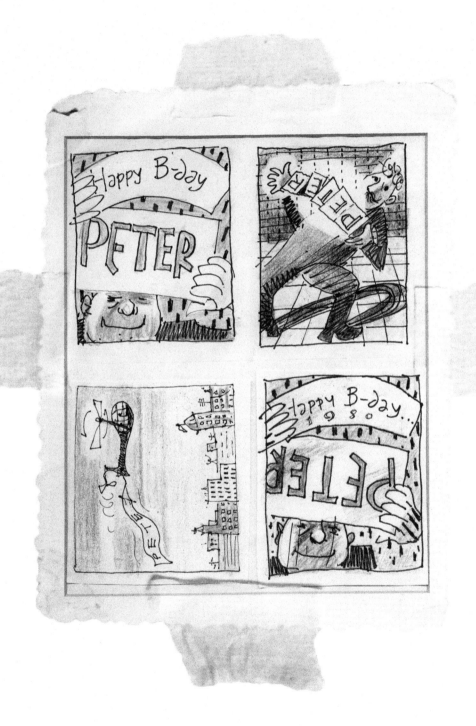

actually looks neat."

That night before dinner—with my now married sister Liz in Philadelphia soon having a baby; brother John, a medical resident, listening to people's heartbeats at New York's Montefiore Hospital, and brother Gene at Walt Disney's Institute of the Arts throwing paint on huge canvases in California—my father entertained Peter by playing Scott Joplin tunes on the piano; his fingers did a twinkly rendering of "Ragtime."

And then it was time to head to the family table, for Mom's ham-studded Scalloped Potatoes Gratin. Its topping used crunchy crumbs from Dad's bread. For me, Peter liking the dish or not was in its own funny way a test of his loyalty. The savory combination of potatoes and ham, some sautéed onions, all baked slowly in béchamel sauce, was true comfort food for our family, and if he didn't agree, it was like a red flag… something might be off.

A sense of unease hung around the table. It circled like a hungry seagull at the beach waiting to swoop in. Would Momma make some glad-you-are-here remark? Would Peter be a burping bad boy? Would he like the scalloped potatoes? And would Dad tell another embarrassing-to-me story? Before long Peter was talking about Canadian politics. But even that was one of those topics, wasn't it, along with religion and money, that rule books caution people to avoid in polite company? My breath-holding continued.

"Did you know that Canada's Prime Minister Pierre Trudeau was once blacklisted by your government?" asked Peter. "About twenty years ago Trudeau was prevented from entering the United States, basically because of having once attended a conference in Moscow and some left-leaning magazine subscriptions."

Was this a dig at the U.S. government, I wondered, trying to get a better sense of the dynamic. We knew, of course, that "Trudeaumania" had taken hold recently, and Canada's dashing, French-speaking jet-setter was frequently in our news.

"Fortunately," my father said, "the U.S. government isn't as restrictive as it was then."

"And Trudeau's more responsible now," added Peter. "Under his Just Society, the country passed legislation providing universal health care and making the country bilingual. Yet his personal motto, Reason Before Passion, must have been popularized before he dated Barbara Streisand and married high-spirited Margaret Sinclair this past March, a woman thirty years his junior….

"Oh, and I'd love more ham and scalloped potatoes," he continued. "Your casserole is delicious."

Mom beamed. "It's a favorite meal here—so simple and easy to make ahead of time." And then she voiced one of my concerns: "If someone doesn't like it, I might wonder if he is difficult to please, you know, finicky."

Despite my initial worries I sensed Peter was creating a positive impression. He was temperate, yet engaging and lighthearted—in some ways like my father. But my loyalties still felt yanked unevenly: parents versus new boyfriend.

Soon Peter swung into a high storytelling gear. He told us about his real passion, sports… playing golf with his older brothers Stu and John; teaching tennis to middle-age women; dashing off to play hockey, with the emphasis on the subzero temperatures growing up in western Canada. We remained tableside long after finishing thick slices of Grammy Chloupek's chocolate cake hidden under a thick layer of chocolaty frosting.

And, thank goodness, no burping from well-mannered Peter.

The next day I noticed that my father put aside Jansen's *History of Art*, the textbook for his summer introductory art class, and opened the *Durham Sun's* sports section, nearly a first. "Do you ever go to baseball games?" he asked Peter. And after more "chewing the fat," as the expression goes, after Peter read a draft chapter of Dad's book on UNC's architecture ("Your country's oldest state university has really cool history!"), Peter must have felt at home because, without asking, he headed to the refrigerator for a snack. That awkward first encounter of a new boyfriend meeting the parents was thankfully, blessedly, over.

Loyalty, I realized, isn't an either-or thing. Just fill your life with people, lots of them, who are full of integrity and fun—and crazy about your mother's (or father's) cooking.

VIRTUES COOKING TIP:

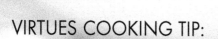

loyalty

A virtue in short supply, **loyalty** needs to be nurtured with time devoted to standing up for family, friends and one's beliefs.... Encourage these discussions over a dinner with Scalloped Potatoes Gratin, which creates loyalty in its own right.

SCALLOPED POTATOES GRATIN

serves 4 to 6

1 tablespoon good olive oil
1 medium onion, *sliced*
1 bunch green scallions, *diced*
2 cloves garlic, *minced*
2 tablespoons butter
2 tablespoons flour
2 cups milk
1 cup sour cream
1 cup Gruyere cheese
2 pounds russet baking potatoes *(about 6)*
1 pound prebaked ham *(optional)*,
cut into chunks

Preheat oven to 350 degrees. In a large skillet, heat the olive oil and lightly sauté the onions, scallions and garlic. Add the butter and then the flour, stirring constantly over medium heat for a minute or two. Pour in the milk and continue stirring until the "roux" thickens. Add in the sour cream and cheese, until it melts. Set aside. Peel the potatoes and slice thinly. Butter a medium-sized microwavable baking dish *(9-inch square, for instance)*, layer with potatoes, ham and sauce. Repeat for 2 to 3 layers. Microwave the dish for 10 minutes to speed up baking and then place in the oven for an additional 45 minutes. Pass under the broiler, if needed, for a golden brown top.

This dish is even better
the second night.

16) love

THE WEDDING BELLE

The postal truck circled the oak tree at the end of Chase Avenue and dropped a postcard in my parents' mailbox. "It's from France, from Elinor," said my mother, yelling over to my father who was mowing grass. "She says… she says, 'Isn't it wonderful—Peter and I got engaged as we biked in France along the Mediterranean. We're heading next to Switzerland and will stay with Suzi and Gil and their kids before flying home.'"

My postcard about getting married had them shaking their heads, puzzled. "A postcard?" Mom remarked. "For something this important? No details? Nothing about a place or date for the wedding? What's gotten into her?"

Dad was equally vexed. Although unconventional, he had a very conventional side when it came to *his* daughter, the quasi-Southern belle, scooting off to Europe with a young man from Toronto they hardly knew. "I told Elinor if she was going to marry Peter then she should do it before she left," he said. "Her response? She told me not to go bananas... they were only good pals. Do you think she might get married without us?"

Little did they suspect that a week earlier I'd sent a euphoric description of Peter's proposal. All the details! Since phoning was expensive, I'd packed everything into that letter, starting with my love for this handsome Canadian, eh. How he'd asked me to marry him on a sunny day while we biked between Nice and Monte Carlo. We'd stopped for lunch on a rocky ledge, I'd written, the shimmering sea lapping hundreds of feet beneath us; his proposal came during our picnic of *pâté* and cheese, a crunchy baguette. I added that two months earlier Peter first shared his feelings of deep affection when we'd biked to Chartres, the church's distant spires and flying buttresses seeming to spring up from French mustard fields as we pedaled up a hill and vanishing then as we went into a valley, and springing up again....

My letter described how in the ancient Gothic cathedral he'd whispered, "I believe you and I are meant to be together. Me, your skinny Canadian. You, my brown-haired, granny-glasses-wearing American. All this eating and biking and exploring is something we couldn't do easily back home; we're having such neat experiences... like Chartres. It's our own pilgrimage to this 800-year-old church and its famous *Sancta Camisa*. I mean really, can you believe that tiny relic over there is supposed to be a piece of the Virgin Mary's tunic worn at Jesus's birth? And this is how we're starting off together."

Mushy-eyed from writing the letter, I'd ended by saying Peter and I hoped to receive the blessings of both families and marry later in the winter in Chapel Hill. I'd popped the letter in an old rusty postbox in Nice, not far from the youth hostel where we were staying. I was happy as a lark in love and had no idea the French postal service might not do its Cupid's best.

When we arrived at Suzi and Gil's home in Switzerland, a short letter awaited us. "We are deeply disappointed," wrote my mother. "How could you be so cavalier about your wedding, one of the most important moments in your life?"

Confused and upset, I didn't know what to do. Her response didn't make sense. Dad had wanted us to marry; she thought Peter endearing. Why not their usual enthusiasm? Again, I debated phoning. But with only a few days before we were to leave, me to Carolina and Peter to Canada, he urged me to wait and talk face-to-face.

"El-e-a-nor All-cott," said Suzi two days later, pronouncing my name the European way, "you have a let-ter." I ripped open the envelope and found it stuffed with a crayoned drawing. Dad had sketched a grinning bear, his alter ego, standing next to what was clearly a caricature of Mom, their arms outstretched to a bicycle-riding, mustached Peter. And I was there, too: the long-haired, muscled gal on a bike next to him. (Not exactly the image of a Southern belle.) Their acceptance came in the form of a drawing.

It was a head-scratcher, though, why so upset and then so delighted. (That puzzle would only be pieced together upon my return with news about the delayed letter.)

Alas, my parents' elation didn't apply to Peter's family. He'd decided not to tell them. "Not now," he said quietly. "It's not that they don't like you; they do. It's just they think I should get my MBA at night and date more and that, at twenty-three, I'm too young to settle down. You know, my four brothers and sisters were all older when they got married."

An icy unease now wrapped around my love for Peter. No matter what, the reserved Griffiths would likely see me, a mere five months older, as a cradle-robber encouraging Peter to make this rash move. But parental blessings or not, we decided to remain firm on our decision to marry and settle in Montreal, where Peter could get a hotel job and French would be an asset.

In early November, we made one last bike ride. It was the thirty-five-mile trip to the Geneva airport. We tried to keep our spirits high. "This will work out somehow," said Peter, tenderly kissing me before I boarded my plane.

Weeks passed, and he didn't have the conversation. Instead, Peter immersed himself in his job search. In late November he phoned. "I told my parents tonight.

" Marriage is not merely sharing the fettuccine, but sharing the burden of finding the fettuccine restaurant in the first place. "

—Calvin Trillin

They aren't happy, but they didn't kick me out. Dad said if this is what I really want and I'm really sure, they'll go along with it." Appropriately, it was around the Griffith's dinner table when his sister Pat and her husband Hans were visiting, everyone seated. A good meal, wine and... his surprise.

We set a date: Saturday, February 17. Peter started his new job in the sales department at one of Montreal's grand hotels, the Queen Elizabeth. And before long a letter arrived for me. Not just any letter, but a much-thought-about letter bearing the distinctive cursive penmanship of Peter's father, James Stuart Griffith (a.k.a., Mr. Griffith):

> *I think it is about time I dropped you a note to wish you much happiness now and in the years ahead as Peter's bride. While no doubt you are aware of our very normal wish for Peter to have a few years of carefree bachelorhood before knuckling down to the responsibilities and restraints of the married state, no doubt you and Peter have made a sound decision. From the little I have seen of you I feel sure you two have a better than average chance of happiness....*
>
> *I expect too that you're both realists enough to recognize that you are not entering a state of everlasting bliss. My own mother used to say that one should be pretty much a saint to be successfully married to a Griffith in order to put up with his idiosyncrasies.*
>
> *Most important, we firmly believe that this is a permanent state of life, and that the 'til death do us part agreement is for real in the eyes of God, and not just a conventional platitude. Grayce and I feel sure you will work out your everyday disagreements and difficulties in a mature and intelligent manner.*
>
> *So Elinor, for better or for worse, welcome to the clan.*

The letter's tone was half welcome, half somber lecture (e.g., "a better than average chance of happiness"... really?). It was so unlike my dad's colorful sketches. But I had clarity on one point of human behavior. Most people act with restraint, not like the arms-flung-wide, crayoning Allcotts.

*F*inally, the wedding countdown began in earnest. A snowstorm hit Montreal midweek, and Peter phoned me in Chapel Hill. "I'm not sure I'll be able to fly out tomorrow," he said. I felt flutters of anxiety. Such a big chapter in my life was about to start, and no Peter Griffith.

Calls streamed in, though, from Peter's older brother in nearby Durham. A doctor at Duke University, John told us of each arrival: parents from Toronto, sister Pat from Sudbury and older brother Stu from Puerto Rico. At our chartreuse house, the seams were also popping: my sister Liz, her husband and two boys (Philadelphia), brothers John (New York) and Gene (California), and our grandmother (Washington, D.C.), along with Peter's three golfing groomsmen from Toronto, in the basement. At least Aunt Ruth (Madison) was staying wisely at the quiet and elegant Carolina Inn.

To pass the time and feed everyone, Dad baked Friendship Bread. He formed two loaves into a large *E* and *P*, and displayed them on the table. (For my sister Liz's wedding, he'd planted grass seed in the lawn out front with her and her fiancee Bill's initials, which sprouted into a vibrant green *L* + *B*.) Grammy Chloupek made her well-loved chocolate cake. Always pragmatic, Mom lined up a fourteen-foot-long U-Haul truck for our "honeymoon," a two-day trek to Montreal.

"Well, you already had a three-month pre-honeymoon in France, Italy and Switzerland," she said. "This short trip in a truck, Mrs. Soon-to-Be Peter Griffith, won't be bad."

At last, Peter called again. A few planes were taking off from Montreal; apparently he'd told just about everyone in the airport he was getting married. He had managed to switch flights and was arriving via New York. "It's been too long," he said. "Can you meet me at the airport, just you?" The soothing sound of Peter's voice, even two plane rides away, restored my sense of calm.

To ring those joyous wedding bells, I'd arranged a Catholic priest for Peter, a Protestant minister for me, Dad's piano playing for all. Finally, on February 17, at two p.m., I was wearing my mother's white silk wedding dress from thirty-one years earlier. We had scripted our own ceremony (considered daring at the time) and were in front of our families and friends saying words about love and commitment that danced deeply in our souls:

" Don't hide love. If you feel it, express it—not to demand that others love you back, but simply to live outwardly the best of what you feel inwardly.

The worst that can happen to your heart is not rejection by another person but failure to act on the love you feel. "

—Martha Beck, The Joy Diet

We stood face to face, eagerly, lovingly. Beside us, as we spoke our vows, were the priest in his long black robe and the minister in his suit. I was reciting Grampa Gene's "Irish Blessing" when a little child's voice rang out. It was my nephew Michael. Despite being only three, his words projected clearly to all 110 guests.

"Mommy," he said gesturing toward the priest, "why is that man wearing a black dress?"

Everyone laughed. The roll of laughter, including guffaws from Peter and my barely contained chuckles, thawed the differences separating our two families. Our love ignited over those laughs, right before we said the all-important "I do." Peter's father then read a telegram from Heather, the missing sister, on behalf of her family in Saskatchewan: "John's wish to you is for many babies. Pat's is for no divorce. Mary Lou's is for no fights. Chantal's is for equal rights. Nancy and the godson Tom ask your blessing. We all send you this traditional but heartfelt wish for a happy and meaningful life together: 'Love bears all things, believes all things, hopes all things, endures all things. Love never fails'—1 Corinthians 13. Love, the Meaghers."

And at our reception, not quite a pot-luck affair, but close, we offered regular and spiked fruit punch ("what, no bourbon?" said a Griffith brother). We had a Williamsburg Orange Cake made by my former high school home economics teacher. There were homemade cookies and Dad's Friendship Bread, and among other delectables, a large bowl of my neighbor Tera White's egg salad, a favorite growing up and now part of our wedding table.

Peter and I kissed. We fed each other nibbles of the Orange Cake. "Mr. and

Mrs. Griffith" was official now, sealed with cake and kisses....

Love is the universe's heartbeat. So why not take time to enjoy one of its many manifestations—celebratory food.

oyage

Father Bear, Feb. 19, 1974

an irish blessing

This blessing was carried in my grandfather Gene Chloupek's wallet from the day he received it during World War II until his death in 1964, and it was read at our wedding.

May the blessing of Light be on you, light without and light within.
May the blessed sunlight shine on you and warm your heart till it glows,
Like a great peat fire, so that the stranger may come
And warm himself at it, and also a friend.

And may the light shine out of the two eyes of you,
Like a candle set in two windows of a house,
Bidding the wanderer to come in, out of the storm.

And may the blessing of rain be on you—the soft sweet rain.
May it fall upon your spirit so that all the little flowers may spring up,
And shed their sweetness on the air.

And may the blessing of the Great Rains be on you.

May they beat upon your spirit and wash it fair and clean,

And leave there many a shining pool where the blue of heaven shines,

And sometimes a star.

And may the blessing of the Earth be on you—the great round Earth.

May you ever have a kindly greeting for them you pass

As you're going along the roads.

May the Earth be soft under you when you rest out upon it, tired at the end of a day;

And may it rest easy over you when at the last, you lay out under it.

May it rest so lightly over you that your soul may be off from under it quickly—

And up and off, and on its way to God.

And now may the Lord bless you all, and bless you kindly.

love

Like the seeds of wildflower, **love** blossoms
when cast wide, and often! What's better for
love than tangible expressions for family and
friends… perhaps some lovely Orange Cake?

ORANGE CAKE

serves 8

2¾ cups cake flour
1½ cups sugar
1½ teaspoons baking soda
¾ teaspoon salt
1½ cups buttermilk, room temperature
½ cup butter, *soft*
¼ cup canola oil
3 large eggs
1½ teaspoons pure vanilla extract
1 cup golden raisins, *cut up*
½ cup fine chopped walnuts or pecans
1 tablespoon grated orange peel

butter frosting

⅓ cup soft butter
3 cups confectioners' sugar *(sifted)*
3 tablespoons concentrated orange juice
2 teaspoons grated orange peel

Preheat oven to 350 degrees; line two 9 x 2-inch round cake pans with aluminum foil. Put all ingredients into the bowl of an electric mixer and blend for half a minute on low speed, scraping bowl constantly. Next beat 3 minutes on high speed, scraping occasionally. Pour into cake pans and bake for 30 to 35 minutes, until an inserted wooden toothpick comes out clean. Frost cake when cool.

Butter Frosting

Blend butter and sugar with an electric mixer. Stir in orange juice and peel, and beat until smooth.

Combine all dry ingredients the day before so you are mainly baking the cake on the day of the event.

17) simplicity

ANOTHER KITCHEN CATASTROPHE, MONTREAL

Everything started off well enough. As newlyweds Peter and I moved to Montreal
and were living in an apartment building near Mount Royal Park. Our tiny home felt
enormous, though, due to the view from the living room. The picture window captured
a truly panoramic sweep of the city and the distant St. Lawrence River, which cut a
silvery path across the horizon. At night, lights twinkled romantically below us.

Our kitchen shared much of the same view. Occasionally as I made
my friend's short-cut recipe for shrimp curry (catsup and sherry were the secret
ingredients) or other easy dishes, I'd see a boat churning its way up the river, or watch
gulls winging through wind gusts off the mountain. I'd find myself daydreaming of
family and friends 700 miles away in North Carolina, or Peter's parents, a little closer,
but still 300 miles off in Toronto. So to fill our new home with laughter (and chip away
at loneliness) we urged friends to visit us in our little aerie on the mountainside.

"Come and check out Quebec," I'd say. "This French-Canadian city is called
La Belle Province for good reason. Lots of attractions make it 'the beautiful province'

such as a popping good nightlife, awesome food, hiking and fishing. And even though Premier René Lévesque is spouting off about the Parti Québécois separating from Canada that won't likely happen."

Immediately taking us up on the offer was Gil, a young Swiss doctor who was giving a speech at an international conference for psychiatrists. Several years earlier a family friend had arranged for me to spend the summer in Switzerland where I had looked after his and his wife's two kids. When I was a university student studying in France I continued to see them during long school breaks, and each time my French would improve dramatically. Later, on a three-month biking trip after college, Peter also met them. Thanks to Suzi and Gil, I'd experienced a lot of "food firsts": my first cheese fondue, my first rabbit stew (not bad) and my first mouth-melting... well, for now let's call it an extraordinary Swiss dessert.

*The virtue of **SIMPLICITY** keeps things simple and straightforward, unpretentious.*

On that memorable day Suzi had asked, "El-e-a-nor my dear, after dinner might you join us for a car ride?" She thriftily served noodles and sausages that night, and then everyone got dressed up. Amidst great whispering she and Gil then strapped their two sleepy kids next to me in the back of their old Citroën Deux Chevaux. Gil wound the car through the hills of Lausanne, drove along Lake Geneva and pulled through the massive iron gates of a vine-covered restaurant. The moonlit lake, the shimmer of the distant Swiss Alps, the surprise of going into such a splendid restaurant all left me awestruck.

Speaking quickly and quietly to our waiter in French, Gil did the ordering. I could hear only one word, "spé-ci-al-i-té."

What a sight soon arrived at our table. Four mountainous meringues! Each filled an entire plate. Each sported white peaks that jutted up through mounds of whipped cream, mirroring our view across the lake of the snow-covered Alps. It took only my first spoonful—a delectably crispy and mouth-crunchy sugary confection with a smooth, creamy finish—and then another and another, and that soulful meringue sprinted up my list of desserts and staked an everlasting claim near the top.

"You like it?" asked a smiling Suzi, breaking the fourth meringue into two portions for her now wide-awake children.

"*Oui,*" I said, the sound muffled by another bite. And that evening, done quite affordably and with lots of whispered fun, was my unforgettable introduction to Swiss meringues.

So now four years later in Montreal, a teenager no longer, I wanted Gil's meal in my first home to be equally memorable. I hoped it would be seen as a reflection of my appreciation for his family's hospitality. There was just one problem. I didn't have a lot of experience preparing gourmet meals, and that gourmet part was especially important to Peter. His job as a sales director at the Queen Elizabeth Hotel meant he entertained clients at the hotel's legendary Beaver Club, where a wave of Béarnaise sauce lapped at the edges of our seared-to-perfection porterhouses; or he'd host dinners at the Salle Bonaventure and we'd slurp oysters, clams and mussels while everyone watched high-kicking (yikes, topless) can-can dancers. He expected fancy culinary creations without the chorus-girl prancing.

The St. Lawrence, seen from Ellie's and Pete's apartment-balcony.

I talked with Peter about the all-important menu. "I think you need to keep the meal real simple," he stressed. We decided that an easy recipe from my former French landlady in Lyon for *pâté de campagne* was an ideal hors d'oeuvre. A solution for the other end of the meal, dessert, leapt out, too. A family favorite, which I jokingly called "Tart Apple Tart," would have a gourmet appearance if I slivered the apples uniformly and took extra time to arrange the slices into artistic, symmetrical portions. Both recipes could be made ahead without any pressure.

Now with hours to spare before Gil's plane arrived, the *pâté* was in the fridge and the tart cooling on the kitchen counter. I walked leisurely to a market on Sherbrooke Street and gathered the remaining items for dinner: salad greens, fingerling potatoes and a one-and-a-half-pound fillet of halibut. To spice up the fish, after all it needed to look snazzy, I picked up ingredients for a fiery sauce diable. I'd tasted it on trout once at the Salle Bonaventure.

"It's not hard at all," the chef had explained. "Sauté shallots and garlic, add a shake of red pepper flakes and, after cooling, stir in Dijon mustard, a squeeze of lemon juice and some butter."

Soon this devilishly delicious sauce was in the fridge chilling. So far, so good for my first fancy dinner party, never mind that there would only be three of us....

When Gil arrived we stood at the apartment door for several minutes and talked "Franglais," that half-English, half-French spontaneous combination of languages. Each of us wanted the other person to feel at ease. He noticed that the 21-speed Mercier bikes leaning against the entryway wall were the same ones we'd used in Switzerland. The back and forth between languages, though, remained awkward until English won out.

"I need to be more fluent," said Gil. "This practice, it is needed for my conference."

All was going well... the *pâté* a hit, the potatoes steaming and the salad already on the table. I pushed the broiler on the kitchen's ancient gas oven to its top setting, 500 degrees (not a good idea), and placed the roasting pan with the halibut on the top rack. Ten minutes later I carefully removed the pan with oven mitts and lightly touched the warm flesh for doneness. Not quite ready, so back it went.

"It's already 7:30, way past midnight in Switzerland," said Peter anxiously minutes later. He walked over from the kitchen door, where he and our friend had been hovering, and whispered, "Can't you hurry things up?"

I stuck my arm back into the oven and began to pull out the fish. In my haste the roasting pan sizzled up against my wrist. My hand shot upward, knocking the pan back into the oven. But then in a confounding, once-in-a-lifetime acrobatic maneuver, the now perfectly broiled halibut somersaulted upward and outward and landed, *splat*, on the floor.

Our dinner's centerpiece then skidded ingloriously across several green linoleum tiles before coming to a halt near Gil's right foot. I was mortified. I was aghast. I wanted to flee to the bedroom and hide in the closet. Peter did not look happy either. "I'm so sorry," I stammered as I grabbed several ice cubes to cool the red welt on my wrist.

And what did Gil do? He laughed. A robust hah-hah-hah noise came from deep inside him. Grabbing the fish platter from the countertop, he scooped up our errant dinner and bounded with it to the table. "*Si la cuisine est bonne, on peut manger sur terre*," he said. "Please, not a moment of worry."

His kitchen wisdom was rather silly, "If the cuisine is good, you can eat on the floor." It was the Swiss version of the five-second rule.

And that's when I had a flashback of an earlier kitchen catastrophe. After a hurricane knocked out power at my parents' home, Mom had salvaged a stewing hen from the thawing depths of the old freezer and was fixing it for soup when suddenly the valve on the pressure cooker had a meltdown. The force of the explosion flung chicken bits to the ceiling—"a most unexpected cosmic encounter with primordial soup," said Dad—and it rained back down on the floor below, and even the dog refused to eat it. The situation so comical, Dad wrote up the story for his weekly family letter, his own personal, wondrous experience with the Big Bang.

A sense of wonder and fun, I realized, was what had turned that happening into an oft-told family story. I'd forgotten to smile when facing my own culinary disaster... until Gil stepped in and laughed. And with that realization, I pulled the chilled sauce diable out of the fridge, cut off a bit and mustered up a smile. I tried to appear casual as I placed the slices of sauce on our still-steaming, clean-off-the-floor halibut.

"*Bon appétit*," I said, my voice high, my cheeks red. I was thinking of my kitchen idol, Julia Child, and her masterful performances when things in the kitchen went kaput. Fortunately, the rest of our dinner was already made and went smoothly, so by the time we forked into the fruit in the Tart Apple Tart, everyone was relaxed. And there was no question, my first dinner party would long be memorable—though not in the way initially envisioned.

This is why, when new to giving dinner parties (or planning a big event), it's wise to keep things simple, real simple, and embrace any kitchen catastrophes that happen along the way.

Epilogue for Foodies:

French-Canadian neighbors—Gerard Blackburn and Ruth Croft—soon befriended us. Gerard was a culinary maestro and I became his assistant working on my skills. After hunting and fishing excursions in Ungava Bay, a thousand miles to the north, he'd return with prized catches and ask us for supper: Arctic char, wild duck, venison steaks and roast goose; the goose always prompted him to whip out his lighter mischievously for some flambé-ing of the cherry sauce.

We joined them for trout-fishing on remote lakes and met Henri, the editor of a French hunting and fishing magazine. (No specifics, however, will be forthcoming about a short-lived friendship with a nefarious Quebecois who used sticks of dynamite to "urge the fish to come to the surface, eh eh," as he said, then skimmed off a few to eat.) One day Henri asked if we'd like to join his magazine's team-building outing. By then I was an editor at *Reader's Digest* and liked the idea of an adventurous weekend of skeet shooting on an island in the St. Lawrence River. My husband and I helped with dinner: an everyone-take-a-turn-twirling-the-lamb-on-a-spit extravaganza. Before long Gerard asked us to join North Lake, his fishing club near Ottawa—its cook known for lemon meringue pie. And by the next summer we were visited by many family and friends, all quick to reserve advance pieces of the much-coveted pie.

HALIBUT (OR SALMON) WITH SAUCE DIABLE

———

serves 4

4 *(6 oz.)* halibut or salmon fillets

sauce diable
2 tablespoons shallots
2 cloves garlic
2 tablespoons olive oil
¼ teaspoon red pepper flakes
2 tablespoons Dijon mustard
1 lemon *(rind and 2 tablespoons juice)*
4 tablespoons butter, *room temperature*

Preheat oven to 400 degrees. Butter a 9 x 13-inch baking dish and add the fish, skin side down. Bake for approximately 10 minutes, or until fish flakes with a fork. Carefully top with several rounds of Sauce Diable and put back into oven for another minute or two.

Sauce Diable

After chopping the shallots and garlic, lightly sauté them in olive oil, adding the red pepper flakes. Turn off heat and work in the mustard, lemon rind and juice, and butter. Once cool, place on a large piece of plastic wrap, shape into an-inch-wide roll and refrigerate.

If you need a simpler apple dessert, consider **Apple Crisp**. Just grab the same 9-inch square baking dish and heap in 6 cups of diced tart apples, 1 tablespoon flour, ½ cup sugar, 1 teaspoon cinnamon, a little salt, 2 tablespoons lemon juice and 2 tablespoons water. Toss the ingredients. For the topping, blend: 6 tablespoons butter (softened), 6 tablespoons flour, ½ cup light brown sugar and ¾ cups rolled oats. Spread over the top and bake in a preheated oven at 350 degrees for 40 to 50 minutes. The top should be golden and bubbly.

TART APPLE TART

_____

serves 6

½ cup soft butter
¾ cup sugar
2 large eggs
1 lemon, *grated for rind*
4 teaspoons lemon juice
1 cup sifted all-purpose flour
⅛ teaspoon salt
5 tart apples,
peeled and cut into ⅛-inch slices
2 tablespoons melted butter

Preheat the oven to 350 degrees. Line a 9-inch square baking dish with aluminum foil. With an electric mixer, beat butter and ½ cup sugar until creamy. Add eggs one at a time, beating. Add lemon rind and 1 teaspoon of the juice. Mix again. Sift flour and salt together, gradually adding to the batter and beating thoroughly. Pour the batter into the baking dish. Toss apple slices gently with the remaining 3 teaspoons lemon juice and arrange evenly over batter in three rows with a slight separation in the middle. (This forms the six pieces, with each grouping of apples sandwiched in a tightly packed line.) Drizzle melted butter over apples and sprinkle with the remaining sugar. Bake for 1 hour until apples are golden brown and batter pulls away from the sides.

VIRTUES COOKING TIP:

simplicity

When anxieties and worries pile up, the virtue of **simplicity** allows your family to stay calm. For stress-control at meals, keep things simple, as in "Fish with Sauce Diable and Tart Apple Tart" simple, especially when guests are coming for dinner.

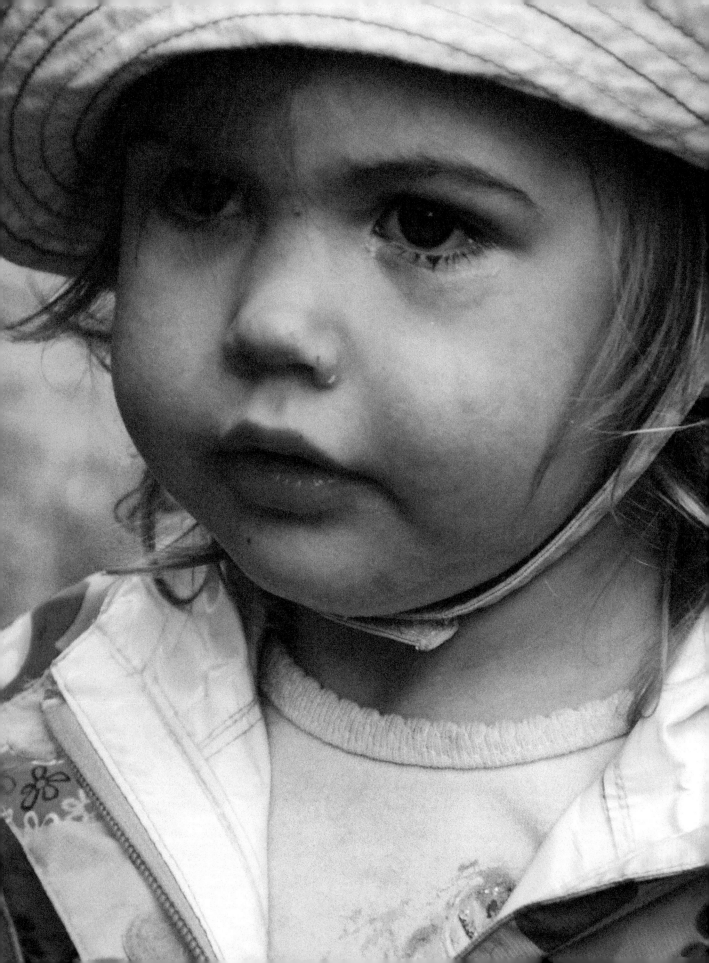

18) gratitude

PARENTING? AS EASY AS PIE

I was fixing chamomile tea in my kitchen in Millwood, N.Y., when I heard the buzz of a chainsaw. My energy sagging, I was two weeks overdue for my first child. I climbed gingerly down the hillside toward my neighbors' home to investigate, slow step by slow step, my stomach preceding my body by a good foot. A man was slicing at the base of a towering Norway spruce, while another workman kept tugging at the end of a rope that was attached about fifty feet up, to direct the tree toward a clear patch of lawn.

"How's it going?" yelled my neighbor Georgette, spotting me as I emerged from the bushes and stood along the far side of her pond. "Hot enough yet for you and your big belly?"

"I can't believe my labor hasn't started yet," I said. "I'm exhausted."

My body was tense from the roar of the chainsaw. The tree's

position was dangerous—my neighbor's house only thirty feet away on one side and a four-car garage on the other. Bobbing unsteadily, the spruce snapped and careened toward the garage. The assistant yanked at the rope again and again to change its direction. With an earth-quaking thud the tree smacked the lawn, its branches swishing dangerously against the garage.

"Good golly," said Georgette shaking her head, "that was close."

"I... I think I just had a contraction," I said. "That tree got my heart racing, my tummy jumping, and now a little pain comes and goes."

"Let's phone your obstetrician and get Peter home. Your baby's going to arrive soon. And when you're back from the hospital, I've planned a special treat."

"Oh that's so thoughtful, but don't worry for a moment about us," I replied. "We'll be fine, and our parents will be visiting in a month or two. You really shouldn't."

*An attitude of **GRATITUDE** makes a virtue out of sharing words of thanks.*

My doctor wasn't overly concerned about the mild contractions and suggested waiting longer. So, when Peter returned from his job in New York City, we had a light snack and around nine at night drove to the Northern Westchester Hospital. The windy road took us past the headquarters of Reader's Digest. I'd worked for the company in Montreal and now, after transferring to the "mothership," was a senior editor for the magazine. With a new baby there would be less time for article-editing and magazine-reading, which involved scanning up to 200 different magazines and newspapers for reprints, story ideas and humorous jokes.

Peter checked me into the hospital's maternity wing, constructed with money donated by Dewitt and Lila Acheson Wallace, the founders of Reader's Digest. "Ice chips," I blurted. "My mouth is so dry. I'd love a Dixie cup of ice chips."

I began to pace the floor, Peter in step beside me. That evening turned into morning and morning into afternoon and still no baby. We stopped often to gaze into the nursery and take in the recent arrivals. Girls with delicate pink-and-white striped stretchy caps. Boys wearing blue-and-white ones. After a while I couldn't look any longer. My doctor soon gave me a hit of Pitocin, a drug to quicken contractions, and Kathleen Grayce arrived finally.

Black tufty hair, a tiny rosebud of a mouth, all the requisite fingers and toes, Kathleen was perfect. We couldn't believe our good fortune. And then the cells in her tubby baby belly must have fired up a message to her already active brain that alerted her ready-to-be-tried-out vocal cords, and she let out a monstrous cry that meant, "FOOD! FOOD NOW! FOOD RIGHT NOW!"

Tired as we were after her birth, an immense feeling swelled up, so powerful that we—new parents in our thirties—would have given her anything at that moment... our home, our meager bank account, our old yellow Toyota Celica sports car. Yet all Kathleen wanted was food.

"Remember, you're eating as a team," said the lactation nurse. "No wine or alcohol. No garlic, onions, chili or pepper. And forget greasy foods like French fries." After pausing and with deliberate emphasis she added, "and no chocolate."

Okay, I realized, this baby-business was going to separate me temporarily from my gastronomic pleasures. But no chocolate, really? Meanwhile, my colleagues at The Digest were keen on Kathleen's birth and sent around a memo proclaiming, "Another Baby Boom Seems Near":

In a move widely expected by experts to bring an end to her nine months of pregnancy, Elinor Griffith delivered a baby (she had hoped for a teenager) on Thursday, July 22, at 7:45 p.m.

After twenty-three hours of labor Kathleen Grayce "Ziggie" Griffith made her appearance in the world, looked around, asked for some French fries, whined for several minutes to go back in, then settled down in bemused contemplation of her Dad, to whom emergency staff were simultaneously applying resuscitation measures and Gestalt therapy, his customary aplomb lying in tatters on the delivery-room floor.

The newcomer weighs eight pounds, eight-and-a-half ounces and wears a size 11 shoe. Doctors attributed her 23-hour malingering to a virulent systemic dismay brought on by her mother's daily reading aloud in the past few months of particularly pessimistic Evans and Novak political columns. However, the doctors were amazed at the couple's mastery of the Lamaze natural childbirth methods, in which the father calculates the cost of college tuition, while the mother wipes his brow, and the doctor practices his putting and the baby begs for drugs in order to forget the whole drawn-out delivery.

Before Peter and I knew it we were walking up our driveway, Kathleen snuggled on his shoulder. We spotted two large brown paper bags wedged against the back door. "Guess what?" said Peter peering at a note. "The Mapes left us a heap of goodies."

I was ravenous. After days of so-so hospital food and a pile up of missed meals, I hungered for home cooking. What did we find? Roasted rosemary chicken. Mashed potatoes. Fresh baked bread. A zucchini tart with veggies from their garden. Rusty-red heirloom tomatoes. A sea of blueberries peeking out from under the pastry strips of a homemade pie. Even a bottle of champagne. And, truth be told, I was ready for a small celebratory glass. I felt euphoric, my gratitude soaring. Kathleen was our miracle.

Food! Drink! For our late lunch we scooped into the bags, dove into the blueberry pie. And Peter, the proud father, popped open the champagne and gave a toast, "To our family."

I could hardly wait to phone the Mapes and convey thanks. "That pie has five pints of berries I picked at a farm up the road in Yorktown," said Georgette. "I loved making it for you. You know, we wanted to help out." And soon Georgette was at the door, her arms welcoming Kathleen.

I'd always been a "giver," I realized, like my parents. We were energized by doing things for others. Dad delighted in dropping off loaves of his Friendship Bread and fun sketches. Mom loved to share Mason jars of homemade pickles, dilly beans, or pink applesauce from North Carolina mountain apples. She would give away funky baskets she'd woven out of wisteria and grape vines. She'd overnight boxes of spring's first daffodils to northern relatives still shoveling out from under wintery snows.

" When eating fruit, remember who planted the tree; when drinking water, remember who dug the well. "

–Vietnamese Proverb

But when it came to letting other people put themselves out for us, we were reluctant. We didn't want to be a bother. And we always protested with quite a few "you shouldn'ts."

As a new mother, my response to offers of help changed dramatically. Along with the notion of "give," I warmed to the notion of "give-and-take"—a more balanced arrangement allowing friendship to thrive. And what a profound sense of appreciation came in accepting those offers. My friend Fran, soon to be Kathleen's godmother, offered to watch her while a doctor checked out my lingering mammary infection. "Yes," I said immediately. Later Fran confessed that she spent the entire time bent over Kathleen's bassinet watching every inhale... "just to be sure she hadn't stopped breathing." I felt such gratitude.

And when my parents proposed flying up earlier from North Carolina than planned, I said another relieved "yes." More gratitude. Peter and I then made quick plans for Kathleen's christening so her other grandparents—Stuart and Grayce Griffith; yes, that grandmother was her namesake—could also join us.

Upon Dad's arrival he headed to the grocery store right away. Picking through the Granny Smith apples, he told the other shoppers: "My daughter just had a baby, her first, a beautiful little girl named Kathleen. This afternoon I'm going to make my granddaughter her first Circus Tent Apple Pie."

Ten Granny Smith apples, a small container of cinnamon and a five-pound bag of all-purpose flour were among Dad's treasures. He also found a rare treat, Long Island duck breasts. A little later, over a celebratory dinner of roast Duck Breasts with Green Peppercorn Sauce, my parents, Peter and I relived our exciting recent events, starting with how the near-calamitous crash of the tree had precipitated Kathleen's birth. And then, my feet up in a cozy stuffed chair, Kathleen snoozing, her head nestled near my heart, I most gratefully accepted a piece of Dad's pie—its golden crust towering like a tent over the cooked apples.

New parenthood was, at that shiny moment, as easy as pie. The sleepless nights; the infection; the fog in my head mid-afternoon, still unshowered, still nightgown-wearing, had vanished from mind. Instead, I felt blissful as I spooned into the apples. From across the living room I heard Dad say, "I've been reading up on cinnamon, the spice I sprinkled on little Kathleen's pie. From tree bark, it was once a gift for kings and queens, and used in Egypt since 2000 BC. Supposedly it was added to Moses's holy anointing oil. Now Kathleen knows of its enticing fragrance, its history recorded somewhere in her brain. She'll grow up loving its distinctive sweetness in pies and cinnamon rolls."

Tiny as she was, my daughter was already experiencing some of the same culinary scents and sights of my childhood in Chapel Hill. My deep gratitude embraced the BIG (her healthy birth) and the little: this glorious Circus Tent Apple Pie; Georgette's blueberry pie and champagne chaser, Fran's eagle-eyed babysitting....

Astronomer, astrophysicist and author Carl Sagan said, "If you wish to make an apple pie from scratch, you must first invent the universe." The miracles of the universe are manifested in everything around us. Illumination comes when we pause in gratitude, in stillness, our eyes opening in appreciation for these most wondrous creations, big and little, like babies and pie.

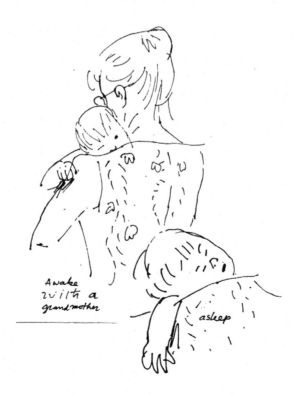

Awake
with a
grandmother

asleep

VIRTUES COOKING TIP:

gratitude

Gratitude is the moment of pause, the reflection of thanks, that enhances the day, the week, the year. Practice gratitude by saying a family blessing at dinner or starting a robust discussion when everyone says what he or she is grateful for. Apple pie-eating, hopefully.

CIRCUS TENT APPLE PIE

serves 8

Store-bought crust *(Or use French Pastry Dough; see recipe for 7 Frog Blueberry Pie.)*
8 large tart apples *such as Granny Smith*
1 lemon, *for zest and juice*
¼ cup all-purpose flour
¾ cup sugar
1 teaspoon cinnamon
¼ teaspoon nutmeg *(optional)*
4 tablespoons butter

Preheat over to 425 degrees. Place a pie crust on the bottom of a 9-inch ruffled round pie dish. Peel the apples, cut into chunks and put in a bowl. Squeeze in lemon juice to keep apples from turning brown and for a citrusy taste. Mix the flour and ½ cup of the sugar, and then sprinkle ¼ cup of it on the pie bottom. For the rest of the flour-sugar mixture, add more sugar—¼ cup—as well as the cinnamon, nutmeg and lemon zest. Next put half the apples into the pie dish, dot with butter and add a generous amount of the flour-sugar mixture. Repeat. Top with the second crust and seal the edges using the tines of a fork. Place on a baking sheet *(to deal with spillovers)* and bake for half an hour at 425 degrees, and then turn to 325 for another half hour.

For a special touch, use a fork and prick the top of the pie to form the initials of someone you love—your spouse, a child, grandparent or visiting friend. This vents the pie and shows gratitude. Also, a gift of an apple pie in a beautiful fluted pie dish will be long treasured.

DUCK BREASTS WITH GREEN PEPPERCORN SAUCE

serves 4

2 duck breasts *(1 pound each)*
½ cup chicken stock
1 teaspoon corn starch
½ cup creme fraiche
2 tablespoons mashed green peppercorns
1 teaspoon sea salt

Preheat oven to 450 degrees. With a knife cut a crisscross pattern on the duck skin and use a fork to prick a few tiny holes, then place skin side up on the rack of a small roasting pan so fat can run off. Broil for 20 minutes (the flesh should still be pink), remove from the oven and cover with aluminum foil. After skimming off the duck fat, use the chicken stock to deglaze the pan, scraping in pieces of duck for the sauce. Pour this juice into a small saucepan, add corn starch, creme fraiche, green peppercorns and salt. For approximately 10 minutes cook over a moderate heat until the sauce thickens. Carve duck breasts, fan pieces on the plate and puddle sauce around each serving. It's elegant and simple.

To carve duck breasts, cut on the diagonal into thin slices, thus avoiding toughness.

19) Flexibility

HOLA PAELLA

My sister Liz's letter from Seville, where her husband was doing research in the National Archives of Spain, was tempting: "Why don't you fly over for a week or two this August and we can go from castle to castle and see the country as it was hundreds of years ago. The food is so amazing... paella, tapas, ceviche, calamari, also olives like you've never tasted before. My kids would love it, too."

And *my* kids? How would they fare mommy-less? With Kathleen having turned four earlier in the week, on July 22, and my new baby Alex toddling about as he approached his first birthday, I felt conflicted. Who would wake them in the morning? Who would make them all those special "mommy meals" and tell them nightly stories and do tuck-ins? Even knowing they'd be fine with my husband and our sitter Charlotte, a drama still played out in my head with lots of scary "what ifs" and always ending with worries that my children might feel abandoned.

Timing wasn't great for work either. At Reader's Digest, I had only recently undertaken a new assignment to turn around the Editorial Correspondence Department, an area with a dozen employees overseeing thousands of reader letters annually and 25,000 author submissions. I needed to modernize and streamline the department. But my body kept rebelling from the long, tense hours and would toss me a migraine. Not painful, not like when I was a child, but still thirty-minute episodes every month or so with disorienting auras of spinning, blinking lights and scotomas, or the partial loss of vision.

As circumstances change, **FLEXIBILITY** *is the virtue that helps you cope, adapt and grow.*

Always on the run, always trying to do my best for others, always juggling, I deeply craved restorative "me" time. I wanted a better work-family-me balance—and, most important, to have more fun. Later that afternoon I discussed the trip with my husband. "I don't think I should go," I told him. "But my migraines are like a wake-up call that things aren't right. I'm always racing around doing the same things. I know getting away could be a smart move... for me. But I'm not sure about it for everyone else. "

"Don't worry about us or your work," said Peter. "You need time off for yourself and have never been to Spain. This is a rare opportunity. Liz and her husband speak Spanish and know the country. Really, no worries."

With that, I pushed at my stuck "flexibility" switch—that ability to go with the flow. An imaginary button went from the "no" position to "yes." Opening to new possibilities, I purchased a plane ticket. And now as the jet raced faster and faster up the runway, an intense feeling of elation overtook me. Not to permit myself a moment of anxiety (*really*, was this trip a smart move?) I opened up *Iberia*. I'd brought James Michener's book along for his colorful look at Spanish history, much of it, I was told, organized around specific towns. I started to read the introduction:

> *I have long believed that any man interested in either the mystic or the romantic aspects of life must sooner or later define his attitude concerning Spain. For just as*

Alexander John Griffith

August 21

8 lbs. 15 oz.

Joy!

this forbidding peninsula physically juts into the Atlantic and stands isolated, so philosophically the concept of Spain intrudes into the imagination, creating effects and raising questions unlike those evoked by other nations....

Romance, well, that wouldn't be in store for me, but a more mystical experience sounded enticing. I plunged deeper into the book....

I was greeted at the Madrid-Barajas Airport with lots of "I can't believe you really did this" back-clapping. Lots of swinging around of my niece Heather (eleven) and hopping up and down with nephews Chris and Mike (fourteen and sixteen). Our first stop was the medieval walled city of Avila. We took two small rooms in what was formerly the sixteenth century Piedras Albas Palace, now a parador, or a government-run historic hotel, built into the city's massive protective walls.

That night at an "early" eight p.m. dinner of roast chicken at a local restaurant, Bill started to read to us about Avila from his own well-thumbed copy of *Iberia*:

> *Most visitors who come to Avila do so to pay homage to a remarkable woman whose piety made the city famous. The woman was Santa Teresa de Avila (1515-1582), foremost of the Spanish mystics. She was born of a good family and at the age of eighteen unexpectedly announced her intention of joining a convent.... At the age of forty she chanced to see a statue of Christ that had been left accidentally in her path and in a moment of divine inspiration she saw through to the reality of God.... [As Saint Teresa writes in the opening of her book Interior Castle] "I began to think of the soul as a castle made of diamond or very clear crystal in which there are many rooms, just as in heaven there are many mansions....*
>
> *"For if we consider the matter, the soul of the righteous is but a paradise in which, as God tells us, He takes delight....*
>
> *"Let us then consider the many mansions of this castle, some up high, others lower down, still others along the sides, and in the very center of all the principal one, where takes place the most secret intercourse between God and the soul."*

A member of the Quaker faith, Bill stopped occasionally to answer questions from his children about souls and paradise. At one point Heather asked solemnly, "Is this woman a real saint?"

"Yes, she is the patron saint of Spain," I said, wondering if my young niece thought Santa Teresa was someone who got thunderbolts of information directly from God. "I heard that sixteen years ago, in 1970, she was one of the first two women in Catholic history to receive the title of Doctor of the Church—that was a big deal. Let's look around tomorrow for the Convento de Santa Teresa, which was built over the house where she was born."

Seeing our pleasure talking and eating, our waiter asked if we'd like to come back the next night. "We could make you a magnificent paella," he said. "The dish is prepared as if you're in Chef Jorge's home. He gets the freshest seafood from the coast and uses his family's special recipe from Barcelona." A warm handshake, and we were all set. (More on this memorable paella and Santa Teresa a little later.)

Much of the rest of the week was a journey through history. We had fun investigating the area's Three *C*'s—castles, churches and convents—always on the lookout for special food. Totally flexible, off we went to explore....

In the city of Salamanca, for instance, while sharing *churros*, or long cake-like pastries that are cooked in olive oil, we spent hours poking around the old city. Considered by many to be the heart of Spanish culture, this historic area was home to dozens of churches, many having fallen on tough times. To illuminate the altar in one church for a few minutes, we had to stuff 60 céntimos into a money box so the electricity would be turned on. "Just a few streets away is the country's most famous center of learning, the University of Salamanca," said Bill. "It was founded in the 1200s about the same time as the Sorbonne."

Another day in Penafiel, from the lofty central tower of its castle—which stretches 200 yards in length and is among the country's most impressive medieval fortresses—we surveyed the Duero River and the town below. The kids laughed about the "gopher holes" dotting the hillside; actually, the holes were vents for the caves deep

Be a Flexitarian... Try to be flexible when it comes to eating. Eat healthy, but enjoy the occasional indulgence and meals in the company of friends without scrutinizing ingredients or feeling guilty.

—Darina Stoyanova

underground that keep Ribera del Duero wines at a constant temperature. At a store I selected a hand-smocked dress with delicate pink and green flowers for Kathleen, and then spotted two, ten-inch-tall silver medieval soldiers.

"I'll take them, too," I said.

Overcome suddenly by tears I asked my sister, "Can you tell the shopkeeper in Spanish that today, August 21, is my son's first birthday? I deeply miss him and my daughter."

Liz gave me a comforting hug as the shopkeeper wrapped up the packages. My sister knew that marrying Peter and having high-spirited Kathleen and my bright-eyed, already inquisitive son were the best things that had happened to me. And as a mother, she understood that my heart, bumped around by thoughts of Alex's birthday, was awash with concerns about their well-being and happiness. But she also very much supported time off from mothering, for me.

"Let's get lunch and a glass of Ribera red," said Liz. "We'll celebrate Alex over food."

Our next historic town was Valladolid. We emerged from a divine chocolateria and found ourselves viewing a rare event, the running of the bulls through the city's streets. Firecrackers snapped and popped, and my nephews Chris and Mike were among dozens of boys chasing the animals. Suddenly, Chris was pushed accidentally from behind, and I gasped as he tumbled and rolled toward the stomping feet of one of the beasts.

Fortunately, there was no life-threatening slash of a bull's horns. No goring of Chris. Just a messy skinned knee. Very fortunately, the bulls weren't real, though the city did sponsor an actual bull-running in September. Instead, these bulls were life-sized paper-mache creations, each supported by two men who ran the beast this way and that, and occasionally swooped into the crowd.

On we went to Segovia and Toledo, and then back to Madrid. At an annex to the Prado I was standing with Liz's family in front of Picasso's twenty-five-foot-long *Guernica*, showing the bombed Spanish city. My sister and I felt a sense of time-travel, as a strong memory overcame us from our childhood. "For years this masterpiece was

| *The Virtues of Cooking*

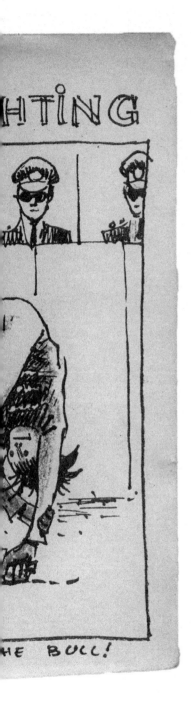

in safekeeping at New York's Museum of Modern Art," said Liz to her kids. "Aunt Ellie and I viewed it there with our parents. It was one of the paintings most admired by Grampa John."

"Grampa told us," I added, "that following the artist's instructions, *Guernica* was to be held outside of Spain until General Franco was gone, and liberty and democracy restored. Only then could it be sent to Spain. That happened, finally, in 1981."

"I can't believe we're all seeing it here in Spain," I said. "Dad will be pleased."

Unsettled after seeing the painting and wanting to pause, we spotted a bar nearby… food would get us reenergized. Among an assortment of tapas were *chopitos*, or batter-fried baby squid, and shrimp *ceviche*, and dishes using green Manzanilla olives. "I read last night that King Alfonso X, the King of Castile, came up with the idea for tapas," I said. "Supposedly back in the thirteenth century he was recovering from illness and needed many small meals to return to good health. A few tapas sound perfect for us right now."

All these experiences with Spanish food and history intruded into our imaginations, as Michener verbalized so well, and started to reshape our thinking. But among all the happenings, the paella in Avila was the most memorable.

Maybe it was the anticipation of my first taste of Spain's national dish. Maybe it was the excitement of returning to a nice restaurant, after an afternoon in the hot sun exploring the area where Santa Teresa was born 500 years ago. Or maybe it was just knowing that I was actually, really, finally, fulfilling my commitment to renew myself, to relight the candle within. When Chef Jorge proudly presented his paella—a cloud of steam swirling over succulent chunks of lobster, tiny clams, mussels, pink roasted shrimp and morsels of white fish—it seemed to whisper "enjoy this rare time in Iberia." I nearly clapped in delight.

The seafood carried the scent of the sea, familiar to the chef growing up in Barcelona, and a hint of exotic yellow saffron. I tried the lobster, so delicious, and had to restrain myself from taking another mouthful of the paella immediately, a warm clam already on my fork. The rice, speckled with local peas, tomatoes and red peppers, complemented the seafood, the same underlying hint of saffron, but with its own delectable, chewy appeal.

The paella was incredibly satisfying.

"Aunt Ellie, Aunt Ellie," cried Heather. "What did Mr. Michener say about paella? Did he eat it too?"

Once again out came *Iberia*. In Michener's search for that "golden moment" of having a perfect Spanish paella, a process that "would yield compensations other than the discovery of the moment itself," he admitted to never being satisfied. "I am convinced," he wrote, "that in Spain I shall never hear a good flamenco, nor eat a decent paella... but I would always be eager to return for the effort."

And so in mystical Avila—the six of us dipping into seconds of a decent (but admittedly *not* perfect by Michener's standards) paella, only a few streets from Santa Teresa's birthplace—came clarification. It was something I'd heard but never fully understood or experienced, until then.

Life is truly a quest, a journey, where getting there, wherever the "there" may be pulling you... a vacation, a promotion, a new home, another child, a new language... is not as important really as what you make of the day-to-day as you proceed. All the more reason then to latch onto flexibility so unexpected adventures— and fun—can happen along the way.

Paella, anyone?

5 steps to resiliency

All 28 virtues in this book, including flexibility, help instill personal resiliency. John A. Calhoun, the founder of HopeMatters and former president of the National Crime Prevention Council, gives a snapshot of what else works well. These are his top five suggestions for children and teens:

- *A goal.* You are determined to complete something. It can be small, like making the soccer team, passing your English class. Or it can be larger: graduating, getting a job. The point is this: you are determined to make your goal. You are focused. Nothing is going to stop you. If you don't have a goal, anything can knock you down.
- *An adult who is always there.* Can be a parent, a coach, one of your teachers, an uncle, a grandmother. Someone you can go to always, especially when you're hurting.
- *A skill.* Something you can point to: "I can sing. I can shoot hoops. I can make people laugh. I am a brilliant mathematician, and can I ever act!" Discover what you're good at and celebrate it.
- *Optimism.* It can be a form of hope: "I have hope. I know things will get better." Or optimism can be described in a theological way as in "I know God holds me in his hand."
- *Altruism.* This means you have a responsibility to help, that real living means being there for others, too. It also means you know you have good stuff. If you share it, it means you feel good about yourself, that you have something someone else needs.

VIRTUES COOKING TIP:

Flexibility

Flexibility opens up new possibilities.
Champion this virtue in the kitchen! Consider
adapting the paella recipe with your family,
based on vegetables in season.

CHICKEN PAELLA

serves 6

5 tablespoons olive oil
1 medium onion, *sliced thinly*
3 medium tomatoes,
peeled, seeds removed and diced
6 deboned chicken thighs
1 teaspoon salt and pepper
½ cup thinly sliced Spanish chorizo
sausage
1½ cups short-grained rice
(preferably Valencia)
3 cups chicken stock
5 to 6 stems saffron
(or substitute ½ teaspoon paprika)
¼ pound fresh green beans, *ends removed*
1 medium red pepper, *cut into strips*
12 medium cleaned shrimp
10 green olives
1 *(14 oz.)* can artichoke hearts

Preheat oven to 400 degrees. In a 15-inch paella dish or paellera *(a round flat pan with handles)* heat half the olive oil and cook the onions and tomatoes for 5 minutes on top of the stove, mashing and stirring with a spoon. Salt and pepper the chicken and then, after adding the remaining oil to pan, sauté the chorizo and chicken until browned. Push to the side. Now add the rice to the pan and cook for several minutes; if needed, add a little more olive oil. Meanwhile, heat the chicken stock in a small saucepan and add the saffron, then pour gently over rice. Arrange chicken pieces around the pan. Add green beans. Place in the oven and cook for 15 minutes.

Now it's time to decorate. After removing the paella dish from the oven and lowering the temperature to 300 degrees, create a colorful artistic top: red pepper, pink shrimp, green olives and artichokes. Back into the oven for 10 minutes more, or until all liquid is absorbed. Remove the paella, cover with aluminum foil and let sit for 5 minutes.

Serve paella family-style on the table so everyone can scoop in for more. And be flexible on the toppings. My Colombian sister-in-law Lucero Arroyo Griffith sometimes substitutes mussels for artichokes. "What's important is the rice, which is the heart of a Paella Valenciana," she says. "The rest is personal taste. Virtually each town in Spain has its own paella recipe."

20) generosity

KEEP STIRRING, FOR ART

My younger brother Gene was "Atlanta's most popular artist"—self-proclaimed, mind you. His phone message ended with his infectious laugh and these words: "Just send a check or leave a message." A grown man now, Gene had settled in this fast-growing southern city with its excellent public-transit system, which was perfect for someone considered blind but who could still, somehow, see enough to paint.

"I've a deal with one of the city's coolest restaurants, not far from the Emory campus," said Gene one day on the phone. "I bartered a painting in exchange for hundreds of dollars of food. You've never been to Atlanta before so why don't you visit? You could meet my friends, stay in my new digs on Curran Street and we'd stop by to see the painting. You know, get a free meal."

The promise of that special meal in "HOT-lanta," as Gene called the city, was the clincher. And besides, since a recent trip to Spain I'd continued to cultivate more work-family-me flexibility. This was the perfect time for a mini-restorative break; my husband could look after our two children, and I could see how my brother was doing.

Appropriately, the restaurant was called Chow. On the Friday night when I arrived, my socks were knocked off, to use a favorite family expression. Gene's colorful eight-foot-long artwork, "Uptown Couple," depicted a well-heeled couple making a champagne toast with friends, and his distinctive Gene Allcott signature—half-scrawl, half block letters—was prominent in the bottom right corner. My kid brother had frequently mentioned his one-man shows and group exhibits, even in faraway Sweden; but, as another favorite expression goes, the proof is in the pudding. And this commissioned "pudding" was awesome.

I was in for more surprises. The waiters' black t-shirts sported Gene's "Uptown Couple." And the same painting was imprinted on the menus. Always generous, he was pleased to have the image used elsewhere… "at no extra cost, guys." Everyone seemed to know him, and I decided he must have adopted the owners and staff into his fun-loving circle—a group of friends called "Gene's People."

The virtue of GENEROSITY shares time, talent and treasure. There's a bonus, too: a feel-good boost.

"What ya'll wanna eat?" asked the waitress, flashing Gene an ear-to-ear smile. "Of course, it's on the house."

"HEEEY there, thanks," billowed Gene taking charge. "My sister, the BIG TIME magazine editor, is keen on France so I bet she'd like the tarragon chicken salad with crunchy walnuts and apples, and that French bou-let bread. I'll have a blackened chicken sandwich with a double order of Chow fries."

His thick glasses practically poked at the menu as he rocked his head back and forth to read everything. "And for my favorite part of the meal, DES-SERT, we'd like those malted Belgian waffles. Oh, and don't forget extra Vermont maple syrup."

Lowering his voice only slightly, Gene turned to me and asked, "What do you think of my new fixer-upper on Curran Street?" But before I could respond, he said, "My home is owner financed since no bank would take me on." Chuckle. "There's no heat so winters may feel, you know, a tad chilly." Chuckle, chuckle. "But painting the place won't be a problem. I can paint 'er up! My lawyer friend Harry closed the deal, and in exchange I'm painting his portrait."

By the time I had finished the last bite of my maple-syrup-covered Belgian waffle, Gene's homespun philosophy about art had tumbled out. It came out rapid-fire like this: "When you're hot, your shipping bill is a lot. Remember to wear the smock and beret when you paint. Keep that full-time job as a waiter or janitor, entering the slides as often as you can to shows. The scene in Atlanta is just right for your own dash of salt and pepper. But remember, a watched pot never boils. Keep stirring, for art...."

Gene was a character, an original, just like his art. Every wall of his home displayed colorful paintings: Russian school girls, kids on skateboards, a ballerina in a pink tutu, football players and bicyclists, a preacherman....

That Saturday evening, many of Gene's People popped over for a backyard party where he served up platters of Shrimp and Grits, alongside a bowl of extra sauce for more of the dish's addictive hot spiciness. The shrimp were garlicky and scalliony, with red pepper flakes and a hint of Tabasco, a squeeze of lemon. And then a thought flashed through my mind: this Southern dish was like generosity, Gene's helping out of others: deeply satisfying, spicy and fun.

And Gene was Mr. Generosity....

An elderly former neighbor, for instance, said he used to walk with her to the food market and carry back her packages. Nothing too unusual there. But after he moved to this new home, my nearly blind brother would haul his little gas-powered lawn mower onto the city bus, ride several stops and then bop the mower down the stairs and push it over to her house. Knocking on her screen door he'd say, "I'm ready to mow your lawn, Ma'am."

Once finished, he would stick around, nodding his head vigorously, appreciatively, up and down, at her reminiscences of Atlanta. Appreciatively nodding over oven-hot cookies, too. "Yes, Ma'am," Gene would say with a southern gentleman's charm. "I couldn't refuse such a tasty treat. Yes, a few more would be might-y nice to take home. I'm an eligible bachelor, you know." Chuckle, chuckle. Invitations to upcoming art exhibits soon filled her once-empty mailbox. In large crayoned block letters, he'd write: "See you there, darlin'!"

He generously hosted parties. I learned about a recent "exclusive" event for his male neighbors. Over potato chips and six-packs ("a real man's dinner"), the group talked of how cool it would be to turn Gene's new place into the headquarters for a regular "important men's gathering."

"Sure, my door is open, the red carpet out, the salt and pepper yours to use," said Gene, with a characteristic chuckle.

"What if we formed a group of manists?" someone asked. "If there are feminists, there must be room in this world for manists, and our Washington lobbyist could be Gene."

Puffing up his chest in mock self-importance, then hooking the thumb of his right hand onto his shirt to indicate a pair of suspenders, Gene said loudly: "I would be proud to... ah, ah... represent my contiguously in the great state of Geor-g-ia."

"That's constituency," said a neighbor, then remembered how Gene had a way of using words and expressions improperly for humor.

"It could be a gentlemen's club," Gene said amidst laughter. "Sort of like a country club or the Chamber of Commerce." Then he had an even better idea: "I know, let's create The Curran Street Men's Club."

And there they were, Gene's People: an attorney, an art director, an architect, a photographer, a landscaper and several others, leaving behind their lives as fathers, husbands, responsible providers... for a few silly and very precious hours at his bachelor pad. It was long enough to let the club's unanimous choice for its leader, Gene, hold court in his paint-splattered, multicolored jeans. His crown was his ever-present baseball hat, and his manner was irreverent and joyful.

For one of their meetings, at a construction site, the invitation read:

> *Gentleman, once again it is time for the Curran Street Men's Club meeting. The theme this year is "Be a Real Man." Those of you with welding torches and backhoes know exactly what I mean. If anyone shows up in a Volvo, they won't even make it to*

> " *Establish yourself in a flow of generosity, giving without concern whether it will return something back to you.... Whether you are rich or poor, whether you are educated or not, you can always share a little bit of what you have.* "
>
> *—Swami Kripalu*

the front door. And please dress like a real man, even if you look like a sissy most of the time.

Evidently, Gene and his friend Doug had a grandiose idea about how to arrive. They made plans to land on a nearby vacant lot in a Grasshopper, a small helicopter. But when the copter owner saw the site, he said, "No way, not with a $200,000 helicopter. It's too risky." Instead, Gene and his buddy showed up in a Chris Craft boat pulled by a semitrailer truck. Gene was waving the whole time and had on a white jumpsuit that said "Mr. President" on it.

A sense of generosity (and more fun) prompted Gene to teach painting to kids in the tough Peoplestown area of Atlanta. One afternoon he said to Jim, the organizer, "Hold on, I've something for you." Gene reached down, fumbled around and pulled out a long, green-and-black snake—a plastic one. "Here," he said. "I want you to have this!" Well, Jim was surprised. And the snake went back to his office, where he put it in the bottom of a large potted tree and soon had his own fun moments with it.

Over seconds of shrimp, I heard how Mr. Generosity had jumped to assist Ernest Norwood, a custodian at the Atlanta College of Art, when Gene was an art student. One night while painting late, he bumped into Ernest.

"HEEEY there my good sir, I'm sure you can paint better than I," he said to Ernest, feeling an immediate connection. "You've watched us students all these years. Just give it a try."

Gene bought Ernest some canvas and paint, and got him started. Encouraged thus, Ernest had his first exhibit... in the janitor's closet. Soon an article in an Atlanta magazine about self-taught artists spotlighted Ernest, and there was a show of his art up at the Woodruff Arts Center cafeteria. Ernest would pep up discouraged students by saying, "If I can learn to use a brush, you can, too."

Stories abounded of Gene's generosity... of how he'd had the good fortune of selling a batch of paintings at once and feeling flush made a beeline back to his alma mater. He stopped at the office of administrator Libby Mohr, another friend, and flipped a $50 bill on her desk.

> " *I've never given a hug where I didn't get one back. So I'm giving in part to give it, and I'm giving in part to get it.* "
>
> *–Danny Meyer*

"There," he said. "Now what do I get named for me?"

Libby disappeared to discuss this with Ofelia Garcia, president of the college at that time. Ofelia suggested naming the bottom drawer of her filing cabinet for him, The Gene Allcott Drawer—that "important drawer on which the other drawers rest." When Libby reported this to Gene, he was delighted and wanted to see his eponymous drawer. That day happened to be the day of a college board of directors meeting.

"Ofelia is busy and is not to be disturbed anymore," Gene was told. And as he bounded toward the college president's closed office door, Libby admonished him repeatedly, "Don't disturb her." Before long she heard laughter. As Gene left, Libby commented that he must not be afraid of danger. Gene was still laughing, but he stopped, rubbed his eyes and replied in a more somber, reflective tone, "You know, you can't be afraid of danger if you can't see danger coming."

These stories came as I talked to his friends over generous platters of Shrimp and Grits. I could tell my brother was having more fun than a barrel of monkeys.

And now Gene and I were back at Chow... chowing down on another free meal, a Sunday brunch of pancakes and mimosas. Gene wanted to be sure I hadn't missed a thing before I flew back later in the day to my home near New York City. He asked if I would like to see his tattoo... a small mole, just above his right ankle. "For Mole Studios, my nom de palette," he said. Chuckle. Chuckle. "Because moles are sorta blind. You know, I'm awfully lucky to do what I'm doing with a boatload of friends. I sell paintings for a quarter and for thousands of dollars, depending on my cash flow. I wish you could see the world as I see it."

I could peak into his world, though. My brother—with his warm "HEEEY there" and a barrel of friends known as Gene's People—was redefining Southern generosity.

SHRIMP AND GRITS

serves 4

6 slices bacon, *diced*
2 cups white mushrooms, *sliced*
1 tablespoons olive oil
1 pound large shrimp, *peeled and deveined*
1 cup green scallions, *sliced*
2 to 3 cloves minced garlic
6 teaspoons fresh lemon juice
1 teaspoon Tabasco
$\frac{1}{2}$ teaspoon sea salt
$\frac{1}{2}$ teaspoon freshly ground pepper

cheese grits
1 cup stone-ground grits (*Adluh white grits are excellent*)
4 cups water
1 cup Cheddar cheese
$\frac{1}{4}$ cup Parmesan
4 tablespoons butter
1 teaspoon salt
1 pinch cayenne pepper
$\frac{1}{4}$ teaspoon Tabasco

These recipes can be doubled and tripled easily, for parties with friends.

Brown the bacon in a skillet and blot on paper towels. Set aside. Remove most of the grease, then sauté the mushrooms about 4 minutes in the same pan and set aside on a plate. Clean the skillet, add the olive oil and now sauté the shrimp. As they start to turn pink, add the scallions, garlic and previously sautéed mushrooms, and stir for another minute. Season with lemon juice, Tabasco, salt and pepper. On each plate serve a puddle of Cheese Grits; spoon shrimp mixture on top and crumble on bacon.

Cheese Grits
Follow the instructions on the package for 1 cup of grits. Stir in remaining ingredients and cover on the stove for 10 minutes.

VIRTUES COOKING TIP:

generosity

What's better for cultivating the virtue of **generosity** than inviting people over? With a little help, each child can host a dinner and serve Shrimp and Grits. It's really cool, generosity.

21) honesty

After dozens of disasters involving food, I started to wonder if our family has a "calamity in the kitchen" gene. Years earlier while cooking a once-frozen chicken in a pressure cooker, for instance, my parents had an explosive experience with soup showering the ceiling or, as my Dad described it, "the Big Bang all over again." At my first dinner party, steaming halibut splatted across the floor. And other occasions signaled our kitchen-calamity DNA might be afflicting a third generation. My son, Alex, as a teenager, became entangled with an upside down Coconut Cake….

Nancy and Camilla decided to organize a birthday luncheon for our girlfriend Harmony. I volunteered to bring a Coconut Cake, one of my favorite desserts. It has a heavenly frosting, a five-minute boiled southern confection with coconut. And my friends wouldn't know the cake itself was a doctored store-bought mix.

The only problem was the timing wasn't great. Harmony's birthday was in October, right in the middle of my new work assignment at Reader's Digest. For the first time I'd been tapped to be a check editor for an issue of the magazine; meaning I had to polish a constant stream of articles that other editors had, ostensibly, put into shape... each needing a snazzy title, the right tone and length, and all the best anecdotes and examples.

I started to feel conflicted. My work self didn't have time to bake a cake, or leave for lunch. My social self, though, was tossing jelly beans at the windows and wanted to be sure I took time for friends... like my cool brother Gene, Mr. Generosity.

HONESTY or truthfulness, not lying or cheating, governs this virtue.

What should I do? At work and at home, I tried to make everything appear effortless. Like the poster "Keep Calm and Carry On," the wording used by the British Ministry of Information in 1939 and now often attributed (falsely) to Winston Churchill, I put a sense of calm on the surface and paddled like a duck, and worked like a dog, to keep up. Somehow I'd squeeze in cake-making and catch up with friends.

On the night before Harmony's birthday I started work at six in the morning and didn't get home that night until eight. The house was quiet. My son Alex, in high school, was still at a New York state team soccer practice across the Hudson River, my husband as his driver, and daughter Kathleen was a student at the University of North Carolina. So for dinner I nibbled on chunks of Cheddar cheese and started to make the cake. Heaping a generous teaspoon of almond extract into the mix would give the cake its distinctive flavor; extra baking powder would make it fluffy light. I filled two, eight-inch-square cake pans with the batter and put them in the oven. Next I went on to the frosting, whipping egg whites, whisking them into a boiled sugar syrup and sprinkling in coconut.

Just as I took the perfectly golden cake out of the oven, Alex walked in. "Mom," he said, still sweaty from soccer, "we haven't had cake in a long time. What a great surprise."

"It's, ahhh, it's actually for tomorrow," I replied softy. "It's for someone else,

Honesty - Cake Nibbler | 205

for Harmony's birthday that I'm attending with Nancy and Camilla."

"A gigantic Coconut Cake for four women? You only need a little one. Just cut each square in half and now you've enough pieces to make two small cakes, frosting them as usual. We can keep one for ourselves." And then, in case I might be hesitating, he added, "This is a no-brainer."

I looked at the cooling cake, looked at him, looked at the frosting ready to smear across the top, and without a heartbeat of hesitation I caved. What was I feeling—honestly? Guilt. My working-mom barometer was spiraling with guilt over a stream of long days and so-so meals.

"Good idea," I said. "Of course, I can do that."

Shortly before ten o'clock that night, Alex, my husband and I forked into Coconut Cake No. 1. A divine crunch came from the slightly hardened frosting, a sweet chewiness from the coconut, and then almonds danced through each airy bite of the yellow cake.

"The cake is awesome," said Alex. He began to tell us about a cooking experience he'd had several summers earlier on Nantucket when he and his buddy Pete had each made a kid's fortune, over $100, selling homemade chocolate chip cookies on one of the island's bike paths.

As we ate and talked, I thought of my father's cherished tradition of Second Desserts, essentially another sweet several hours after dinner. And so we lingered for seconds. More conversation. For the first time in months, we weren't focused on transactional business... of who would drive where, or do grocery shopping, or make (or buy) dinner, or take the dog to the vet for shots. Forkful by yummy forkful, I felt the ticking taskmaster in my head become quiet. The treadmill stopped. I felt happier, lighter. And I could tell Alex and Peter felt carefree, too.

That's the truth about food—it can be transformational. Coconut Cake No. 1 delighted the palette and shifted perceptions. The same aggravations were there, but the enjoyment from the cake dissipated anxiety and stress, and created space for joy.

As for Cake No. 2, it would cause a kitchen calamity. For now, it was in the refrigerator. Six well-placed toothpicks hoisted a plastic-wrap tent to protect the fragile frosting.

" Why is a birthday cake the only food you can blow on and spit on and everybody rushes to get a piece? "

—Bobby Kelton

*F*ast forward to the next day, around mid-morning. At work since seven a.m., I almost ignored the incoming call. I wanted to finish editing a short article before leaving for what could turn into a long lunch. The tiny screen on the phone console, though, blinked with my home phone number. It was probably Alex, his classes for the day not yet started.

"The Coconut Cake should be okay," was the first thing out of his mouth. Not his normal, "Hi, Mom."

"It sorta somehow slipped out of the fridge and landed top down on the floor," he continued solemnly. "The cake almost ended up on my feet." Then his voice perked up. "Fortunately, the plastic wrap held everything together. Well, mostly. Only one side got smushed. I've already flipped the cake back over."

I tried to respond. But the sounds from my mouth were more like that coming from an orange koi lifted out of a fish pond... small gulping noises. No words, just little smacks. I was, well, unmotherly mad. Certainly, not calm and collected. I needed to get my act together quickly because Alex was doing what I'd encouraged always, telling the truth.

He must have been nibbling on Cake No. 2 when out it tumbled. Should I dash to a local bakery, I wondered, and pick up a cake for $20—perhaps one shaped like a ladies hatbox? Or one sporting orange carrots on top? No, I decided. My cake was something I'd baked, even if it started out as a mix. I'd try to make the best of things, knowing the cake was protected by plastic wrap and hadn't likely acquired kitchen floor dust, dog hair or worse.

"Thanks for telling me what happened," I said, this time without the gulping. "Just place the cake back in the fridge, and I'll fix things when I pick it up. I appreciate honesty."

Around noon I was knocking on Nancy's door, a mostly repaired cake in hand. I was having second thoughts, though. One edge banged in, the top slanting to that side, my cake now had a large bump-out of coconut frosting to conceal damage. I felt uneasy. Very uneasy. I should have bought a fancy cake.

All I could think of was a *Winnie the Pooh* story I'd read as a child—and reread many times with Alex and Kathleen. Heading to Eeyore's birthday, little Piglet was excited to be bringing his friend a large balloon. But what happened next left Piglet discombobulated:

> *Running along, and thinking how pleased Eeyore would be, he didn't look where he was going, and suddenly he put his foot in a rabbit hole, and fell down flat on his face. BANG!!!???***!!! Piglet lay there, wondering what had happened. At first he thought the whole world had blown up.... And then he thought, 'Well, even if I'm on the moon, I needn't be face downwards all the time.*

As Piglet picked himself up, he discovered that the small piece of damp rag he was clutching was actually the exploded birthday balloon. "Oh, dear, oh, dearie, dearie, dear!" he uttered, not unlike my own current sentiments.

So there I was, exposed, when three smiling friends opened the door. I presented the Birthday Girl with the small and pathetic, once-upside-down Coconut Cake No. 2. Knowing that honesty *is* the best policy, I forced myself to confess... like my son. I told her that Alex's cake-nibbling had accidentally flipped her cake, "fortunately covered in plastic wrap," onto the floor. I explained how the night before our family had hungrily devoured half the original cake. "You know," I said starting to feel a bit more confident, "it definitely was a case of having one's cake and eating it, too."

My friends were now chuckling so loudly I decided it was time for more confessions. I whispered my closely guarded cooking secret: the cake was a mix. I even shared my insecure Piglet-type feelings for giving a smushed cake and not replacing it.

The three women hooted and hollered. Their cheeks trickled tears. No store-bought perfection, I realized, could have caused such laughter. After lunch and singing "Happy Birthday," we indulged in big slices of cake, delighting in the almond flavoring, the crunchy-chewy coconut frosting. Harmony told me it was "the best birthday cake ever." (That's a girlfriend for you.)

The experience reminded me of my parents' rules for dealing with culinary mishaps:

Rule 1: If you are in the kitchen, you've got to be able to take the heat. Chin up!

Rule 2: Should soup, dinner or dessert fall calamitously on the floor or shoot to the ceiling, have plates and silverware handy.

Rule 3: And, most important, try to get a bang—a BIG BANG—out of whatever happens.

So don't despair if you or someone in your family appears to have a "calamity in the kitchen" gene. Instead, chin up and use honesty—a virtue well worth cultivation—to fess up to whatever happens. And then Rule 3 can come into play, for some unbelievable fun!

HONEST-TO-GOODNESS COCONUT CAKE

serves 8

2 large eggs
½ cup butter, *room temperature*
½ cup margarine
1 "super moist" yellow cake mix *(Duncan Hines or Betty Crocker)*
1 teaspoon baking powder
1 cup milk
1 teaspoon pure vanilla extract
1 ½ teaspoons almond extract

boiled icing
2 egg whites
1 cup light brown sugar
1 cup white sugar
⅓ cup + 2 tablespoons water
½ cup coconut

Preheat oven to 350 degrees. Line two 9-inch round cake pans with aluminum foil. Using an electric mixer, blend the eggs, butter and margarine in a large bowl. Add the cake mix and remaining ingredients. Follow the cake instructions for mixing and baking *(e.g., beat at high speed for 2 minutes, etc.)*. The cake is ready when it bounces back to the touch. Frost when cool.

Boiled Icing

Beat the egg whites until stiff and set aside. Combine the sugars and water in a small saucepan and boil gently for 5 to 7 minutes until the syrup reaches 250 degrees on a candy thermometer or forms "drips." Drips are firm little balls that form when a drop of hot syrup is put into a cup of cold water. If no drips, boil a little longer and test again. *(To avoid runny frosting, be sure the consistency is correct.)* Remove from heat. Using an electric hand mixer, add a third of the egg whites to the hot syrup and whip on high speed. Whip in another third; and repeat once more, for a foamy consistency. Stir in ¼ cup coconut, reserving the rest to decorate the top of the cake.

By using square pans, you can easily make two small cakes and give one away; just cut each layer in half and frost two stacked pieces for each cake masterpiece.

VIRTUES COOKING TIP:

honesty

To encourage the habit of **honesty**, what's better than making Coconut Cake (honestly, one of the best-tasting cakes ever!). And don't hide the packaging in the trash, but fess up to your kids... this delicious treat is actually from a doctored, time-saving cake mix.

22) acceptance

FLOUR POWER: HOMAGE TO THE BAKER

Four bread pans sit in a row on my granite kitchen counter. Nearby, seemingly out of place, is an empty, eight-inch-wide clay flowerpot. Sunny daffodils or a clutch of tender herbs could grow there. Instead, its well-season blackened sides hint at a much different use....

In a flash my thoughts take me to Chapel Hill, N.C. I was in junior high and, after walking home from school, I often helped Dad bake bread. He'd been prodded by Mom to take up bread-making when she returned to work, and was surprised to find the process so enjoyable. Soon baking became part of our weekly routine, and the dough hook got quite a workout. Over the years he made hundreds and hundreds of loaves of oatmeal bread in those four pans. The flowerpot? Well, it wasn't for gardening (though Mom did buy the pot at a garden store). An unusual choice, the flowerpot was also for baking bread; mother claiming it was much like old-fashioned French clay bakeware.

One day Dad started to give his bread away. Someone had a new baby. Someone was sick. Someone got a promotion. Someone was new to town. A loaf of what was soon called Friendship Bread, beautifully browned and oven toasty, found its way to their homes.

Truth was, the round flowerpot loaves were the beginning of a family tradition. Dad loved how these creations served as a conversation starter. "You've got to be kidding," people would exclaim. "You, an art professor, baked this yourself? You used a clay flowerpot?"

It always made Dad beam with delight, almost as if he couldn't believe the results himself.

As a virtue, ACCEPTANCE involves learning that when things cannot be changed, peace can still be found.

Memories catapult me to 1985 and Millwood, N.Y. I was married and living over 500 miles from my childhood home, and had a three year old and a new baby. After my maternity leave ended, I was back at my job editing magazine articles; I walked wearily up the driveway, trying to wish away the deep fatigue that stuck to every thought, every step. All my husband and I needed was one uninterrupted night of sleep, just one night.

A faint smell of butter and molasses stirred the air. Fortunately, my parents were helping out for the week, and so as I neared the house I glanced through the glass porch door to see what everyone was doing. Mom was reading to Kathleen, wedged tightly beside her in an overstuffed living room chair. Only several months old, Alex was on a soft blanket stretched across the butcher block table in the kitchen and was snoozing. Dad occupied a corner of the same table. He absentmindedly patted Alex, stopped and picked up a blue crayon, and vigorously colored something. It must be the birth announcement he was making to announce Alex's arrival.

Still looking in, I saw it then, the smell of butter and molasses explained. Flour was everywhere. Dad's telltale baking trail ran from counters and cabinets over to the wooden chair where he sat. And there on the countertop were two hot-out-of-the-oven crusty masterpieces. Dad's tradition of making Friendship Bread was now embracing our young family. I bounded inside, suddenly refreshed. "Look, Kathleen," I exclaimed. "Grandpa found time to bake for us!"

Special moments always surrounded his Friendship Bread.

December 1989, Chappaqua, N.Y. I was dashing from the Grand Union supermarket to Key Food. "Do you have any yeast?" I asked anxiously. No luck. At our town's small village market, I tried again and upon hearing "No, we're out," I couldn't hold back any longer. I burst into tears.

The big-hearted Italian owner put his arms around my heaving shoulders and rocked me gently, as if this happened every day and there was nothing extraordinary about a woman crying because his small specialty store didn't have yeast.

"I've got to bake... bake some bread," I stammered finally.

"There, there," the owner said as my weeping continued in his comforting arms.

"My Dad... he just died, age eighty-four," I choked out. "He was a professor but he baked our bread growing up and continued to make his Friendship Bread to give away. I've gotta bake now like him."

"I'm so sorry, lady," he replied. "I get you yeast by noon. No problem. How much you need, a pound?" And suddenly we were both laughing over the thought of a pound of yeast when I only needed two small tablespoons.

"I can never thank you enough," I said. "This means so much to me."

The act of making Dad's bread later that afternoon—and defrosting a large dish of another favorite comfort food, Spicy Chicken Enchiladas (delicious on the first day and even better the next day, and fabulous to freeze for the proverbial "rainy day")—surrounded me with wonderful recollections of my Professor Baker Dad. For dozens of years, I realized, my own DNA for baking had remained dormant, much like dry yeast awaiting warm water and sugar to activate. Now in a few simple steps I was re-creating his bread. I took extra time to knead it, exactly as he'd taught me as a teenager: *Push, flip 'n turn, push, flip 'n turn.*

And it was seven-year-old Kathleen, watching me, whose sweet words were repeated many times over the next weeks, "Grandpa is up in Heaven today baking his own fresh bread."

Like a warm hug from afar, a sense of acceptance for his passing gently settled over me.

Back in Chapel Hill. My sister Liz and I were on Franklin Street and paused in front of the "Flower Ladies" to enjoy their tin cans full of miniature roses, daffodils, and red, orange and yellow zinnias. Buckets of daisies, too. We then ducked into NCNB bank. We'd flown in to help our mother get some of Dad's documents out of the bank vault. Down the stairs we went, back into the windowless basement. It felt increasingly airless. We entered a bare-bones office and signed our names in a registry book on a stark metal desk. Even after a year, Dad's death could occasionally spin me into sadness, and I just managed to hang on.

"I'm Velma," said the bank assistant. She peered closely at our names and our driver's licenses. I anticipated trouble. Our identification wouldn't be sufficient somehow and another trip would be needed, another hurdle; our time was tight and already filled with a long list of bureaucratic chores to sort out Dad's modest estate.

Instead, we heard the woman say warmly, "You must be the Allcott girls."

Liz and I nodded, puzzled. The woman's wrinkly brown face broke into a grin. "Wasn't Dr. Allcott the old teacher who came here with his gray dog, the one with blue eyes? He was your father—right?" she asked. We nodded again, thinking of how Dad went everywhere with his Weimaraner.

"Dogs aren't allowed in the bank," she continued, "but they always arrived together. I never said anything. He often brought me homemade bread, from a flowerpot, he said. He even copied out the recipe. Step-by-step, he told me how to make it."

Wow, I thought. Our father's oatmeal bread was etched deeply in her memory. And if Velma at the bank got his Friendship Bread, so did the postman, the accountant and the vet, and probably the newspaper delivery guy.

Ever the artiste, Dad had seen the whole picture. With grace, he had accepted changing family roles when my mother reentered the job market; he wanted to help out by using what was then her recipe. Ever-so-quickly he then discovered that bread-making was not just about food for our family and the incredible taste of fresh bread. There was more... the magic of "flour power." And so he used bread baked in the whimsical flowerpot to add spark to people's lives and scatter joy, in his own heartfelt way.

These days in my kitchen. I lightly rub butter on the inside of the four bread pans and flowerpot, and shake around some flour, readying them for use. Every time now I pull yeast from the cabinet or hear the dough hook beating its lively rhythm in the electric mixer, the same trusty KitchenAid he'd used, every time I knead the warm mixture, Dad comes to mind. It's a peaceful feeling. Meditative.

And like him, I tap into the magic of flour power, in baking for friends... a girlfriend opens an art gallery, a yoga teacher has a birthday ("Leading with your heart," Osi insists, "is key to living up to your potential."), a neighbor not seen in months. My own roll call of gifted loaves now stretches to over a hundred people. And Friendship Bread goes on road trips. My brother John uncovers a flowerpot loaf tucked into his daughter's suitcase when she returns to Oregon after visiting me. Heading to Toronto to see my mother-in-law Grayce, I split the trip into two days, spending a night in upstate New York with my sister Liz and her husband—and have bread for everyone. (My mother-in-law, though, gets the flowerpot one.) When my husband and I drive to North Carolina, I carry two loaves: one for a stopover in Washington, D.C., with my nephew Mike's family, and the other is saved for Chapel Hill.

Chapel Hill? Friendship Bread has come full circle. It's back in the town where my parents first baked it. Another golden loaf—from that same blackened flowerpot—is for Peg and Phil Rees who'd received Dad's bread from the same pot over forty-five years earlier. So widespread was his bread-giving over the years that when UNC dedicates the new Allcott Gallery for undergraduate art in my parents'

"Finish every day and be done with it.... You have done what you could; some blunders and absurdities no doubt crept in; forget them as soon as you can. Tomorrow is a new day; you shall begin it serenely, and with too high a spirit to be encumbered with your old nonsense."

–Ralph Waldo Emerson

honor, the brochure includes the recipe for John & June Allcott's Friendship Bread. This injunction appears at the recipe's end: "Share with Friends!"

Acceptance—that feeling of serenity that comes from the realization that life is the way it should be for that day, for that moment, no matter what is happening—is easier if coupled with making, eating and sharing Friendship Bread.* For back-up comfort food, the Plan B for acceptance, have Chicken Enchiladas always ready in the freezer.

The recipe for acceptance can be that easy, really.

* Instructions for Friendship Bread can be found in Chapter 1, "No Loafing Around."

food facts:

LOVE AND TIME

My friend Laura Mogil has this recipe on her blog, "The Inspired Chef," for healing with "Love and Time":

Ingredients

2 pounds of passage of time

1 cup of acceptance

3 drops of sweet memories

4 tbs. full of hope and faith

2 cups of patience

Tears as needed

Condiments

Calm, prayers and smiles

Preparation: Warm your feelings slowly. Add the sweet memories, faith and hope. Mix with patience. Gradually add in acceptance, life must go on. Add tears and sadness as needed. Season with calm and prayers of your personal choice. Sprinkle with smiles as you can. Add the passage of time.

A note from the chef: Move gently through the days. Be good to yourself. And simmer this recipe as long as needed and notice sorrow will slowly begin to dissipate. Eventually sweet memories will provide a special seasoning to your life.

SPICY CHICKEN ENCHILADAS

serves 6

3 cups shredded cooked chicken
1 cup sour cream
1 cup fresh cilantro, *chopped*
2 red peppers, *chopped*
1 cup shredded cheddar cheese
1 *(16 oz.)* jar green salsa
½ cup water
2 cloves garlic, *minced*
1 teaspoon cumin
1 package 8-inch flour tortillas

Preheat oven to 350 degrees. Butter a 9 x 13-inch baking dish. In a large bowl, mix together the cooked chicken, ½ cup sour cream, cilantro, red peppers and cheese. Using a blender or food processor, puree the remaining ½ cup of sour cream, salsa, water, garlic and cumin. Spread a small amount of sauce over the bottom of the baking dish and put a cup of it in the chicken mixture and then stir. *(The remainder is for the top of the enchiladas.)* To make the enchiladas: spoon ½ cup chicken mixture onto a tortilla, roll it up and put it in the baking dish seam-side down. Continue and form a long row, putting remaining sauce on the top. Bake uncovered for 50 minutes until bubbly. Brown for a minute or two under the broiler for a golden color.

For a time-saver, debone a store-bought roasted chicken. Also, you can make the dish a day in advance and refrigerate or, better yet, freeze.

VIRTUES COOKING TIP:

acceptance

Who'd think that **acceptance** is a
virtue? Yet so much time is lost in going
over, again and again, unchangeable
history. So cultivate Zen-like acceptance
and de-stress over delicious, defrosted
Chicken Enchiladas, prepared with
children when time was plentiful.

23/consideration

SPILLING THE BEANS ON THE MARRIAGE SECRET

At thirty-six, still describing himself as "Atlanta's most popular artist," my bachelor brother loved to chow down on pizza and burgers and beer—that was, until he met Miss Mary Alice Giblin. She was the charming and high-spirited woman of Gene's dreams. Soon they started to date. Before long she was seen at his new home on Chandler Street.

Both were used to being on their own. So Mary Alice explained to Gene that they needed to "learn to do things together." That meant such things as shared cooking. Not exactly a tough fifty-fifty split required for Gene, but still a push-up-the-sleeves, let-me-help-you-a-little kitchen assistance.

One day Mary Alice decided to make a pot of healthy 15 bean soup before she headed off to her job as an emergency room nurse. She chopped up onions, parsley, celery and garlic. She tossed in an armload of beans—red beans, kidney beans, lima beans, green and yellow split peas, lentils, cranberry beans, chickpeas and small white beans (okay, so maybe it was only a 9 bean/pea soup)—and seasoned with smokey, fiery Cajun spices. All it needed was to simmer for several hours in the Crock-Pot.

"Babe," she called out to Gene as she headed out the door, "when you come back from Kinkos, can you stir the soup every now and then? Make sure it doesn't burn."

Off she went. And off he went to print up invitations for his upcoming exhibit, one of several art shows in Atlanta that year. When Gene returned he started his soup-stirring. He even remembered to stir it again several hours later. But he wasn't quite sure about the hot five-alarm taste.

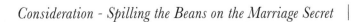

CONSIDERATION of others, through thoughtful actions and deeds, guides the path of this virtue.

That night Mary Alice arrived home from an intense day at the hospital, entered the kitchen and gave Gene a hug. "How was your day?" he asked. With only a hint of exaggeration, she said, "Not bad; I pulled someone from the jaws of death."

"Baby," he said then ever so proudly, "we have a secret recipe."

Immediately suspicious, she asked, "What did you put in my soup?"

"Well, it was spicy hot, so I cooled it down with some... ah, well ah... well, some wheat germ."

"Wheat germ? Wheat germ!" she shrieked. "You've got to be kidding!"

Normally a sweet-as-pie gal, what she said next wasn't very ladylike (and so I won't repeat it here). She didn't think wheat germ had a small place, even a cameo role, in her soup.

Gene was confused. He was upset. He had explained what he'd done and thought his creation tasted better. "Maybe you should take a chill and be more considerate," he moaned. "You know, try the soup before becoming so hostile. You might like it."

As it turned out, the soup had, as Mary Alice explained later, "the consistency of watery cream of wheat. Then out popped something hard, maybe a bean, or maybe a lump of wheat germ. It was hard to say."

My bachelor brother was walking on eggshells, and Mary Alice, without a nod to his culinary ingenuity, said, "Why don't you take a little time downstairs in your art studio? You know, put your creativity on canvas, buddy, and please, please, please, keep it out of the kitchen."

Fortunately, Gene lived in the moment. He shrugged off gaffs and goof-ups, such as the inedible and spicy 9 bean/pea + wheat germ soup.

After this kitchen calamity, Gene tried to steer clear of cooking. With a sudden aversion to soup, he even developed a dislike of pop-artist Andy Warhol's paintings of the Campbell tomato soup can. But occasionally in "a manly outdoor

undertaking, no sissy indoor stuff," as Gene described his effort, he would barbecue skewered chicken pieces marinated with his own concoction of soy and honey, and huge "man-sized" chunks of garlic and ginger. He called his creation yakitori. The recipe was based, very loosely, on a meal the two of us had eaten a year earlier in Tokyo when visiting our sister Liz and her family. (Her husband had set up a branch of an American university and I'd jumped at the opportunity to visit Japan, once again part of seeking out a better work-family-me balance.)

Luckily, Gene and Mary Alice's other efforts proved more successful. So successful that he decided to take the nuptial plunge... to marry Mary. He'd needed more than three and a half decades to get to this point, and they settled on the most romantic of days possible: Valentine's. And while saints named Valentine have been recognized since the third century, Gene told me that it wasn't until around 1380 that the first sentimental association was paired with the word. "It was by Chaucer," he said proud of knowing the fact, "the father of English literature."

I'd looked up what Chaucer wrote and found his *Parlement of Foules* virtually incomprehensible, even that key passage: "…For this was on seynt Volantynys day, Whan euery bryd comyth there to chese his make.…" But then I saw this Middle English wording translates to, "For this was Saint Valentine's Day, when every bird cometh there to choose his mate." And so 610 years later Gene embraced Chaucer's idea: he chose his mate on Valentine's, a smoochy, hand-holding, heart-thumping Red Letter Day.

The look: Gene was spiffed up with a red paisley tie (borrowed) and wearing his only suit. Mary Alice had a better handle on the red theme; she was wearing a crimson dress with white piping around the collar and sleeves.

The place: Gene's home on Chandler Street full of his paintings, including "Hot Lips" of a smiling woman with electric red lips.

The food: Pepper-encrusted roast beef (pinky red) and Virginia ham, salads of every sort, homemade breads, and baskets of fragrant strawberries (the red theme, again) from a farmers market in Atlanta. No "secret recipe" soup, thank goodness.

The ceremony: With the selected verses read, their "I Do's" done and wedding stresses behind them, Gene and Mary Alice eyed their cakes: a traditional white-layered wedding cake and a chocolate confection for the groom. (Nowadays Chocolate Party Cupcakes—such as Grammy Chloupek's recipe using buttermilk for moist, dreamy bites—are a good substitute for a groom's cake.) Alas, nobody could find the photographer.

While we waited, Gene's closest friends, known as Gene's People, shared stories of his pre-wedding adventures. His friend Geddes, an architect, told about once waiting for a parade to start and Gene standing next to a stiff military man and his pretty wife. "I always enjoy watching Gene interact with people," said Geddes. "Well, the woman became fascinated as Gene played with some of the kids, strutting and dancing around. The man, though, was standoffish, not wanting anything to do with this free-spirit. Finally, the parade came and Gene was still cutting up and laughing, and the man started to warm up. When the parade ended, his wife pulled me aside. 'You know,' she said, 'your friend was more fun than the parade itself!'"

Ann Stallard, president of the YWCA of America, said she'd first met

> *Being considerate of others will take your children further in life than any college degree.*
>
> –Marian Wright Edelman

Gene when he was a student and had seen an article about her running a graphic communications company. She got one of his impromptu telephone calls. "I'm an upstanding citizen," he said. "Can you teach me to silk-screen?" Ann did not take him up immediately. After all, as a Southern lady she'd been taught "not to fall for the promises of strange young men right off the bat." But a few days later a package of Gene's greeting cards arrived. Scrawled across the top of a large sheet of paper in purple inch-high letters he began, "Dearest Ann."

"Now I hadn't met this man," explained Ann, "but he took up the rest of this oversized note to tell me what he intended to do to accomplish his goal of becoming 'Atlanta's Most Popular Artist.' And with his earnest charm, I found myself on the way to the Atlanta College of Art to teach a man, who could barely see, how to silk-screen." Before long Gene painted her portrait while she read to a group of inner-city children; the YWCA, she said, sold cards of the painting to raise money to support reading programs. As for Ann, she became a charter member of Gene's People.

Another friend, Margaret, confided, "When we're not doing stuff together Gene constantly checks up on us. Years ago after I lost my job he'd call every morning at 8:15 and say, 'Hello, it's your buddy. I'm checking on you.' And at the end of each conversation, Gene would always say, 'I love you.'"

Speaking of love, at long last the photographer was located and the two lovebirds were ready for the cake-cutting. But, just as they raised slivers of cake to the other's mouth, another delay happened. A deep southern voice rang out, "Do you know the most important words for wedded bliss?"

A chuckle came from Gene, then silence.

We turned around. Who was it, we wondered, who knew the marriage secret? The voice was coming from a bow-tie wearing gent, our Cousin B, as in Dr. B. Rogers Beasley. He was a retired medical missionary who had lived all over the world—in India, Africa and Indonesia, as well as directed the Frontiers Nursing Service in the Appalachian mountains—and served as a health-policy expert for the Rockefeller Brothers, in Manhattan. All to say, he had treated and talked to thousands of couples. He had stitched them up after accidents, knocked out their fevers, delivered their babies, looked after their diseases such as leprosy and always listened to their stories.

"Just two words," he said mischievously.

Now everyone was thinking, laughing, as if all guests had jumped into a game of wedding charades. What were those two words? Any hints? Meanwhile, the pieces of cake for the newlyweds still floated, uneaten, mouth-level.

"Well," said Gene who was known for his appetite, "I do want to eat my cake, and I can't stand the suspense. Guess it's time to learn those words."

"It's easy, really, and it's all about doing what your spouse wants," explained Cousin B. "It's about consideration for the other person every day of your married life. The words are 'yes dear.'"

"Yes dear, yes dear," Gene and Mary Alice repeated loudly. And, finally, amidst much laughter and photo-taking, they munched their cake.

In mulling over Cousin B's international recipe for a successful wedded life (advice equally valuable for family life), the other person is put first. What an affirmation! What a vote of confidence to act on things from your partner's (or child's) perspective and needs, not yours. That opens a two-way opportunity for the other person to reciprocate.

So remember consideration, notably in the kitchen. And to get started, all that's required is to say those two simple words: "Yes dear."

CHOCOLATE PARTY CUPCAKES

yields 24 cupcakes

1 cup white sugar

1 cup light brown sugar

¼ teaspoon salt

⅓ cup cocoa

(Hershey's unsweetened is good)

½ cup butter, *room temperature*

2 large eggs, *room temperature*

1 teaspoon baking soda

½ cup hot water

½ cup buttermilk, *room temperature*

2 cups sifted cake flour

⅓ cup Maraschino cherries,

chopped and no pits

frosting

8 oz. cream cheese

(in a block, not whipped)

8 tablespoons butter

(1 stick, room temperature)

1 teaspoon pure vanilla extract

⅓ cup unsweetened cocoa

2 cups sifted powdered sugar

Preheat oven to 350 degrees. Put 24 paper liners in cupcake pans. With an electric mixer, cream the sugars, salt, cocoa and butter. Add the eggs and beat thoroughly. Meanwhile, put the baking soda into the hot water and let cool; then combine it with the buttermilk. Now alternate adding the cake flour and buttermilk mixture to the batter. Add Maraschino cherries and stir gently. Fill each cupcake liner with batter, about half full. Bake for 20 to 25 minutes until the tops spring back to the touch. Cool and frost.

Frosting

Using an electric mixer, combine cream cheese, butter, vanilla extract, unsweetened cocoa and sifted powdered sugar. Mix on high until the consistency is light and spreadable. If still runny, add more powdered sugar.

You can adapt this recipe for a cake. Merely use two 9-inch round cake pans lined with aluminum foil and bake for 25 to 30 minutes, until the center springs back.

VIRTUES COOKING TIP:

consideration

The kitchen invites **consideration** at every turn. Like baking
soda, an ingredient that puffs up Chocolate Party Cupcakes,
this virtue flourishes once activated. So ready, set, make
cupcakes… and watch kids manifest consideration.

24) wisdom

MOTHER'S DAY IN MOROCCO

Not long ago, I pulled out the Moroccan wallet given to me by my mom on Mother's Day. I remembered the significance of the wallet's timing. Heralded in splashy newspaper ads and Hallmark cards, in enticing displays in jewelry stores, in colorful construction-paper creations from school kids, Mother's Day is the time when 85 million women in the United States are saluted for 365 days of mothering. Many are hard-working, independent, adventurous women like my mother, June Allcott. Madre, mère, mutter or mother. The word for the woman who gave us life starts in Spanish, French, German and English (including the folksy "mum-sie" used by my Canadian-born husband) with the same letter—"M"—as in MMMmmm good. MMMmmm, the heart of the family. MMMmmm, the inspiration to live to your full potential. This brings me back to the story of the Moroccan wallet....

One day my mother announced she was planning a Girls Trip to Morocco. "Why there?" I asked.

"Because I know nothing about the country," she said. "I've been to Canada, South America and Europe, to the Middle and Far East, but never to that part of Africa. Morocco has crept into my imagination and I'd like to learn more about it. I've found a tour and am asking you and your sister, and my two daughters-in-law. Want to join me?"

It sounded exotic. Humphrey Bogart's classic 1943 film *Casablanca* was my only taste of the country. Since Dad had passed away, Mom had continued to work part-time as a guidance counselor at the University of North Carolina, and saved her salary for travel. I knew my kids, Kathleen and Alex, both teenagers now, would be fine, even if my husband fixed spaghetti nonstop for the two weeks I'd be gone. Another editor could fill in for me at Reader's Digest where I worked. And, heck, with someone else picking up the tab, it would be easy to give myself permission to go.

As a virtue, WISDOM combines knowledge and experience with insight, humility and, hopefully, humor.

Still, Mom was seventy-eight and had only recently recovered from a scare with lymphoma, as well as taxing rounds of chemotherapy. She had a fused right hip, an artificial left hip and walked with a pronounced limp. Moreover, she had a severe allergy to pine nuts, an ingredient common in Mediterranean cooking. I was concerned about her health, her stamina, and a flutter of "red-flag" warnings arose in my head; meaning, good medical care should be close by.

I telephoned my sister Liz. "Do you think the trip would be too much for Mom?" I asked. "She could run into problems, and I wonder if it's really wise." We were both uncertain.

Surprisingly, it was our sister-in-law Mary Alice, an emergency room nurse in Atlanta and the young widow of my artist brother Gene, who strongly encouraged us to go. "Remember, there are no guarantees in life for anyone," she said; she was referring to Gene who had died, age 38, when he fell accidentally from the back of a truck. "Who would have thought Gene would be gone, off painting sunsets in Heaven, or so I like to think. Let's support June if she wants to do this. I'm an ER wonderkid, remember? So if June happens to eat Moroccan baklava made with pine nuts, I'll have an EpiPen handy and will watch over her wheezy allergic reaction."

Three "yeses" later, Liz, Mary Alice and I agreed to be her companions. (Our sister-in-law Beth, a psychologist with a busy practice in Oregon, couldn't get away.) We still felt worries, justifiably so, but this trip would be a kick-up-our-heels way to celebrate Mom's return to health.

That May, as Mother's Day approached, we left my home in Chappaqua, N.Y., for Kennedy Airport. It was just as the cherry tree hugging my kitchen burst forth with pink fluttering buds, as if waving us off. And at the other end of the plane ride welcoming us to Casablanca were colorful mosques, minarets and mosaics. Such a world of differences! On our first night, we—some eighteen Americans and Europeans—sat at low tables next to Moroccans wearing colorful kaftans and hooded djellabas, trying new-for-us foods having Berber-Moorish influences. We sampled tantalizing dishes of vegetable and chicken couscous.

"Couscous is considered the national dish of North Africa," said Mom who'd been reading up on Moroccan food. "It's made from grains of durum wheat.

"And over there," she continued, "is a meat tagine; it was cooked in a vessel bearing the same name. See how the beef and zucchini, carrots and other vegetables were placed in the pie-pan base of the tagine and the cone-shaped lid nestles on top, lots of moist steam to cook everything? Many of the seasonings and condiments are also from Morocco: saffron from Tiliouine, olives from Meknes and oranges and lemons from around Fez. Let's dig in while it's hot."

We sampled our first Moroccan baklava (no pine nuts, fortunately). And, again, Mom was full of wise facts: "Walnuts are brain-boosters and heart-protectors, thanks to omega-3 fatty acids, and offer quality protein. And honey contains an array of antioxidants, and is a good source of vitamin C and energy. This dessert is exquisite—and healthy.

"Can you believe we're doing this?" she added, grabbing more baklava. "Our passports are stamped in confirmation. Pinch me."

As our tour bus traveled from town to town, with unusual names like Ouarzazate (imagine, a town with two Z's in its name, known for making movies such

So long as you have food in your mouth, you have solved all questions for the time being.

—Franz Kafka

as *Lawrence of Arabia* and, more recently, *The Mummy* and *Gladiator*), we were offered frequent cups of green tea with mint. Mom delighted in drinking the super-sweet tea—up to ten cubes of sugar in a pot, a sign in North Africa of wealth. We'd heard a Berber proverb that says, "He who rushes is already dead," so the mint tea gave us reason to slow down and pause, talk, live in the moment... and so we did.

In Fez, founded in 789 and the oldest of the country's Imperial cities, Mom proved she was not going to be left behind. Using a foldable cane on uneven, stone-paved streets and grabbing occasionally onto Liz or me as our group wove through the souk, or market, she kept up. And later in the day, while some of us bartered and haggled over carpets, she headed off solo.

"But not for long, or too far," I shouted after her. I kept thinking of how good she looked, her eyes so sparkly. Despite the crowded passageway, I couldn't resist yelling out one more thing: "I love you, Momma."

The oldest in the group, Mom waved her cane and smiled. I watched her retrace her steps up a hill and then disappear into the darkened labyrinth of twisting alleys. She evidently located a stall selling leather goods that she'd seen earlier. Noticing light coming from its second floor she climbed up, creaky stair by creaky stair, and looked out the window. A collage of brilliant colors popped out from the surrounding white roofs, all backing the souk. It took a moment for her to realize what she was seeing: dozens and dozens of waist-high clay vats containing brilliant dyes. Dazzling reds, oranges, yellows, blues and greens. And flapping on clotheslines were hundreds of colorful drying leather skins that would be turned into wallets and belts, hats and jackets.

Mom then eased back down the stairs. She accepted the owner's offer of tea and asked in English about his leather goods. Excited to learn that he made the items himself ("no import from India, China"), she carefully selected three wallets.

That Sunday was Mother's Day. At dinner—tender chicken with preserved lemons and salty olives and, on the side, more couscous—Mom told us about her initial unease in exploring on her own, then the exhilaration of the adventure, the unexpected view over the souk. "It was like a brilliant impressionistic painting," she

Lives of great men all remind us
We can make our lives sublime,
And, departing, leave behind us
Footprints on the sands of time.
Footprints, that perhaps another,
Sailing o'er life's solemn main,
A forlorn and shipwrecked brother,
Seeing, shall take heart again. "

—Henry Wadsworth Longfellow
("A Psalm of Life" was found in the journal of my great, great grandfather, Carl Zander, in 1849)

said. She talked about her pleasure in shopping for the wallets. Mine was the color of sun-scorched Moroccan sand. It had delicate white stitchery across the top and a mosque tooled onto its surface.

"I can't thank you enough for this wallet, for the trip," I said, reveling in her high spirits. I lifted the wallet to my nose and inhaled the leathery smell. "This is like Mother's Day in reverse, with you treating us, your daughters."

Over the next days our bus driver wheeled east toward the Sahara. One morning we awoke to loud knocking at our doors at three a.m. Another adventure! Quickly, we stuffed breakfast rolls into our daypacks, jumped into Land Rovers and set off into the star-filled desert—soon miles and miles of sand dunes surrounding us. I felt a shiver of unease. Medical facilities were now many hours away. But as we sat in the chilly dunes and watched the sun shimmy up over Morocco's border with Algeria,

nature in all her majesty, I could see that Mom was truly having the time of her life—living without fear.

And then, seemingly out of nowhere, Berber men approached, riding in a small camel caravan. They stopped. The camels squatted, a most awkward movement, and the men got off. They indicated we should take a ride. Mary Alice, Liz and I took turns... very bouncy and unrhythmic... as mother watched.

Around the neck of one of the turbaned men was a stunning necklace: multiple twisted strands of shiny black beads and a tiny silver flask at the center. I pointed at the necklace. Very persuasively, very earnestly, he said in broken English: "Beads rare... black coral. This for...," and he pointed to his eyes, indicating the flask was for a black powder called kohl, used for eye makeup. "My father make it week before die."

The necklace was beautiful, the tale moving. "Could I possibly buy it?" I asked.

By then I had the hang of Moroccan bartering and so I offered him all the cash in my pockets (the equivalent of $35). He took it and pointed at the inexpensive Timex on my wrist (done). On my own I pulled two clips out of my hair and passed them along. He indicated he wanted my black sweater, and now warmed by the rising sun I turned it over. But still he looked at me. Obviously, he wanted something more, an object truly worthy of his necklace.

"Show him the blowing bubbles for kids," Mom suggested. "Just don't give him any more clothing; this isn't strip poker." As we laughed, I pulled a small pink jar from my daypack, took out the wand and blew a few bubbles into the air. The bubbles swirled skyward, then turned downward and blew around before popping eventually on the sand. He smiled. Bubble magic turned out to be perfect for sealing the exchange, and I put on the black beaded necklace.

On the last afternoon of our trip, in Marrakesh, Mom's face was flushed as we roamed the city's congested market; she clung to Liz's arm. I hoped it was just the heat. We bought cumin and curry powder, prized packets of saffron. Argan oil for cooking. Seeing a crowd gathering, we worked our way through a maze of open-air sellers and watched little monkeys dance. A few feet away several cobras undulated, unrestrained. After several minutes the handler poked at the snakes with a forked stick and forced them back into large round baskets.

"I've had enough of this," said Mom quietly. "Let's take a horse-drawn carriage over to La Mamounia Hotel. It's tea time. If there's one thing I've learned, it's that Moroccans value their tea, the ritual of making it and sharing it, and the lift that comes with drinking it with friends. I need tea."

Among La Mamounia's orange and olive trees, and its hot pink bougainvillea hedges, among twenty-seven soothing fountains, Mom ordered tea. Soon we were sipping from dainty china cups. No overly sugared green tea or cobras, here. Our oasis was the elegant hotel's twenty-acre garden where Winston Churchill once painted.

"I'll hate to leave tomorrow," Mom said. "I can see why Churchill called this hotel, 'the most lovely spot in the whole world.'"

In this uncharted and uncertain time of her life, Mom had rolled out an adventure. No familiar food or sights. No husband to carry bags, handle bills or ease

If parents want to give their children a gift, the best thing they can do is to teach their children to love challenges, be intrigued by mistakes, enjoy effort, and keep on learning. That way, their children don't have to be slaves of praise. They will have a lifelong way to build and repair their own confidence.

–*Carol S. Dweck, Mindset: The New Psychology of Success*

the way. No time for worries or fear. No safety net of nearby doctors "just in case." Her cup of tea, as the expression goes, was clearly in discovery with us, her girls—of couscous and camels, and tea. And now as she cradled the china cup, the color of her face back to normal, Mom said, "The wisest thing I ever did was to ask you to join me. We're having such a riotous good time."

Wisdom is more than passing on little jewels from one's knowledge. It's in also sharing one's best example, one's actions, in how to live life boldly and expansively.

Postscript

Shortly after the trip, Mom's cancer roared back. It was just as she'd started dreaming of the Lost City of Petra, in Jordan. That trip had to be postponed. With my mother in mind I created a new healthy recipe for a Moroccan-inspired Cranberry Couscous Salad, which is a "wise" choice for a hot, busy day. And my Egyptian friend gave me her family's baklava recipe to try… delicious. As for my treasured wallet, it is still full of what I call "mad money from Mom." I use it to pay for special treats inspired by her—for restaurants, specialty cookware, other things, too—and refill it as needed, all thanks to that Mother's Day in Morocco.

the building blocks of character

Scientists are now studying the development of "character" and how people can take certain character-building actions to have a more meaningful life. In their ground-breaking work, psychologists Christopher Peterson and Martin Seligman identified and classified various positive human characteristics. Their 2004 book, Character Strengths and Virtues, categorized six core virtues—wisdom, courage, humanity, justice, temperance and transcendence—that are comprised of 24 character strengths. Focusing on these attributes, they maintain, can lead to happiness and well-being.

And in her recent film, "The Science of Character: Shaping You and Your Community's Strengths," Tiffany Shlain shows how by focusing purposefully on certain parts of who you are, your character, you can reap great personal rewards. Shlain asks: "What are your top five strengths?" So be sure wisdom is among your favorite virtues.

CRANBERRY COUSCOUS SALAD

serves 4

1¼ cups water
1 cup large pearl couscous
½ cup dried cranberries
2 tablespoons flat-leaf parsley, *chopped*
1 tablespoon lemon zest
2 tablespoons lemon juice
4 tablespoons good olive oil
1 teaspoon sea salt
¼ cup slivered almonds, *toasted*

In a small saucepan, bring 1¼ cups of water to a boil and add the couscous. Cover and simmer on low for 8 minutes. *(Grains should be firm, not mushy.)* Cool and mix in cranberries, parsley, lemon zest and juice, olive oil and salt. Place in a serving bowl and top with almonds.

For a super-healthy variant, make **Quinoa Salad**. This ancient wonder-food, grown in Bolivia, is packed with protein (as much as in meat). Just substitute 1 cup of quinoa for the couscous and cook a little longer, about 15 minutes.

wisdom

Wisdom needs its voice heard. As a
starting point, prepare foods from other
countries—Moroccan couscous, Bolivian
quinoa, Egyptian baklava—and learn with
your family about those places and each
food's health benefits.

BAKLAVA

---

yields two dozen "diamonds"

syrup

2 cups sugar

1½ cups water

filling

½ lemon

1 tablespoon butter

1 tablespoon flour

¾ cup sugar

1 teaspoon cinnamon

1 pinch ground cloves

2 cups hazelnuts

1 package phyllo dough, defrosted

(follow instructions on package)

1 *(16-oz.)* can Crisco

"Cover baklava lightly with aluminum foil," says my friend Mireille who grew up in Egypt. "It can remain at room temperature for several days, and any leftover filling is great on yogurt, cereal or buttered toast."

Make the syrup at least 2 to 3 hours but up to a day before assembling the baklava. In a small saucepan combine 2 cups sugar and the water, and stir; when the sugar dissolves, add the juice from half a lemon. Cook for half an hour over low heat until thick but not caramelized, stirring frequently. Cool completely and place in fridge. For the filling, cook the butter and flour in a small saucepan until pasty and brown *(not soggy)*, stirring constantly. Set aside to cool. Use a food processor to combine sugar, cinnamon, cloves and hazelnuts. Pulse on and off, leaving some nuts coarse. Stir in the butter-flour paste.

Preheat oven to 200 degrees. Grease the bottom of a large *(9 x 13 x 2-inch)* pyrex baking dish. Count the phyllo sheets and remove half, placing them under lightly moistened paper towels, ready for use. Melt a cup of the Crisco. In the baking dish, place two sheets of phyllo, then baste with Crisco. Repeat process until the sheets are finished. Add the nut mixture and repeat layering with remaining sheets, brushing each twosome with Crisco.

Before placing in oven, re-baste edges and cut into diamonds. To do this, with a sharp knife cut parallel lines the length of the pan, then make diagonal lines for perfectly sized two-bite diamonds. When necessary, wipe the knife with water to clean. Bake for 1½ to 2 hours until the bottom is rosy. Remove from oven and top immediately with syrup.

25 / curiosity

CHANCE ENCOUNTER IN A TRATTORIA

You're dining out and sense the people at the next table are listening to your conversation.
Eavesdroppers. After a few moments they approach. Don't turn away. That encounter can have
surprising results.

*F*amily friends were eating at a small trattoria in Florence's Piazza del Carmine,
not far from the Ponte Vecchio, when a well-dressed woman at the next table
spoke in English. "Where are you from?" she asked curiously as her husband looked
on.

"Chapel Hill. That's in the United States, in North Carolina," replied our
friend, Larry Slifkin.

The husband smiled. He spoke rapidly in Italian as his American wife
translated. "I knew someone a long time ago from there," he said. "I was eighteen;
Mussolini had overtaken Italy; the Germans had come down and I was in an
underground unit. Just after the war a professor from Chapel Hill came over.

He taught in Florence." The Italian went on to explain that he had no shoes so the professor found him a pair of boots. After a pause, he added, "He drew portraits of me and my brother and sister. I still have those sketches framed in my home."

"I wonder if it was John Allcott," said Larry, referring to my father, a former art professor at the University of North Carolina.

"I think so... yes," was the excited response.

Before leaving, Larry jotted down the Italian man's name, Marcello Perugi. He promised to pass along news of the conversation.

That winter I visited my mother in Chapel Hill several times. She was living alone, Dad having passed away six years earlier, and now she had a rapid-spreading cancer. I felt heartsick, but Mom didn't dwell on her illness. The Italian was on her mind. She mentioned how the Slifkins had phoned and told her about Marcello. "I feel like a detective trying to follow clues to put the story together. Could his lost friend really be John?" asked Mom, her face puffy from prednisone. "Hearing this story is like an unexpected visit from a person in another time and place. After all these years, this would be so amazing."

The virtue of **CURIOSITY** *discovers things... with gusto!*

Her curiosity engaged, Mom directed me to a bookcase stacked with several rows of large black sketchbooks. Most had white lettering on the book spines: Paris 1980, China 1981, Scandinavia 1987.... Off to one end was a small leather volume, its spine bespeckled with tan age marks. "I wonder if John's early sketches from Italy are there," she said.

I opened it. On the inside cover was a handmade blue bookmark with the words "John Allcott 1938." That was a little after my father's first stay in Florence when he received a certificate from the Royal Academy of Art.

"It looks promising," I said, handing her the sketchbook. Drawings of people popped out. A cluster of bathers, a young kid in overalls, a man eating at a lunch counter... and pages and pages of soldiers. "Oh, my gosh," said Mom, stopping suddenly. A simple ink drawing of a teenage boy faced us. He was sitting in a massive wooden chair and wore shorts, an officer's hat perched on his head—*and* he was barefoot.

"Think it's Marcello?" she asked.

A light cotton blanket covered her frail body, her eyes widening in merriment. The dates didn't quite match up, we decided, but perhaps Dad had the sketchbook when the Army sent him back to Europe at the end of World War II. He and a group of other professors taught short courses at the GI University in Florence and educated hundreds of soldiers waiting for aircraft carriers to transport them back home.

"Given the assimilated rank of colonel, John got a jeep with a driver and cans of gasoline," explained Mom. "When he wasn't teaching he'd go off to the hill country around Florence to sketch. I remember him saying he gave some of his scarce gasoline allotment to monks at Assisi who for years had been unable to clean grease out of their cassocks, until the gasoline helped them remove it. Maybe he met Marcello around that time."

To please Mom, I wrote up her little story and called it "The Wonderful Tale of Larry Slifkin." The sketch of the shoeless teen ran down the left side of the page; the story was on the right, and on March 8, I made dozens of copies. I left them on a table in her room at a health-care center, where she had moved recently.

Though not overly religious, Mom felt an intense spiritual sense of cosmic tilting. At this crucial crossroads, as the advance of cancer diminished her days with pain, sudden fevers and bone-weary fatigue, Dad seemed to reenter her life in a delightfully whimsical way. And as odd as it may sound, Scott Joplin's "Ragtime" was often on her radio, the same twinkly music that Dad once played on the piano in our home.

When a friend would visit Mom in the health center, she would smile and hand over a copy of the story. With a look of contentment, she'd say, "Wouldn't John have loved this?"

Mom died on March 19, 1996. My sister Liz brought 100 small rosemary plants to the Community Church (the same church that Reverend Charlie Jones had started during the Civil Rights Movement) and shared them with friends at her memorial service. She gave them out and said with a hug, "Mom always loved plants, and for centuries rosemary has been considered a symbol of remembrance at weddings

A fruit is a vegetable with looks and money. Plus, if you let fruit rot, it turns into wine, something Brussels sprouts never do.

–P.J. O'Rourke

and funerals." We also passed around the story about the Italian, knowing our friends would find this chance encounter—and its timing—quite curious.

I decided to mail a letter off to Florence. In my mind I could picture Dad and Marcello as young men, strangers at first, soon sharing stories and food, boots and sketches. If only I could have watched Marcello as he read my letter and be able tell him so many things about my father and our family....

Nothing happened for the longest time. But later that spring a long tan mailing tube arrived from Italy. Rolled inside were photocopies of six sketches. One was eerily familiar: a young man sat pensively in a chair, wearing shorts. Yet this man's face was broader, the hair slicked back... and he had on shoes. Marcello was not the mystery man after all in Dad's sketchbook. It was some other person, but clearly Dad was the artist of both drawings. I showed the photocopies to my siblings, and the circle connecting the Allcotts and Perugis felt complete, or so I thought.

A few years passed. Our daughter Kathleen, then attending the University of North Carolina, talked of going abroad. "I want to study in Florence," she said. "It would be so interesting to live in another country."

"Sounds great," I replied. "Grandpa John would certainly have been pleased." And then it hit me: The connection with Marcello—which started after World War II and popped up years later, during the chance encounter in a trattoria—wasn't over. Another chapter, a third act, was about to begin. I pictured Kathleen in a tiny apartment in Italy, her small window overlooking aged tile rooftops and the orange dome of the Duomo, the Perugis not far distant. We would visit her, and them.

Homesickness. The invasion of Iraq. The health scare of SARs. In the early months of 2003, this menacing threesome swirled around Kathleen, chipping away at her confidence. Her dream semester in Florence wasn't initially what she—or we—had anticipated. Moreover, the view from her apartment was of a dingy building. Our conversations often got snapped short when the connection with her cell phone went dead. Redialed numbers resulted in incomprehensible recorded messages, in Italian.

Then one morning, she called sobbing, "I was held up at knifepoint. My purse was slashed, my wallet stolen."

The cure for boredom is curiosity. There is no cure for curiosity.

—Dorothy Parker

I asked if she wanted me to call the Perugis. There was a pause. "No, I went already to the police," said Kathleen answering slowly. "I'll… I'll be okay."

Despite the robbery, I sensed my daughter had somehow reached deep within to steady herself. A mental barrier now seemed to keep this scary stuff more out there, not close to her heart. She was becoming self-sufficient, and resilience buoyed her voice as she said, "Let's meet them all together when you visit Florence, this March."

Five weeks later, Kathleen, my husband and I wove our way through the cars and scooters lining Piazza del Carmine. We knocked on a stately oak door. I wondered what Marcello must be thinking as he awaited John Allcott's family… nearly sixty years later. The front door burst open and there he was, arms flung wide, welcoming, still quite handsome in his late seventies. Dressed in a black high-necked sweater, black pants, his leonine hair combed back, he hugged us warmly many times… "*Benvenuti, benvenuti!!*"

We never sorted out which language to use. Sometimes he spoke in Italian with his wife Lisa translating; sometimes we used French; sometimes he tried a little English. "John Allcott, I tried to find him. I looked for him in phone books. I wanted to write and make him a visit."

As we drank Italian wine in the peaceful courtyard of his home, Marcello showed us faded black and white photographs. Dad had given these family treasures to his friend who'd carefully safeguarded them.

"You take this one," Marcello said. He handed me a picture of my mother standing with my brother Johnny, then a toddler, and my sister Liz in a pinafore, holding a clutch of daffodils.

"But I don't have a photo of John," he said wistfully. "I wish I could see him again." He went on to explain how he'd met my father at the Galleria dell'Accademia, the museum that housed Michelangelo's famed *David*. "John Allcott lectured there… He visited my family's home, many times… We often had dinner."

Wow, I thought, Dad lectured in the same building as Michelangelo's *David*. I supplied key highlights of my father's life during the missing years. How he became head of UNC's Art Department, wrote a book about campus architecture and, until shortly before his death, volunteered frequently to give tours of the campus

to incoming freshmen and their families. Fluffy white hair, sparkly brown eyes, megaphone in hand, he would say with pride to visitors, "UNC is the oldest state university in the country, and I can't wait to tell you about its remarkable history."

Soon we headed with Marcello and Lisa to a nearby trattoria—the same restaurant where they had met the Slifkins—and stories continued. He told us he'd once lectured at Columbia University about his plans to put roads and parking areas under Florence's Old City, a way to lessen car congestion and corrosive pollution. "Marcello was an architect ahead of his time," said Lisa proudly. "But his plan, alas, was too costly."

Risotto, sautéed spinach, crispy chicken and crusty fish, and sublime eggplant parmesan. (Curious about re-creating this dish, I turned to the English-speaking chef at the Don Alfonso 1890, one of my favorite restaurants in Italy, and he kindly gave me the recipe for his signature eggplant parmesan.) Always Chianti. More talk of Dad over food.

"You, beautiful girl, do not put off the little and big things your heart wants," said Marcello, nodding at Kathleen. "One day passes into next and it's too late." But his eyes, those warm brown Italian eyes, indicated that it wasn't too late—not really for him, not for the rest of us. And before we hugged many more times and whispered our good-byes, not wanting this wonderful time to ever, ever end, I said to him, "Your meeting our family friends; Mom hearing the story; us being back here. Unusual, isn't it?"

Call it a coincidence, serendipity, or something more. But as Marcello smiled I knew one thing with certainty: there was still unfinished business.

Upon my return I addressed a large envelope to Marcello Perugi. As I did so I could hear my Dad's music—that spunky, tap-your-toes strut of "Ragtime"—playing in my head. Inside the envelope, I tucked some special photos so Marcello could see his friend again: my father as a young man in the 1930s, him and Mom at their wedding, and a more recent one of Dad sketching; a few other favorites, too.

Friends, soon reunited—all because curiosity sparked a chance encounter and more curiosity kept the story unfolding. It's an ingredient that keeps life fascinating.

Italian Food

Oh, how I love Italian food.
I eat it all the time,
Not just 'cause how good it tastes
But 'cause how good it rhymes.
Minestrone, cannelloni,
Macaroni, rigatoni,
Spaghettini, scallopini,
Escarole, braciole,
Insalata, cremolata, manicotti,
Marinara, carbonara,
Shrimp francese, Bolognese,
Ravioli, mostaccioli,
Mozzarella, tagliatelle,
Fried zucchini, rollatini,
Fettuccine, green linguine,
Tortellini, Tetrazzini,
Oops—I think I split my jeani.

—Shel Silverstein,
Every Thing On It

VIRTUES COOKING TIP:

curiosity

Curiosity jumps up and down, a lively presence. Encourage curiosity in your children by turning everyday ingredients into exciting new dishes, like an elegant Eggplant Parmesan.

EGGPLANT PARMESAN

serves 4

1 pound long Japanese eggplants
1 cup vegetable oil for frying
7 ounces mozzarella cheese
¼ cup chopped basil, *plus a few leaves*
10½ ounces tomato sauce,
preferably homemade
pinch sea salt

Preheat oven to 350 degrees. Cut the eggplant into very thin slices, fry in hot vegetable oil and drain on paper towels. Slice the mozzarella into thin rounds. In each of four small ceramic dishes with straight sides alternate two slices of eggplant with a slice of mozzarella, a pinch of chopped basil and a tiny dollop of tomato sauce. Repeat for five layers. Bake approximately 10 minutes. For the presentation, center an eggplant stack on each plate, nap with warm tomato sauce and decorate with a basil leaf. Top with a pinch of salt. Serve immediately.

This dish from the Don Alfonso 1890, a Michelin-starred restaurant in Italy where I've held cooking groups, will stun company. So simple, so elegant.

RUSSET BAKING
POTATOES
U.S. NO. 1
NET WT. 10 LBS.

PACKED FOR: COUNTRY FOODS
DIV. OF AGWAY INC., HAUPPAUGE, N.Y.

26) caring

7 FROG BLUEBERRY PIE

I set off in a blue kayak dipping through the swells on Lake Skaneateles, one of the Finger Lakes in upstate New York. In a yellow kayak my sister paddled nearby. I felt uneasy. On this early morning outing, we were two tiny bobbers on the lake, shoreline fast receding, and could barely see our destination—a long stone dock on the far side, about a mile away. Waves were high, white crests curling the tops.

"I'd like to make dessert for tonight," I said, trying to distract myself from the chop of the waves and wondering if our kayaks might flip. "I need to organize some blueberry picking. Also, can I use the ice-cream maker? I promise not to use soy milk, not a drop."

The summer before, our brother John—known affectionately in our family as a "barbecue vegetarian" (normally a tofu type of guy, he couldn't resist spicy pulled pork on occasion, a carryover from growing up in the "cradle of the 'cue," the name for barbecue-crazy North Carolina)—had volunteered to make ice cream.

I'd dreamed of a creamy dulce de leche, with finger-licking-the-bowl deliciousness. But, alas, his health-conscious beliefs had prevailed. John made a concoction with pasteurized soy milk and canned mandarin oranges. Using the ice-cream maker he had purchased as a house present, he'd poured the watery mixture into the metal canister, turned on the paddles, and half an hour later, *voilà*—sorbet. Heart-friendly it was. Tasty it wasn't.

A good sister, I'd heartily praised his culinary creation and dutifully cleaned my bowl. Cooking might not come easily to John, a busy doctor, but I give him credit. He always practiced our parents' Rule No. 1 for Being a Houseguest: show you care by making something special to eat. (Rule No. 2 was to clean up all the messed up pots and pans.)

This virtue, CARING, is best shown through kindness, courtesy and compassion.

And now, despite the side-to-side rocking of the kayaks, Liz and I pushed through the splashes and continued across the lake. Dip, dip, dip, dip—our paddles churned through the white caps into the teal-colored water below. After half an hour we glided into a protected bay, made our ritual thump against the dock and u-turned back into choppy water. Guiding our return was Liz's white clapboard lake house and a burst of yellow from a gardenful of brown-eyed Susans. Glancing around for more distractions, I noticed both kayaks had names stamped on the front: Perseverance and Serendipity. Maybe all this persistent paddling, I thought, would end up leading to some serendipitous fun along the way.

And it did. "Look," said Liz. "There's a white gull in the distance trying to balance atop the swells, and, and... what's that?"

It was an athletic brown muskrat doing its own early morning paddle. Didn't it know the middle of this glacial lake was 315 feet deep? Wasn't it concerned the closest shore was still a quarter mile away, no food in sight, no muskrat taxi service available? Wouldn't it like a rescue? As we approached, the muskrat dove underwater, then popped up behind us to watch again.

"Guess he doesn't need a lift," Liz said. And before long we reached her dock, exhilarated and safe.

A SPECIALTY RESTAURANT
MANY COOKS
ALL AT THEIR SPECIALTIES

*E*ach summer, family and friends gathered at the lake house from across the United States: Eugene, Red Lodge (Montana), Tucson, Oklahoma City, Chapel Hill, Greensboro, Washington, D.C., Manhattan, Chappaqua, Ithaca and Boston. India and Australia. Elsewhere, too. It was a time to embrace and celebrate family, and reconnect. Motor boating and hikes. Bird-watching. Naps. Fossil-hunting. Making stepping stones for gardens back home—with the feet of the youngest baby pressed into the wet concrete and almost all containing the word "PEACE."

All this good stuff was the backbone of our days. The real "caring" heartbeat of these summers, though, revolved around food and conversation. Eat, eat, eat and talk!

Sweet corn and sun-warmed tomatoes. After kayaking, Liz and I scooted to a vegetable stand several miles up Route 41A and served ourselves since the owner wasn't there. As we talked, we counted out two ears per person of "butter and sugar" corn. Grabbed extra tomatoes. It was the honor system so we stuffed money into a small box with a teeny, tiny lock.

Thyme. Lots of thyme. In the garden, a niece and nephew, and their high-octane offspring, joined me to swish leisurely through silvery patches of lemon thyme, for no reason other than to enjoy the herb's fragrance. We had thyme on our hands for fun, for love. Plenty of time.... Jabbering away, the kids collected sprigs of thyme, dill and basil; our senses floating off on an olfactory adventure. We shot our hands through vines to discover pea pods; we dug potatoes, scooped up zucchini, picked lettuce, clipped zinnias....

Buckets of blueberries. Before lunch two carloads of us went to Grisamore Farms, about half an hour away. A summer tradition of berry-picking! Large bowls and buckets overflowed soon with plump blueberries and raspberries. More conversations, often food-centric and with different relatives: "While in Alaska researching my dissertation, I could catch salmon, your favorite fish, right from my kayak"... "Candy sales for my church's fund-raiser are at a record high" ... "I brought wine from the vineyard where I work. Wouldn't you like to try the organic pinot gris and pinot noir?" ... "I'm leading an Outward Bound trip again this summer; we carry in, catch or pick our food."

Later that afternoon I was in the kitchen practicing Rule No. 1 of Being a Houseguest. To show caring, I was making an old-fashioned blueberry pie. Into a bowlful of freshly picked berries I mixed sugar, lemon zest and juice, and corn starch. I rolled out pie crust for the bottom and settled it in the pan. As I started on the top, I realized suddenly that insufficient dough remained.

Aha, I thought, spotting a cookie-cutter shaped like a frog on the window sill. The kids can punch out as many frogs as possible from the remaining dough and festoon the pie's top with the silly critters. And so freshly washed little hands soon made a pile of frogs. They placed them on the top, and amidst much laughter said, "Auntie Ellie, are we really going to eat frog pie?"

Just then my nephew Hunt came into the kitchen to see why everyone was laughing. "Frogs... for dessert?" he said in mock seriousness as he counted them up; some sporting funky, out-of-shape heads or legs. "I guess that means we'll be having, 7

Cooking is at once child's play and adult joy. And cooking done with care is an act of love. "

Craig Claiborne

Frog Blueberry Pie." And so a new summer tradition started, of making Frog Pie.

Next, the ice-cream-making. Two young nephews broke up chocolate squares and toasted the almonds. They separated eggs. I couldn't resist and told each boy, "You're such a good egg, helping make dessert." They added cupfuls of cream for the custard and the frothy mixture was soon in the fridge before its even bigger chill in the ice-cream maker.

Tender chicken. My nephew Chris and I made Roast Chicken with Goat Cheese, using thyme from the garden. He asked about any Bill Clinton sightings, since the former president and his wife live in my town, Chappaqua, N.Y.

"Last winter Uncle Peter and I were out walking when President Clinton came up King Street hill toward us," I said. "We exchanged hellos, and I was able to thank him personally for agreeing to be the honorary chair of the New Castle Historical Society's Antique Show, something I'd arranged through his office. Just then I noticed Peter's paint-spattered sweatpants. An uncool wad of pajama was sticking out the bottom, an underlayer for extra warmth. At least the president didn't laugh...."

*F*inally, the evening food feast. At dinner, after a minute of silent prayer for each to pause and think of our blessings, everyone holding hands, it was time to eat: a dill-filled garden salad; steamy sugar snap peas; corn on the cob and tomatoes from the roadside stand; buttery fingerling potatoes; and platters of Roast Chicken with Goat Cheese.

As for dessert, the still hot 7 Frog Blueberry Pie and the homemade ice cream produced fireworks—an experience worthy of the Fourth of July displays on Lake Skaneateles. (Okay, I exaggerate.) But the still warm berries in the pie exploded in our mouths with exciting flavor-bursts, quickly joined by crunches from the crispy frog pie crust and the chill of chocolaty ice cream; the flavors cascaded over our tastebuds in a delightful swirl. Alas, the gustatory spell was broken when my grinning, then-five-year-old niece, having finished first, had to show everyone her now blueberry-purpled tongue....

Caring manifests itself best in helping hands (preferably washed!), and in a stir up of silly new family traditions, like 7 Frog Blueberry Pie.

ROAST CHICKEN WITH GOAT CHEESE

---

serves 8

8 chicken thighs with legs attached *(about 4 pounds)* or 16 thighs
5 ounces soft goat cheese
½ teaspoon grated lemon peel
2 sprigs fresh thyme, *leaves only, chopped*
2 sprigs fresh basil, *leaves only, chopped*
2 tablespoons olive oil
sea salt
freshly ground pepper
kitchen string

This recipe has one of my favorite spices—fresh thyme—and making the dish ahead leaves you with that most precious gift... free time. "The chicken can also be stuffed with leeks or truffles, or a mixture of fresh and sun-dried tomatoes and black olives," says chef Kathie Alex who taught the recipe at her cooking school located in Julia Child's former home in the South of France. No matter the stuffing, this chicken is delicious for a picnic.

Preheat oven to 350 degrees. Bone chicken thighs *(leaving leg attached, unboned)* and lay on a baking sheet, skin side down. Set aside. Place goat cheese in a small bowl and add the lemon peel, thyme and basil. Mash with a fork until smooth. Add the olive oil a little at a time, mixing after each addition. Season the chicken with salt and pepper; divide the goat cheese into 8 portions and spread in an even layer over the boned side of the thigh. Fold over the attached leg *(or roll up, with skin on the outside)*. Tie in place with kitchen string, forming an "X." Arrange chicken in roasting pan, skin side up. Drizzle with more olive oil, and season with more salt and pepper. Bake for 1 hour or until the juices run clean. Snip and remove the strings before serving.

VIRTUES COOKING TIP:

caring

How many times a day do you say "take care" and then what? Anything tangible? Put the virtue of **caring** into action by organizing activities with family and friends—like blueberry picking—and everyone can heap the berries into a zany 7 Frog Blueberry pie.

7 FROG BLUEBERRY PIE

serves 7+

filling
½ cup sugar
2 tablespoons cornstarch
2 teaspoons lemon zest, *finely grated*
2 tablespoons lemon juice
½ teaspoon salt
6+ cups blueberries

french pastry dough
2 cups all-purpose flour
½ teaspoon salt
2 tablespoons sugar
1 teaspoon baking powder
10 tablespoons cold unsalted butter,
cut into pieces
6 tablespoons heavy cream,
beaten with 1 egg yolk

This pastry can be made in advance and frozen. Just wrap dough tightly in plastic wrap and aluminum foil, then freeze. When ready to use, defrost for several hours in the refrigerator. Or if really short on time, use a ready-made pie crust.

Preheat oven to 425 degrees. Stir sugar, cornstarch, lemon zest and juice, and salt together in a large bowl; add the blueberries and toss to coat. Place one crust (see recipe for French Pastry Dough, below) on the bottom of a 9-inch pie pan, add the blueberry mixture and get ready to have fun with the second crust.

Using a cookie cutter shaped like a frog *(or dog, or some other animal)*, stamp out as many frogs as possible and place in a circle on top of the pie. I get from 7 to 10 frogs this way. Bake for 40 to 50 minutes, until the frogs are golden.

French Pastry Dough
Place dry ingredients in bowl of food processor and process 2 seconds. Add butter and pulse on/off for 8 to 10 seconds, until mixture resembles coarse oatmeal. Add the cream-egg mixture through the pour-spout with the processor running, just until the dough starts to hold together. Turn onto a flat surface and with the heel of your hand, smear small batches of the dough across the surface to form a pile on the far side. Divide it evenly into two portions, form flat discs and wrap tightly in plastic wrap. Chill for at least an hour before rolling.

27) grace

KATHLEEN TURNS THE TABLES

Go. Stop. Go. Stop. The travel signals in my head were mixed, conflicting. "Are you sure you want to head to Greece in November with Kathleen?" asked my husband Peter. "The weather could be unpleasant. I wouldn't if I were you."

For years I'd dreamed of such a trip, ever since my junior-year-abroad days in France. My college friends had frolicked in the Greek Isles over spring break and feasted on hot-from-the-oven, spinachy spanakopita while I, zipped into a heavy jacket, swaddled with cap, scarf and woolly gloves, had trudged with twenty other students under the slightly lifted Iron Curtain into the Soviet Union. (Alas, we never ate signature Russian dishes like Chicken Kiev, only lots of boiled meat and potatoes, and questionable buttermilk drinks.) Somehow with marriage, two children and a busy job for a magazine company, the thought of traveling to Greece hadn't arisen again until this fall.

The target date: late November. My now-grown daughter could take time off from her job in advertising, and I could also get away. What could be better than sightseeing and eating Greek food? We could go to some of the same places once visited by my parents. And besides, on the way back, maybe I could stop in Paris and have a meal or two with my son who had recently started studies at the Sorbonne.

But I felt uncertain. Was Greece a good choice off-season? What was meant as a fun mother–daughter trip could, with bad weather, turn into a nasty vacation.

My husband wasn't the only one advising us to postpone the trip. A travel agent cautioned me about closed restaurants and hotels, boarded up shops, cancelled ferries and weather woes. "Spring or summer, even earlier in the fall," she said, "would be much, much better."

Kathleen googled November weather for Athens. "Temperatures will be slightly warmer than New York City," she said. "And rainfall for the month—in the two-inch range—doesn't sound like a monsoon. As for rough seas delaying or canceling ferries, let's hop on planes instead. We'll have endless spanakopita, imagine that, and be fine."

As I talked more about Greece, a few people offered encouragement. "You must go," said my art professor friend Larry who raved about having spent Thanksgiving on the island of Santorini. "Sunsets are among the most gorgeous in the world and the island is the legendary location of the lost city of Atlantis. It's a paradise. At that time of year all you need is a warm hooded jacket."

With his words, the travel-to-Greece button in my head switched back to "go." As for the stopover in Paris, that idea was nixed quickly by my son. "I arrived only two months ago and you already want to visit?" said a puzzled Alex when he made his weekly call from a pay phone. "No, that's not necessary."

A bit saddened, but realizing he needed to flex his own wings, not hover under mine, I booked flights, including going to two Greek islands: Santorini (how could we resist such a place?) and Crete. Renowned for beaches and an abundance of ancient ruins that my parents had delighted in seeing such as the Palace of Knossos, Crete was the furthest south of all of Greece's islands. Translation: It has a high sun-warmth factor, a way to increase odds for a successful trip.

Go, go, go....

The virtue of GRACE?
It projects serenity and
peace, despite underlying
challenges and hardship.

*S*unshine and a brisk Saturday afternoon welcomed us to Athens Eleftherios Venizelos Airport. During the next days Kathleen and I devoured the crispiest spanakopita imaginable; we ranked our favorite feta, cucumber, tomato and olive-studded salads, and tried unknown-to-us foods. And in between feasting on Mediterranean food, we saw sights on the Athens "A" list: from the Acropolis and Archeological Museum to the Ancient Olympic Stadium. We poked around the ruins at Delphi, home of the famed Oracle and once considered the center of the universe.

And then came Tuesday. Heavy rain kept us dashing between museums and stores, as a new weather pattern settled over Greece. The next day's flight to Santorini was yo-yoed by wind gusts up to forty miles an hour, our stomachs bumping up and down, our view obscured by squalls. Passing out small boxes of spanakopita, the flight attendant apologized for the four-day forecast. "I'm truly sorry, lots of precipitation," she said. "The storm has stalled."

The cliff-top town of Fira, normally a much-photographed tourist destination, was chilly, rainy, foggy… empty. Only a darker grey fuzziness differentiated land from sea. With rain streaking our faces, wind whipping our jackets, Kathleen and I edged along a cliff to our hotel and checked in for a three-night stay, their only guests. Stepping down steep stairs toward our bungalow dug into the cliff itself, we watched as a gust of wind suddenly whipped the hotel brochure from my hand, almost taking my purse with it, and swept it up, airborne. Just then another gust pushed us toward what we'd been told was a sheer 500-foot drop into the Mediterranean, still obscured by fog.

Unnerved, unsettled, we fled into the cave-like rooms. We tried to read. We heated up tea with honey to settle our queasy stomachs and warm ourselves. Read a little more. We nibbled on the leftover spanakopita and fed a few pieces to five feral cats clawing, damp and hungry, at the door.

"This isn't how I want to spend my vacation," said Kathleen who hadn't smiled in hours. "Maybe Crete isn't experiencing the same storm. Can we fly out later today?"

Her question mirrored my own thoughts, and yet I felt trapped by commitments. We couldn't leave. We'd just arrived hours earlier. Payments for the hotel and rental car would be lost, and costly last-minute plane reservations needed.

And, oh yeah, I could hear myself telling my husband, who'd thought the trip ill-advised all along, that we'd never actually seen Santorini's famous views. Like the photo in our bungalow showing a white-walled Cycladic church with a brilliant blue dome overlooking the sea, one of the more than 250 churches on the seven-mile-long island. "Nope," I'd have to tell him, "we didn't see anything."

"Let's not decide right now," I suggested to Kathleen, trying to put pep into my voice. I poured us another cup of tea. "At least let's give the place a day."

"Okay," said Kathleen, pinching off more spanakopita.

What? Where did her change of heart, her sense of grace come from? To my surprise, and now sounding as cool as a Greek cucumber, she added: "Let's give it a try. I just came to a realization. I want adventures when I travel—not predicable beach vacations like my friends take in the Caribbean. I want experiences that are awakening and exciting, that pull me out of ruts and routines, and move me in new directions. So, if not too cold and rainy, I'd like to explore this island and see what makes people call it a paradise.

"But," she continued pragmatically, "maybe we needn't stay the whole time."

We were a silly sight—our colorful plumage of clothing consisting of long-sleeved shirts under hooded sweatshirts, and puffy vests, pashminas and gloves. And thus warmly adorned and clinging to grace, we sped off on adventures:

… Up a rocky hill to ruins at Ancient Thira. With the rain easing, we drove to the southern side of the island and climbed up rugged switchbacks, past a small rounded stone Christian basilica. Our view of the magnificent sea was ever-expanding. To reach the old hill-topper village with the remains of a few houses and the agora, or market, we had to inch cautiously over a thin slippery land bridge with an unsettling 1,200-foot precipice on one side and a jagged slope on the other.

"Can you believe this?" asked Kathleen, exhilarated by crossing safely. "We're retracing steps Greeks made thousands of years earlier, perhaps daily since their farms were on flat land along the sea far below."

… *To another cliff-side village, Oia.* Despite more showers, we stayed another day and ventured to Oia. A friendly woman corralled us on a deserted street and in

Everybody has to look at his or her own footprint and do the best they can. It's not about being perfect, it's about doing something. If we're looking for perfection, we'll never, ever get there. 🙶

–Laurie David,
The Dinner Table

Kamares Beach, Santorini. June 198

Allcott

excellent English asked, "Would you like to attend my church's feast day?" The tiny Greek Orthodox church she attended was the size of a very large American kitchen. Several dozen black-clad women were singing and talking in one corner, more people than we'd seen in the entire town. They pressed glasses of sweet red mavro wine into our wet hands. Showers lifting, we stepped back outside and marveled at the town's precarious perch on the cliff's edge.

"The earthquake of 1956 caused immense damage," said the woman pointing to several abandoned cliff cave houses, known as *skafta*. "It was the Aegean's largest quake of the twentieth century. It wasn't as damaging, of course, as the volcanic eruption of 1200 BC that blasted out the center of the island, but still homes crumbled, some tumbled into the sea, and yet as before our lives somehow went on."

As we imagined such an unpleasant occurrence, the woman disappeared into the church. She emerged carrying two platters. One held heart-shaped cookies, which Kathleen discovered were a type of brownie covered in a crunchy white chocolate coating. "And try these buns," she said. They were filled with a pocket of crispy sesame seeds. Her hospitality was like a warm embrace of friendship, especially when she added, "The seeds will bring you good luck."

... *To black sand beaches. Red sand, too.* No longer do boarded-up restaurants and villas along the beach bother us. The upside of this emptiness means the beaches were ours alone. In damp black sand our footprints edged deeper.

... *To VERY leisurely meals.* At a restaurant named Poseidon, on our third night (yes, we stayed the full time and did see Fira's iconic blue-domed church), we waited and waited, and waited some more for the food we ordered: artichoke-stuffed squid for me and grilled grouper with a tomato-olive sauce for Kathleen. "The chef is now back," our waiter explained sheepishly as he dropped off more olives and a second basket of crusty bread. "Your dinner will be out shortly. The chef was busy studying something beautiful."

Seeing our puzzled look, the waiter then confessed, "He went out back for a smoke, saw a beautiful girl and began to flirt until the owner started to yell and, and, and...."

Suddenly, Kathleen laughed. Instead of reprimanding the waiter impatiently or jumping up to give the chef a piece of her mind, as she might have done at home in every-second-must-count New York City, she leaned back and smiled, and out came a loud, wonderfully clear and happy sound. A joyful laugh.

An attitude adjustment into grace, I realized, had been happening since our arrival, even at this restaurant. My daughter had shifted into a "going-with-the-flow" mindset. She was the one leading me. As she explained later: "You know Mom, you can't live a positive life with a negative, critical mind. I'm learning that Greek people have their own wonderful sense of time and priorities." The tables had truly turned. After an initial struggle with the messy weather, Kathleen Grayce (her middle name in honor of her grandmother) had helped dispel the layer of gloom clouding *my* thoughts, *my* mood, and she continued to do so. Her own sense of grace contained a valuable realization about the unpredictability factor in travel—and life. Her new view: try to deal gracefully and affably with whatever happens.

Our dinner did eventually arrive. "Your squid is divine," Kathleen said, leaning over to sample my meal. "In restaurants in Manhattan it's often fried and becomes chewy and tasteless so I didn't order it tonight. But with its light artichoke stuffing, some capers, leeks and onions, this squid is really fabulous. Now here try a forkful of my grouper...."

Several days later on Crete, sunny and warm as anticipated, we continued to relish the off-season travel pleasures of uncrowded beaches, museums and historical sites. In driving merely half an hour out of the modern city of Irakleio, for instance, we visited the Palace of Knossos—in essence, time traveling back to around 1700 BC, or so it felt because again we were virtually the only ones there. Greeting us was a solitary ticket-taker. Well, and his animal companions: six cats, several dogs and four strutting, trilling, iridescent blue-green plumaged peacocks.

"Give me a pinch," said Kathleen, again laughing. We were facing a charging bull. The bull was deep red, an ancient fresco on the palace's north entrance. It seemed to look on as we stopped to picnic on a second breakfast, pulled from our backpacks... of thick Greek yogurt, local grapes and apples, salty slices of feta and the freshest bread. Also, more spanakopita; we'd eaten it just about every day as if paying homage to the Greek gods and hoping grace would continue to circle and favor us.

"I can't believe we're in the same palace visited by Grandma June and Grampa John," she said. "I'm so glad we came to Greece."

Grace surrounds us. The challenge is to let go of anxieties and worries, the tendency to complain, that can hover like a Greek fog obscuring this virtue. A sunny disposition—*your* sunny disposition—can let grace shine and clear the air for everyone. That and a hooded jacket!

food facts:

TABLE MANNERS AROUND THE WORLD

If you thought American table manners were tough to remember—"Keep your elbows off the table! Don't talk with your mouth full! Always pass the salt and pepper together!"—think again. Try eating in these countries, where the slightest indiscretion can land you in the doghouse with your host.

Afghanistan: If you drop bread on the floor while dining at a table, pick it up, kiss it, and touch it to your forehead before putting it somewhere other than the floor.

China: Never wave chopsticks at another person, bang them like drumsticks, use them to move plates or bowls, or stab them vertically into a bowl of rice. This last gesture indicates that the food is meant for the dead.

India: In general, eat with your right hand and use your left hand to pass communal dishes.

Tanzania: Do not expose the soles of your feet if you are eating on a carpet or mat. Also, showing up early for dinner is considered rude; aim to arrive fifteen to thirty minutes late.

Japan: Before you commence a meal, wait for your host to tell you three times to begin eating.

Philippines: When you have finished eating, place your fork and spoon side by side on your plate, facing up.

Russia: It is polite to leave a little bit of food on your plate as a tribute to the host's abundant hospitality.

—Annie Tucker Morgan, DivineCaroline

VIRTUES COOKING TIP:

grace

Steady under pressure,
grace is a useful kitchen
companion, especially
when making a difficult
dish. Invoke this virtue by
enlisting family when using
sticky, finicky phyllo, for a
scrumptious spinach pie.

SPANAKOPITA (SPINACH PIE)

serves 8

5 (10-oz.) boxes chopped spinach, *defrosted*
1 bunch scallions
1 medium onion
1 bunch dill
1 bunch parsley
5 tablespoons good olive oil
1 pound feta cheese, *crumbled*
3 large eggs, *beaten*
1 teaspoon sea salt
1 teaspoon freshly ground pepper
1 to 1½ sticks salted butter
1 box frozen phyllo, defrosted *(follow instructions on the package)*

Preheat the oven to 350 degrees. Butter the bottom of a large *(9 x 13 x 2-inch)* baking dish. Rinse and drain the spinach, pressing into a colander and using paper towels to blot up excess water. Put spinach into a large bowl. Finely chop the scallions, onion, dill and parsley, and sauté in a little olive oil. Place in the bowl with spinach. Stir in crumbled feta, eggs, salt and pepper. Pour in several tablespoons of olive oil so mixture is moist. Melt one stick of butter *(more may be needed)* and set aside.

For the phyllo, use two sheets at a time to cover the bottom of the baking dish—extending over the edges. Baste each twosome with the melted butter. Repeat for a total of 4 sets of phyllo sheets, buttering each time. Add the spinach mixture to the baking dish. Now more phyllo: 3 more sets of double phyllo sheets and butter. Fold any sheets sticking over the edge back into the dish and top with a final two sheets and butter. Bake for 50 to 60 minutes until golden brown.

As you assemble the dish, be sure to keep unused phyllo covered with a damp paper towel so it does not become brittle.

28) courage

COOKING IN JULIA CHILD'S KITCHEN

The news that I would lose my job of thirty-one years wasn't completely unexpected. I was soon to be fifty-five, the spring chicken in me aged into a sprightly mother hen, and the editorial offices for the national magazine where I worked as a senior editor had shrunk from a robust 250 people to a frazzled, often-fatigued group of seventy-five. Layoffs like mine were an all-too-common occurrence as American workforces contracted countrywide and, yet, the news still caught me off guard. What I'd feared had actually happened.

Distraught and discouraged, I was relieved my husband and two adult children weren't around when I arrived home. How could I be let go? As a senior editor I'd produced some of the magazine's top-ranked articles, started new features, mentored young employees and played key roles in the editorial powerhouse that put our publication in the hands of 100 million readers worldwide. The magazine had once taken out a full-page ad in *The New York Times*, excerpting an article I'd overseen, and called it, "The magazine article most highly acclaimed by Americans." And now all that hard work and loyalty was yesterday's story, and I had a scary blank page of a future awaiting me.

As I entered my kitchen I turned on the oven, a reflex actually. Dozens of cookbooks including Julia Child's *Mastering the Art of French Cooking* sat squarely on my counter, but I had no recipe in mind. My disappointment was soon nudged, though, by an image from my childhood: of my father hunched over a butcher-block counter vigorously kneading and turning a soft mound of dough. He'd frequently made his Friendship Bread when bad things happened to his friends, knowing that his oven-fresh baking would cheer them up.

*As a virtue, **COURAGE** faces what's happening— adversity, pain, misfortune and fear—head on.*

I could almost hear his voice urging me on, "Elinor, all you have to do is open two packets of yeast and put them in your mixing bowl. Can you do that? Now take out Grammy Chloupek's little silver bowl and measure out a teaspoon of sugar—yup, that's right; mix it in—and add a quarter cup of warm water. Losing yourself in baking this bread will be good for you. Trust me...." As a youngster I'd made so much bread with him, and then delivered the loaves to his friends, especially round "flowerpot" loaves, that I automatically assembled the remaining ingredients: butter, molasses, brown sugar and salt, some leftover stone-cut oatmeal, and a five-pound bag of bread flour.

That evening a smell of comfort permeated the house when my husband Peter opened the door and spotted five well-browned loaves on the kitchen counter. Nonetheless I couldn't hold back the unpleasant news. "I was let go," I blurted. "I realize I'm way too young to retire so I'll figure out something. Not quite sure what, but I'd like to follow my passions."

All I had was a glimmer of an idea about wanting to try something new and exciting. Good salary aside, a rut was a rut. My work had become predictable; my geographic boundaries narrow, with work and home in the same area code. So while I did not know the journalistic "what," "when," "where" or "why" of my next move, the "who" in me had already latched onto the possibility of doing something to match my interests and be on *my* terms.

*M*y search for what to do next was initially much like a troublesome soufflé: lots of whirling around of the ingredients, high expectations and a flop for results. I felt lost and uneasy more times than I cared to admit.

I made a lot of Friendship Bread those first months. Conditioned by decades of early rising, my internal clock rocketed me out of bed at six, and I scurried around making breakfast for Peter. I read the newspaper, took a walk, did yoga, went fishing in the rowboat I'd bought with a friend, volunteered, made more bread and gave it away... and then had no focus. No real overarching sense of purpose. Once precious and scarce, time was now so abundant that its looming weight swung heavily around my neck. Why such guilt in the pleasure of free time, I wondered. Why such anxiety in a maze of choices without immediate answers?

Yet despite giving myself permission—yes, I told myself, after three decades working for the same company, it was perfectly acceptable to take a breather—time continued to be a stern taskmaster, piping up daily: "You wanted me and here I am. Now what?"

Slowly I pealed back the layers of my interests to peek underneath. My sense of identity was conditioned to being "productive," to doing, doing, doing. I busily helped out the historical society, church council, interfaith council and a nonprofit family health clinic, all close-to-my-heart community activities. And I baked and gave away bread. I dove into freelance editing and writing. And gave away more bread.

Then one day when my daughter came for the weekend, she told me about a TV show she'd seen about a grab-a-glass-of-wine cooking school in Italy. "You know," Kathleen said, "you love to travel. You love France and speak the language, and we all know you're nuts about cooking. You'd be perfect leading culinary trips, to France. What a blast that would be!"

"But, but, but...," I sputtered. "I know nothing about French cooking schools. I have no experience leading tours. You're an ad executive in Manhattan with a team of people behind you to accomplish things. Besides I'm fine and can travel occasionally with Dad."

"Just think about it," she said, flashing a sweet smile that indicated I was oblivious to the beautiful pearl she'd dropped in my lap. "You've nothing to lose and fun to gain."

And I did more thinking, as I baked more bread. With limited vacation, my husband was reluctant to travel much overseas; that much was clear. My food enthusiast friends were more encouraging. Still, just as a pearl starts with a grain of irritating sand and only develops into something beautiful over time, I was still thrashing around mentally in the old sandbox, grains of sand flying, not ready to jump into something new. How could I ever summon the courage (and know-how) at this mature point in my life to move into uncharted territory? Leading culinary tours to France would be a true reinvention of myself.

And yet the more I thought about it, the more excited I became. Kathleen had nailed my passions (beyond family, of course): food, friends and France.

Courage can be continuing to tell your spouse what you're thinking, even when his face becomes all wrinkled up. "Really, cooking tours?" he said. "That wouldn't be very lucrative." He didn't understand that money wasn't the point. "These trips would be only once or twice a year," I explained. "My main efforts would remain book editing and writing."

Courage can be breathing into the dream by taking many small steps. Steps with strange initials like EINs and LLCs, for getting a federal Employer Identification Number and setting up a Limited Liability Corporation. Steps that involved a new banking account and credit cards. A website, blast list, flyers, calls to friends.

No courage was needed, however, when it came to choosing the cooking school. In researching options I came across an American chef in the South of France, near Nice, whose name was Kathie Alex. Now I'm no astrologer-consulting, tea-leaf reading, New Age type, but the chef's name was essentially that of my two children, Kathleen and Alex. It seemed like a cosmic sign, a large arrow pointing at her school: GO THERE. Especially when my eyes spotted on the website that this "once in a lifetime opportunity" involved cooking in "Julia Child's former Provence kitchen."

A sense of gustatory excitement overcame me. Julia Child was my culinary hero growing up. What would it be like to cook in her sacrosanct kitchen?

The only real stumbling block is fear of failure. In cooking you've got to have a what-the-hell attitude. **"**

– Julia Child

*N*ow fast-forward to the fruits of my labor. Since 2007, when I organized that first excursion, I've gone back eight times. Trips with friends, or friends of friends. A special trip was in 2012, for instance, the 100th anniversary of Julia's birth. Once again I gathered a group to journey to this virtually unknown culinary mecca and pay tribute to the Grande Dame of French Cuisine herself.

In a rented van filled with five other food enthusiasts, we bumped up the dusty dirt road to La Pitchoune ("The Little Thing"), Julia's name for her rose-covered hideaway. The road was so rutted—and my van so overloaded with people and suitcases—that it slowed to a near stop, then stalled. I tried to gloss over this inauspicious beginning by acting as all-out travel guide.

"The stucco house on that hill is where Julia completed much of the second volume of *Mastering the Art of French Cooking*," I told the group, finally getting the vehicle restarted. "In the 1960s she and her husband Paul were visiting Simone Beck, one of her cookbook's co-authors and whose family owned the old farmhouse across the hillside. A handshake later, no money paid for the property, the Childs were building this simple home, and lived here off and on for nearly thirty years."

We finally made it to the top of the hill, and welcoming us warmly—with a bubbly Kir Royale, slices of dried sausages and crunchy French radishes—was Kathie Alex, La Pitchoune's owner and by now a close friend. An American expatriate, she knew Julia personally and in 1992 had started this cooking school. Everyone leafed through books and articles about Julia and admired the photos throughout the house, including one of Simone, or Simca as Julia affectionately called her friend, wearing a white apron proclaiming "Julia Child Eats TV Dinners."

Ours was a small group. There was a couple from Texas celebrating their fiftieth birthdays, two longtime friends—one a well-traveled New York suburbanite and the other a writer from Florida—and a Michigan gal who confided she was looking for ways to reinvent herself.

"Julia's own second act embracing French food makes for a compelling role model," I said. "She continues to inspire me."

"What do you mean?" she asked.

"Well, at Smith College in the 1930s Julia planned to be the Great American Novelist and then worked in U.S. intelligence in Asia, before her transformative time in France, age thirty-six. Remember how in the movie *Julie & Julia* she and Paul had stopped in November 1948 at La Couronne for their first meal en route to Paris and her oft-described life-changing *sole meunière*? Julia wrote in her memoir that it 'arrived perfectly browned in a sputtering butter sauce... a morsel of perfection... the most exciting meal of my life.' She then went on to attend classes in Paris at the Cordon Bleu with twelve ex-GIs, fell in love with French cooking, took out her typewriter for cookbook-writing and, *voilà*, major reinvention."

"I hope Julia's high-spiritedness and her courage to change rubs off on us," said the Michigan woman.

The next morning that transformative magic was already happening. We felt such warmth coming from the sunny yellow walls of Julia's cozy kitchen; stencils outlining the original location of the pots and pans for her *batterie de cuisine*. It was much like her Cambridge kitchen, now displayed at the Smithsonian Museum. Nearby were Julia's pussycat potholder, her gigantic balloon whisk for whipping egg whites and other cooking paraphernalia. As I looked at her photo on the wall, taken in this very kitchen, I could easily imagine her, a bustling six-foot-two, stirring things up as we gathered for class.

"Is everyone excited to begin?" asked chef Kathie.

On the well-worn, honey-golden wooden counters, she'd placed colorful trays from Provence, each holding the *mis en place* with ingredients for a specific recipe. A tray, for instance, contained duck breasts, unsalted butter, chopped shallots and garlic, veal stock and a half bottle of red wine, as well as garden-fresh thyme and bay leaves. Soon Kathie had us preparing a *Magret de Canard, Sauce Vin Rouge*. Our recipe for mashed potatoes called for truffles and—surprisingly—olive oil, not creamy butter.

Amid the peeling, dicing and chopping, Kathie said, "Have you heard Julia's cooking credo?" Only silence.

"If you can't have fun in the kitchen, don't cook!"

With that, the level of chatter and laughter increased. Covering a small wheel of Camembert with garlic and fine herb Boursin cheese was next. We then patted on puff pastry and browned our creation in the oven. Warm slices of crusty *Camembert en Croute* would enhance a salad of local wild greens. For dessert, a limoncello mousse (a recipe made with generous amounts of cream, egg yolks and lemon liqueur), we julienned and candied lemon zests, without, as Kathie cautioned, "cutting too deeply into the white lemon pith, which can be bitter."

Before long, our cooking finished, our glasses of "bubbly" quaffed on the stone terrace, we were tableside. *Le déjeuner*, the leisurely main meal at noon in France, was about to begin.

"Bonnnn ah-pay-tea," said our token male, his deep Texan voice imitating Julia's well-known singsong voice.

"Yes," everyone chorused, "*bon appétit!*"

Laughing, spirits soaring, we all scooped into the first course: the green salad with a slice of warm *Camembert en Croute* now positioned so elegantly on square green vintage plates, once Julia's. Again, it felt as if she were close, perhaps having merely lingered on the terrace for a second flute of champagne....

As the meal rolled out—the delectable duck and the truffle mashed potatoes—I could tell everyone was enjoying themselves. I reached for a baguette to soak up the remaining sauce. I was thinking about how in *Son of Mastering*, as Julia jokingly called the second volume of her cookbook, she devoted twenty-two pages to making French bread. Given different flours and baking conditions, she said this research effort took her two years and 284 pounds of flour! No doubt Julia—like my bread-baking father—left behind many a floury trail around us as she perfected this recipe. And now the bread finished, my daydreaming done, we awaited the meal's grand finale, a light citrusy mousse.

When not cooking or eating at La Pitchoune, or dining at places like La Palme d'Or, an elegant Michelin-starred restaurant in Cannes overlooking the Mediterranean, I rounded up the group for sightseeing. We checked out paintings by Picasso and Chagall at museums in Old Antibes and St. Paul de Vence; we walked the cobbled streets of Gourdon, the view from the hill-topper village stretching from Nice toward Saint-Tropez, and took time to smell the roses near Monaco, where over 100 varieties perfume the Ephrussi de Rothschild Villa rosary.

And at the end of each day we all bumped happily up the rutted road, for another overnight at La Pitchoune.

*E*ver wake up with a song in your head? I often think about one very special morning when I was staying in what once was Julia's bedroom. I awakened, the early rays of dawn filtering lazily from a high window, with the words of a song by crazy man James Brown spinning around my head: "I feel good, tah-de-dah-de-dah-de-dah, like I knew that I would now; I feel good, so good, 'cause I got you...."

The music was swirling! Twirling! Fast-stepping! This "feeling good" message wasn't coaxed up, reluctantly, from my inner world. It was the first thing in my head upon awakening, like a shout-out of exuberance from deep in my cells. This is where the courage to change my life had landed me.

Truth is, even a soupçon of Julia these days makes me happy. Her cookbooks (around twenty books by my count) and iconic TV show, *The French Chef*, still bedazzle. The pages of *Mastering the Art of French Cooking, Volume 1 and 2*, the emeritus members of my cookbook family, bear more food splashes than others. A framed photo of Julia, a present from the Texas couple, now presides over my stove. And on the table by my bedside are well-read copies of her memoir, *My Life in France*, and *As Always, Julia*. Another prized possession is in that pile of books. New York restaurateur Danny Meyer has inscribed his autobiography, *Setting the Table*—a gift also from a friend—with "For Elinor, the Julia Child of Chappaqua!"

My home has another reminder of my Julia-centric reinvention: a robust stack of recipes. For dinner guests ready to try something new (a type of courage, *n'est-ce pas?*), I love making Goat-Cheese "Surprise" Packages for tossed salad and Salmon in Parchment Paper with Herb Sauce. Other main dishes, too. And each recipe carries special memories of the culinary groups—for instance, among the salivating desserts:

~ Dark chocolate hearts with crème anglaise—much laughter and angst over getting the chocolate to liquefy just right.

~ Lemon verbena ice cream—with two cups of cream and eight eggs, we didn't dare ask about the calories.

~ Raspberry soufflés—triumphant glee as we each made a soufflé that didn't collapse.

~ Three different crème brûlées, with vanilla, coffee cream and lavender—who knew that if used delicately, sparingly, lavender could taste so heavenly?

~ Citrus tarts, upside-down apple tarts, mini-chocolate soufflés and Mona's divine flourless chocolate cake, rose tiramisu.... To everyone's surprise, it really wasn't that difficult to make such elegant desserts.

~ And my all-time favorite, Pavlovas. Eating this dessert, named after a nineteenth century Russian ballerina, left my cooking group speechless, reverential. Its crunchy peaks were covered in a tart and puckery raspberry sauce and soulful whipped cream. The interior was not crunchy like meringues, which I also adore, but called forth a delicate sweet chewiness. Each bite replayed this uplifting experience, and we practically needed oxygen to start breathing again. (My friend Ali mischievously encouraged me to organize a midnight raid on the remaining Pavlovas, which soon disappeared down to the last crumb.) This dessert was—and remains—my own celestial culinary moment like Julia's when she first came to France.

I defy any group *not* to bond over concocting such delights as these. And then there's the dessert I learned of recently, Julia's *Tarte au Citron, La Pitchoune*.

The recipe is in *From Julia Child's Kitchen*, and it's light and lemony—"a little thing" named after her house in Provence. I immediately emailed copies to dozens of my cooking buddies—old and new friends from my trips. I was thinking of how Julia believed in cultivating friends. She liked to say that perfect happiness was "a great meal with dear friends."

And so I met with some of my own dear friends from cooking in France—Sharon, Roma and Yan—at Dee's kitchen in woodsy Connecticut. And while making and sampling the pretty lemon tart, we raised a glass to our illustrious cooking muse on what would have been her 100th birthday.

My daughter, Kathleen, likes to look at my reinvention through the magnifying glass of courage. "Remember when you were let go from your magazine job?" she says. "You thought your life's most rewarding work was behind you. Done! But with your trips and book editing, you've taken loads of risks, courageously, to do

different things. You've turned this period, your sixties, into your best time ever."
Peter and our son Alex, a writer and editor, agree. New possibilities have opened
up, always aligned with what brings me pleasure. And expanding these trips as I've
done—to Paris with its iconic Eiffel Tower and Italy's Amalfi Coast, and with plans for
Istanbul—feeds into more satisfaction.

What could be better than food, friends and France (or just about any travel
destination)? Just think of where courage can take you.

Rue Saint Dominique May 12, 1984

bon courage:
three-course french dinner

GOAT-CHEESE "SURPRISE" PACKAGES FOR TOSSED SALAD

serves 4

2 tablespoons golden raisins
¼ cup water
2 tablespoons pine nuts *(or pecans)*
2 sheets phyllo dough
4 tablespoons unsalted butter, *melted*
4 ounces goat cheese log, *cold*
⅛ teaspoon hot curry powder
parchment paper
tossed salad greens

Put raisins and water in a small saucepan and bring to a boil. Remove from the heat and let soak for 10 minutes. Drain on paper towels. Put nuts on a baking sheet and toast in a preheated 350 degree oven for 2 minutes or until golden brown. Set aside to cool. Lay one sheet of phyllo on a flat surface and brush with melted butter. Cover with second sheet of phyllo and press to seal. Cut sheets into 4 equal squares. Brush each square with butter.

Cut goat cheese crosswise into 4 equal pieces and place in center of each phyllo square. Distribute ½ tablespoon each of raisins and nuts over each piece of goat cheese. Season each with a pinch of curry powder. To form packages, lift the four corners of one square toward the center and gather the remaining phyllo into a purse-shaped package, twisting gently to seal. Place package on a parchment-lined pastry sheet. Chill until ready to bake.

Preheat oven to 375 degrees. Bake chilled packages 8 minutes or until lightly browned. Serve with tossed salad greens.

These "packets" are divine atop a curly endive salad, with orange and avocado slices. Spice up with ginger dressing.

VIRTUES COOKING TIP:

courage

As a virtue, **courage** is
a catalyst for life change.
"Try this, try that," it says
bravely. Your spirit applauds
such fearless behavior. Be an
adventurous role model for
family. For starters, take on
a challenging three-course
French meal for special friends.

SAUMON EN PAPILLOTE AVEC SAUCE AUX HERBES
(SALMON IN PARCHMENT PAPER WITH HERB SAUCE)

serves 4

parchment paper
2 tablespoons butter, *melted*
4 (7-oz.) salmon fillets, *skin removed*
pinch sea salt
1 teaspoon freshly ground pepper
8 thin slices lemon, *seeded and halved*

herb sauce
1¼ cups water
⅓ cup dry white wine
2 shallots, *peeled and finely chopped*
1 cup heavy cream
sea salt
freshly ground pepper
¼ cup finely chopped mixed herbs
*(chervil, chives, parsley, tarragon
or shredded sorrel)*

Preheat oven to 400 degrees. Cut out four 12-inch circles of parchment paper. Fold each circle in half. Open and brush interior with melted butter. Place a salmon fillet on one half of the paper circle, season with salt and pepper, and lay four half-slices of lemon on top. Fold the other half of the paper over the salmon to enclose. Seal the packages by folding over the edges twice and creasing to tighten. Transfer packages to a baking sheet and bake for 15 to 20 minutes. The fish should be firm but not hard when touched.

Herb Sauce

Pour water into a small saucepan; add wine and shallots. Simmer until the mixture has reduced to a syrup. Add the cream and continue cooking for a few minutes to thicken slightly. Season with salt and pepper. Just before serving, stir in the chopped herbs. Serve each person a package to unwrap at the table and pass the sauce.

If preparing the sauce in advance, make the basic sauce and chill; just before serving the salmon, gently reheat and add the cream and herbs.

PAVLOVAS WITH RED BERRIES

---

serves 8

parchment paper
1½ teaspoons pure vanilla extract
1½ tablespoons corn starch
1½ cups granulated sugar
¾ cup large egg whites
(about 6), room temperature
½ teaspoon cream of tartar
pinch sea salt
2 pints fresh red berries
(raspberries or strawberries)
1 cup cold heavy cream,
*whipped with a little powdered sugar added
at the end*

Place rack in the middle of the oven and preheat to 275 degrees. Line a large baking sheet with parchment paper. Pour the vanilla into a small cup. In a small bowl stir the cornstarch into the sugar.

Place the egg whites in a large bowl; add the cream of tartar and salt. Starting on low, beat until foamy. Increase speed to medium until soft peaks start to form, approximately 2 to 3 minutes. Increase speed to medium-high, slowly adding the sugar-corn starch mixture while continuing to beat. When completely mixed, slowly pour in the vanilla. Increase speed and whip until meringue is glossy and stiff peaks form when the whisk is lifted, about 4 to 5 minutes.

Spoon *(or pipe)* the meringue into 8 large round mounds that are three-inches wide on the parchment-lined baking sheet. With the back of the spoon, make an indentation in the middle of each mound to hold the filling. Place in oven. Reduce temperature to 250 degrees. Bake for 50 to 60 minutes, or until meringues are crisp, dry to the touch on the outside and still white *(not tan-colored or cracked)*. The interiors should have a chewy consistency. If the Pavlovas start to color or crack, reduce temperature by 25 degrees and rotate pan. Serve with berries and whipped cream.

The elegant Pavlovas can be served with other delectable toppings such as lemon curd or blueberry sauce.

ABOUT ELINOR

———

Elinor Allcott Griffith has stirred up these bona fides in home cookery: *A Southern culinary pedigree.* She grew up in Chapel Hill, N.C., considered the "Southern Part of Heaven," and can make a wicked-good Shrimp and Grits. *A Julia Child-schooled food enthusiast.* Once a magazine editor at Reader's Digest, she reinvented herself and leads cooking groups to places such as *The French Chef's* former home in the South of France, and elsewhere. World-renowned restaurateur Danny Meyer has even called her "the Julia Child of Chappaqua!" *A skilled cookie-baking "grand" mother.* Just no grandchildren yet. Instead, decades of tasty meals served up to her husband and two children; and *grand-i-ose* outpourings for friends of Friendship Bread, Lemon Bars and Morning Glory Muffins.

She coauthored *First Thing Every Morning* and *The Old Dutch Church of Sleepy Hollow: Legends and Lore of the Oldest Church in New York.*

MESSAGE OF THANKS

———

Special thanks to all the people who guided this book's creation. My husband, Peter, read each chapter and asked me sweetly such things as, "How do you remember details of where we were when I proposed and what we were eating?" Of course, I remembered the food (baguette and brie, a little pâté)… and his proposal in the South of France. My daughter, Kathleen, a superstar in the world of advertising, wrote the Foreword, lined up designer Alicia Tagliasacchi to create the gorgeous layout, and guided the book's marketing. Son Alex made many helpful editorial suggestions. My sister Liz Sharp and her husband Bill suggested I write during summer vacations at their lake house; truth is, I frequently set aside my writing to have real virtues-cooking fun, like gathering kids to bake 7 Frog Blueberry Pie or Circus Tent Apple Pie, both recipes in this book.

Everyone needs a wingman in undertaking a book project. Mine was Laura Kelly. A former VP at Reader's Digest, she offered encouragement and endless ideas, and reminded me of my timetable. I'd worked previously with Lyle Anderson on three undertakings, including a book called *The Old Dutch Church of Sleepy Hollow*, and he scanned my father's colorful sketches, a whole big pile of them.

Other friends tested recipes, including Suzi Hammond. Barbara Eager graciously opened her beach home for some photos. And Lauren Weiss Stever, an executive at TimeOut New York, jumped in with keen insight on several editorial ideas.

Encouragement came from many others: Kathie Alex, John Allcott and Beth Hunt, Nancy Bloch, Jack Calhoun, Lucero Griffith, Shirley Griffith, Mary Ann Hammer, Ali and Jay Klein, Sharon Lawrance and Tom Weaver, Judy McGrath, Heather Meagher, Osi Mizrahi, Laura Mogil, Fran Osborne, Camilla Rafanelli, Harmony Stern, Patricia Strauss, and Nancy and Al Tafoya. Also, thanks to all my wonderful nieces and nephews, several of whom appear in the stories.

RECIPE CREDITS

———

I'm raising a wooden spoon in thanks to the cooks listed below who first made the recipes selected for The Virtues of Cooking.

CHAPTER 1: Friendship Bread—June and John Allcott

CHAPTER 2: Madcap Morning Glory Muffins—Peg Rees

CHAPTER 3: Playful Pancakes—Grammy Chloupek

CHAPTER 4: Inside-Out Toast—John Allcott

CHAPTER 5: Sticky Cinnamon Buns—June Allcott

CHAPTER 6: Pea Soup—June Allcott

CHAPTER 6: Ginger Carrot Soup—Sandra Suarez Sharp

CHAPTER 6: Lemon Bars—Tera White

CHAPTER 6: Toffee Bars—Shirley Griffith

CHAPTER 7: "Going Green" Pesto + Sugar Snap Pea Salad—Liz Sharp

CHAPTER 8: Granola-tivity—Dee Poquette

CHAPTER 9: Worth-the-Wait Turkey Roast—Elinor Griffith

CHAPTER 9: Old-Fashioned Holiday Cookies—Liz Sharp and Aunt Dorothy

CHAPTER 10: Hazelnut Torte—Grammy Chloupek

CHAPTER 11: "Second Desserts" Pound Cake—Trudy Taylor and Miss Effie

CHAPTER 12: Skewered Chicken Breasts with Satay Sauce—Peter Griffith and Chris Sharp

CHAPTER 13: Baked Ziti—Grayce Griffith

CHAPTER 14: Potato Leek Comfort Soup—Madame Loir

CHAPTER 14: French Salad Dressing—Madame Loir

CPSIA information can be obtained
at www.ICGtesting.com
Printed in the USA
BVOW05s1655151216
470758BV00015B/155/P